Contemporary California Architects

Philip Jodidio

Contemporary California Architects

TASCHEN

KÖLN LISBOA LONDON NEW YORK OSAKA PARIS

Page 2 · Seite 2
Eric Owen Moss: IRS Building (detail), Culver City, 1993–94
© Photo: Tom Bonner

**This book was printed on 100% chlorine-free bleached paper in
accordance with the TCF-standard**

© 1995 Benedikt Taschen Verlag GmbH
Hohenzollernring 53, D-50672 Köln

Edited and designed by Angelika Muthesius, Cologne
Cover Design: Angelika Muthesius, Cologne; Mark Thomson, London
Text edited by Silvia Kinkel, Cologne
French translation: Jacques Bosser, Paris
German translation: Franca Fritz, Heinrich Koop, Cologne

Printed in Italy
ISBN 3-8228-8671-8

Contents
Inhalt
Sommaire

Stranger than Paradise

Jerde Partnership, Universal CityWalk, Los Angeles, 1993. Where architecture and the movies meet.

Jerde Partnership, Universal CityWalk, Los Angeles, 1993. Hier begegnen sich Architektur und Film.

Jerde Partnership, Universal CityWalk, Los Angeles, 1993. Une rencontre architecture-cinéma.

Diversity was inscribed in the history of California even before the first explorers arrived in the sixteenth century. From the heavy rains of the Coast Ranges, and the redwood forests of the north, the climate reaches the opposite extreme in the Mojave Desert or Death Valley to the southeast. With an area of 424 000 square kilometers (more than Germany), and a population of 30 million people, California's economy would rank tenth in the world if it were a country. Like a nation unto itself, influenced by climate and history, California's diversity is expressed in its two most important cities, Los Angeles, and San Francisco. More European in its bearing and in its architecture, San Francisco is neither as inventive nor as turbulent as its southern rival. Capital of the entertainment industry, sprawling with its metropolitan area over 88 000 square kilometers, Los Angeles is an extraordinary mixture of the best and the worst in contemporary America. The dreams fabricated in Hollywood or Disneyland, and the riots which shook South Central Los Angeles in May 1992 exemplify the stark contrasts which make up the reality of the second largest city in the United States. Blessed with a mild climate, yet sitting astride the San Andreas Fault, Los Angeles is the paradise of the automobile, where freeways define all movement. It is a place where everything can change unexpectedly, and nothing seems permanent. It is a city where anything goes.

Also subject to severe earthquakes, with a more northerly climate, San Francisco, despite its own turbulent early history, seems to have been formed in a more conservative vein, wealthy and solid. It is hardly surprising that in spite of its penchant for kitsch, or perhaps because of it, Los Angeles has given rise, in the past 15 years, to an inventive school of architecture. As Esther McCoy, an influential architectural writer said, "L.A. always had a larger population than San Francisco, it had more thieves and more speculators, and it was livelier from the beginning. It's always from these lively places that new design comes."

The high visibility and increasing recognition granted architects like Frank O. Gehry has led some to conclude that the "mainstream" of American architecture has shifted from the East Coast and New York to the West. Although

Vielfalt kennzeichnet die Geschichte Kaliforniens – und das nicht erst, seit im 16. Jahrhundert die ersten Entdecker das Land durchzogen. Die extremen klimatischen Bedingungen reichen von den Regenzonen der Küstenregion und den Redwood-Wäldern im Norden bis zur Mojave-Wüste und dem Death Valley im Südosten. Mit einer Fläche von 424 000 Quadratkilometern (größer als Deutschland) und einer Gesamtbevölkerung von 30 Millionen wäre Kalifornien die zehntgrößte Industrienation der Erde – wenn es ein selbständiges Land wäre. Die Vielfalt und Eigenständigkeit Kaliforniens äußert sich aber nicht nur klimatisch und historisch, sondern auch im Erscheinungsbild seiner zwei bedeutendsten Städte, Los Angeles und San Francisco. Im Gegensatz zur südlich gelegenen Rivalin wirkt San Francisco europäischer in seiner Ausrichtung und Architektur, weniger originell und nicht annähernd so turbulent. Als Hauptstadt der Unterhaltungsindustrie, deren Stadtgebiet sich heute über 88 000 Quadratkilometer ausbreitet, zeigt Los Angeles eine außergewöhnliche Mischung des Besten und des Schlechtesten, was das heutige Amerika zu bieten hat. Die in Hollywood oder Disneyland produzierten Träume und die Unruhen in South Central Los Angeles im Mai 1992 veranschaulichen die extremen Gegensätze, aus denen sich die Wirklichkeit dieser zweitgrößten Stadt der Vereinigten Staaten zusammensetzt. Von einem milden Klima verwöhnt, aber rittlings auf dem Sankt-Andreas-Graben erbaut, ist Los Angeles das Paradies des Automobils, wo die Freeways jede Art der Fortbewegung definieren. Es ist ein Ort, an dem sich alles unerwartet verändern kann und nichts von Dauer zu sein scheint. In dieser Stadt ist alles möglich.

Trotz seiner eigenen turbulenten Entstehungsgeschichte hat sich San Francisco – mit seinem rauheren Klima und ebenfalls Opfer großer Erdbeben – in einem eher konservativen Stil weiterentwickelt, wohlhabend und solide. Dagegen ist es kaum überraschend, daß sich in Los Angeles – trotz oder gerade wegen seiner großen Vorliebe für Kitsch – in den letzten 15 Jahren eine originelle Architekturströmung entwickelt hat. Die Architekturkritikerin Esther McCoy sagte zu diesem Thema: »L.A. hatte immer schon eine höhere Einwohnerzahl als San Francisco, es gab mehr Diebe und Spekulanten, und es war von Anfang an aufre-

La diversité était déjà inscrite dans l'histoire de la Californie bien avant que les premiers explorateurs occidentaux n'y fassent leur apparition au XVIème siècle. Des fortes pluies des chaînes côtières et des forêts de séquoias du Nord, à la sècheresse du désert Mojave ou de la Vallée de la Mort, le climat passe d'un extrême à l'autre. Si la Californie, avec ses 424 000 kilomètres carrés (plus que l'Allemagne), et sa population de 30 millions d'habitants, était indépendante, son économie se situerait au dixième rang mondial. Influencée par le climat et l'histoire, la diversité californienne s'exprime aussi dans ses deux plus grandes villes, Los Angeles et San Francisco. Plus européenne par son passé et son architecture, San Francisco n'est pas aussi inventive et turbulente que sa rivale du Sud. Capitale de l'industrie du spectacle, s'étendant, avec son agglomération, sur plus de 88 000 kilomètres carrés, Los Angeles est un extraordinaire amalgame du meilleur et du pire de l'Amérique contemporaine. Les rêves fabriqués à Hollywood ou Disneyland, et les émeutes de South Central de mai 1992, illustrent les violents contrastes qui font la réalité de la deuxième ville des Etats-Unis. Bénéficiant d'un climat doux, mais implantée sur la faille sismique de San Andreas, Los Angeles est un paradis de l'automobile, quadrillé d'autoroutes. Tout peut y arriver; tout peut y changer de la façon la plus inattendue, rien ne semble permanent. Egalement exposée à de violents tremblements de terre, mais jouissant d'un climat plus septentrional, San Francisco, malgré ses débuts mouvementés, paraît issue d'une veine plus ancienne, plus riche et plus stable. Il n'est donc pas surprenant que, malgré son penchant pour le kitsch – ou peut-être à cause de lui – ce soit Los Angeles qui ait donné naissance, au cours de ces quinze dernières années, à une école d'architecture particulièrement inventive. Comme l'écrit l'influent critique d'architecture Esther McCoy: «L.A. a toujours eu une population plus importante que San Francisco, elle compte plus de voleurs, plus de spéculateurs, et elle a été plus animée, dès son origine. C'est toujours dans les lieux les plus remuants que naissent les nouvelles approches créatives.» La haute notoriété et la reconnaissance de plus en plus forte dont bénéficient des architectes comme Frank O. Gehry ont conduit certains à conclure que le «courant prin-

View of downtown Los Angeles. In the city of freeways and low-rise buildings, there are a few tall structures.

Ansicht der Innenstadt von Los Angeles. In dieser Stadt der Freeways und niedrigen Gebäude gibt es auch hohe Bauten.

Le centre de Los Angeles. La ville des autoroutes et des constructions basses n'a pas échappé à la floraison des tours de bureaux.

undeniably influential beyond the borders of California, its architects have yet to demonstrate that the inventiveness they have displayed, partially as a result of the economic boom of the 1980s, can either be confirmed in the West, or imposed in the East. Aside from this note of caution, it is clear that California architects have proven themselves sufficiently to warrant further attention. They have contributed towards a new approach to the relationship between the visual arts and architecture, and they have challenged the existing hierarchies of materials, forms and building types.

Missionaries and Thieves
California was admitted to the United States as the 31st state in 1850, but the history of its exploration by Europeans began more than three centuries before. In 1542, Juan Rodriguez Cabrillo reached San Diego Bay. As the irony of history would have it, in 1579, Sir Francis Drake landed near Point Reyes, north of San Francisco, and claimed the region for Queen Elizabeth I as New Albion. Although this English presence did not prove to be a lasting one in the region, it does symbolize the differences which persist between the north of the state and its southern reaches. It was not until 1769 that Gaspar de Portolá led an expedition and established a colony on San Diego Bay. They also reached an Indian village called Yang-na, at the present site of Los Angeles and named the place "Our Lady Queen of the Angels" (Nuestra Señora la Reina de Los Angeles). The first settlement of the Los Angeles region was made in the San Gabriel Valley in 1771 when two priests founded the Mission San Gabriel Archangel. Although modified in the 19th century, this structure still stands. Together with Mission San Fernando (1797), these structures and other similar ones, adaptations of neo-Classical Mexican churches, represent the earliest California architecture. In 1781, as part of Spain's design to colonize California more thoroughly, the first permanent residents of Los Angeles arrived – twelve humble, mostly illiterate families (46 persons in all) of mestizo (Spanish-Indian), black and Spanish blood. The seeds for the future ethnic diversity of the city existed already in this group. As part of its population of 3.5 million people, Los Angeles today for example

gender. Und es sind immer diese aufregenden Orte, an denen sich neues Design entwickelt.«

Der hohe Bekanntheitsgrad und die zunehmende Anerkennung, die Architekten wie Frank O. Gehry zuteil wurden, verleitete manche Beobachter zu der Ansicht, daß sich die Führung in der amerikanischen Architektur von der Ostküste und New York zur Westküste verlagert hat. Aber obwohl ihr Einfluß unzweifelhaft über Kalifornien hinaus zu spüren ist, müssen die hier ansässigen Architekten erst noch beweisen, daß ihre Originalität nicht nur ein Ergebnis des Wirtschaftswachstums der 80er Jahre ist, sondern eine Strömung, die entweder im Westen tiefere Wurzeln schlagen oder sich im Osten durchsetzen kann. Ansonsten zeichnet es sich deutlich ab, daß die Bauten der kalifornischen Architekten einer erhöhten Aufmerksamkeit wert sind. Sie haben zu einem neuen Ansatz in der Beziehung zwischen bildender Kunst und Architektur beigetragen und darüber hinaus die bestehenden Hierarchien von Materialien, Formen und Gebäudetypen herausgefordert.

Missionare und Diebe
1850 wurde Kalifornien als 31. Staat in die Vereinigten Staaten aufgenommen, aber die Geschichte seiner Besiedlung durch die Europäer begann mehr als drei Jahrhunderte zuvor. Im Jahre 1542 erreichte Juan Rodriguez Cabrillo die Bucht von San Diego. Eine Ironie der Geschichte wollte es, daß Sir Francis Drake 1579 nahe Point Reyes, nördlich von San Francisco, an Land ging und das Gebiet als »New Albion« für Queen Elizabeth I. in Besitz nahm. Obwohl die englische Präsenz in dieser Region nur von kurzer Dauer war, veranschaulicht sie die Unterschiede zwischen dem Norden des heutigen Staates Kalifornien und seinen südlichen Gebieten. Erst 1769 gründete eine Expedition unter Führung von Gaspar de Portolá eine Kolonie in der heutigen San Diego Bay. Die Soldaten erreichten auch ein indianisches Dorf namens Yang-na, das auf dem Boden des heutigen Los Angeles lag, und nannten den Ort »Unsere Königin der Engel« (Nuestra Señora la Reina de Los Angeles). Die erste Siedlung im Gebiet von Los Angeles entstand 1771 im San Gabriel-Tal, als dort zwei Priester die Mission Erzengel Gabriel gründeten. Das ursprüngliche Missionsgebäude

cipal» de l'architecture américaine s'était déplacé de la côte Est et de New York, vers l'Ouest. Bien qu'ils exercent indiscutablement une influence qui dépasse de beaucoup les frontières californiennes, ces architectes doivent encore démontrer que l'inventivité dont ils ont fait preuve à la suite du boom économique des années 80 se confirmera à l'Ouest ou s'imposera à l'Est. Cette réverse faite, il est clair que les architectes californiens méritent d'être étudiés. Ils contribuent à une nouvelle approche de la relation entre arts visuels et architecture, et remettent en cause les hiérarchies figées entre matériaux, formes, et types de construction.

Missionnaires et brigands

Si la Californie devient le 31ème Etat des Etats-Unis en 1850, l'histoire de son exploration par les Européens débute trois siècles plus tôt. En 1542, Juan Rodriguez Cabrillo arrive dans la baie de San Diego, mais c'est Sir Francis Drake qui débarque à Point Reyes, au nord de San Francisco en 1579 et prend possession de la région – la Nouvelle Albion – au nom de la reine Elisabeth Ière. Bien que cette présence britannique n'ait guère duré, elle illustre déjà les différences persistantes entre le Nord et les confins méridionaux de l'État. Il faut attendre 1769 pour que l'expédition de Gaspar de Portolá fonde une colonie à San Diego et atteigne un village indien appelé Yang-Na, site actuel de Los Angeles, et rebaptisé alors «Nuestra Señora la Reina de los Angeles» (Notre Dame la reine des anges). La première installation espagnole dans la région – la vallée de San Gabriel – date de 1771. Deux prêtres y établissent la Mission San Gabriel Archangel. Bien que modifié au XIXe siècle, leur bâtiment subsiste encore. Avec la Mission San Fernando (1797), ces constructions et quelques autres du même style, adaptées des églises mexicaines néo-baroques, constituent les plus anciens témoignages de l'architecture californienne. En 1781, dans le cadre du projet espagnol de coloniser plus activement la Californie, arrivent les premiers résidents permanents de Los Angeles: douze humbles familles métisses de sang noir et espagnol, presque analphabètes, 46 personnes en tout. A travers ce groupe, la future diversité ethnique de la ville existe donc

includes the largest Korean, Mexican, Philippine and Vietnamese communities outside of those countries. On the whole, 22 % of Californians are foreign born, a higher proportion than any other state. This ethnic diversity has a direct bearing on the creativity of the city. As Richard Koshalek, director of the Museum of Contemporary Art (MoCA) says: "The leadership of Los Angeles is going to be Hispanic soon, there is no doubt about it; the mix of cultures we see in this city, from Asia, from Latin America, from Europe, is going to create a new culture."

San Francisco was founded in 1776, when a Spanish presidio and a mission were established. The settlement established by Juan Bautista de Anza was called Yerba Buena, and by 1848, its population had grown to no more than 800 persons. Here too, from the first, history brought varied populations into contact. Russian fur traders established Fort Ross, north of San Francisco in 1812. In 1839, Swiss-born John Augustus Sutter arrived and established his "kingdom" of New Helvetia in the Sacramento valley. It was while establishing a saw mill for John Sutter near Coloma, that James Marshall discovered gold and touched off the California gold rush. The so-called "forty-niners" came in great numbers, spurred by the promise of fabulous riches from the Mother Lode. San Francisco rapidly became a boom city. By 1850 its population reached 50 000 and its lawless coastal area, which became known as the Barbary Coast, gave rise to the vigilantes, extralegal community groups formed to suppress rampant civil disorder. Despite this background, San Francisco also became a very cosmopolitan city. The appeal of gold was not limited to thieves.

By the Treaty of Guadalupe Hidalgo (1848) Mexico had formally ceded the territory of California to the United States, which, by the Compromise of 1850 accepted its entry as a free, non slavery state. Proposed as early as 1845 by Asa Whitney, the idea of a transcontinental railroad was approved by Congress in 1853, but the rail link was only completed in 1869. One side-effect of the necessary work was that Chinese laborers were imported in great numbers, creating the basis for the continuing presence of one of the larger ethnic minorities in California. A railroad

wurde zwar im 19. Jahrhundert umgebaut, ist aber immer noch erhalten und gehört zusammen mit der Mission San Fernando (1797) sowie einigen anderen Beispielen klassizistischer mexikanischer Kirchen zu den frühesten Beispielen kalifornischer Architektur. Als Folge der spanischen Pläne zur vollständigen Kolonisierung Kaliforniens trafen 1781 die ersten 46 Siedler in Los Angeles ein: Zwölf einfache, zumeist ungebildete Familien – spanisch-indianische Mischlinge, Schwarze und Spanier. Die Ursprünge der zukünftigen ethnischen Vielfalt der Stadt existierten also bereits in der ersten Siedlungsgruppe. Zur heutigen, 3,5 Millionen umfassenden Bevölkerung von Los Angeles gehören die größten koreanischen, mexikanischen, philippinischen und vietnamesischen Gemeinschaften außerhalb ihrer Heimatländer. Insgesamt sind 22 % aller Kalifornier ausländischer Herkunft – der höchste Prozentsatz in allen Staaten der USA. Diese ethnische Vielfalt steht in direktem Bezug zur großen Kreativität der Stadt. Richard Koshalek, Direktor des Museum of Contemporary Art (MoCA), sagte dazu: »Zweifellos wird sich in Los Angeles binnen kurzem der hispanische Einfluß durchsetzen, und die Mischung der asiatischen, lateinamerikanischen und europäischen Kulturen in dieser Stadt wird eine neue, eigenständige Kultur hervorbringen.«

San Francisco wurde 1776 gegründet, als auf dem heutigen Stadtgebiet eine spanische Garnison und eine Mission entstanden. Diese von Juan Bautista de Anza unter dem Namen Yerba Buena gegründete Siedlung zählte 1848 nur 800 Einwohner. Auch an diesem Ort kamen von Anfang an verschiedene Bevölkerungsgruppen miteinander in Kontakt. Bereits 1812 gründeten russische Pelzhändler das nördlich von San Francisco gelegene Fort Ross. 1839 gründete der Schweizer Johann August Suter in Kalifornien im Sacramento-Tal sein »Königreich« New Helvetia. Beim Bau einer Sägemühle für Suter in der Nähe von Coloma entdeckte James Marshall Gold und löste damit den kalifornischen Goldrausch aus. Daraufhin drängten in großer Zahl die sogenannten »Forty-Niners« (benannt nach dem Jahr ihrer Ankunft) ins Land, angelockt von der Hoffnung auf den unermeßlichen Reichtum der »Mother Lode«, der Hauptgoldader. Dank des Goldrauschs stieg San Franciscos

en germe dès le premier jour. Aujourd'hui, se trouvent parmi ses 3,5 millions d'habitants les plus importantes colonies au monde de Coréens, de Mexicains, de Philippins et de Vietnamiens. 22 % des Californiens sont nés à l'étranger, proportion plus élevée que dans n'importe quel autre Etat des U.S.A. Cette diversité ethnique joue directement sur la créativité de la cité. Comme l'explique Richard Koshalek, directeur du Museum of Contemporary Art (MoCA): «Il ne fait aucun doute que bientôt notre élite dirigeante sera hispanique; le mélange des cultures d'Asie, d'Amérique latine, d'Europe, que nous voyons dans cette ville, va donner naissance à une nouvelle culture.»

L'établissement d'un presidio espagnol et d'une mission en 1776 marque la date de la fondation de San Francisco. La colonie créée par Juan Bautista de Anza fut appelée Yerba Buena. Sa population n'atteignait même pas 800 personnes en 1848. Là encore, l'histoire met immédiatement en contact des populations d'origines variées. Des marchands de fourrures fondent Fort Ross, au nord de San Francisco, en 1812. En 1839 un Suisse, John Augustus Sutter arrive et crée son «royaume» de New Helvetia dans la vallée de Sacramento. C'est en construisant une scierie pour Sutter, près de Coloma, que James Marshall découvre des pépites de métal précieux et déclenche la ruée vers l'or. Les «Forty-niners» (49, pour 1849) arrivent en grand nombre, attirés par la promesse de fabuleuses richesses. San Francisco connaît alors une expansion incroyable. En 1850, sa population atteint 50 000 personnes, et sa zone côtière «hors-la-loi» est surnommée la «Barbary Coast». Des groupes para-légaux, les vigilantes, se forment pour mettre fin au désordre civil ambiant. Mais l'appel de l'or ne touche pas que les voleurs, et San Francisco devient une ville très cosmopolite. Avec le traité de Guadalupe Hidalgo (1848), le Mexique avait officiellement cédé le territoire de Californie aux Etats-Unis qui, par le compromis de 1850, acceptaient son intégration dans l'Union en tant qu'Etat libre et abolitionniste. Proposée dès 1845 par Asa Whitney, l'idée d'une liaison ferrée transcontinentale est approuvée par le Congrès en 1853, mais le projet ne sera achevé qu' en 1869. Il fallut faire appel à des travailleurs chinois en grand nombre. Cette population allait constituer la base de

connection between Los Angeles (population 11 000) and San Francisco was opened only in 1876, and Los Angeles was connected to the eastern U.S. by train in 1885. Significantly for the local economy, the first trainload of oranges was shipped from Los Angeles in 1886. California today remains the largest American producer of fruits and vegetables. 1886 was also the year of a rate war between the Santa Fe and Southern Pacific railroads. On March 6, 1887, the passenger fare from Kansas City to Los Angeles dropped to only $ 1 and a total of 120 000 people came on the Southern Pacific alone.

From the "Paris of the Pacific" to "Citizen Kane"

People came in large numbers to Southern California because of the promise of a mild climate: hotels, resorts and sanitariums sprang up in Pasadena or Santa Monica at a record pace. By 1887, the population of Los Angeles reached 50 000, and at the turn of the century, 103 000. Mud adobe-style houses gave way quickly to the so-called Monterey style, which mixed local color with New England construction, while subsequent waves of immigrants from the Eastern United States brought each successive fashion with them, a few years behind the times. An Italianate style was followed by the neo-Romanesque popularized in the East by H.H. Richardson. As early as 1893, however one remarkable building was erected in downtown Los Angeles. The Bradbury Building (George Herbert Wyman) is considered by some to be the most significant piece of architecture in Los Angeles, with its skylighted interior, common in Europe, but still rare at the time in the United States.

To the north, the area of San Francisco engaged in more ambitious architectural planning, as seen for example in the Stanford University quadrangle, which was begun 45 kilometers south of the city in 1888 by the Boston firm Shepley, Rutan & Coolidge with the landscape designer Frederick Law Olmsted. This example was followed by the architect Bernard Maybeck for the Berkeley campus of the University of California after 1896, with the patronage of Phoebe Apperson Hearst, the widow of the mining magnate and U.S. Senator George Hearst. At Mrs. Hearst's instigation Maybeck then organized a competition for a

Bevölkerungszahl explosionsartig an. Bereits 1850 hatte die Stadt 50 000 Einwohner, und ihre gesetzlose Küstenregion, die unter dem Namen »Barbary Coast« Berühmtheit erlangte, entwickelte sich zu einer Hochburg der Vigilanten. Diese außerhalb des Gesetzes operierenden Bürgermilizen wurden gebildet, um die immer häufigeren Übergriffe und Verstöße gegen das Gesetz zu bekämpfen. Trotz dieser Umstände entwickelte sich San Francisco zu einer sehr kosmopolitischen Stadt. Die Anziehungskraft des Goldes beschränkte sich nicht nur auf Diebe.

Im Vertrag von Guadalupe Hidalgo (1848) hatte Mexiko offiziell das kalifornische Territorium an die Vereinigten Staaten abgetreten, die nach dem Kompromiß von 1850 den freien, keine Sklaven haltenden Staat Kalifornien in den Staatenbund aufnahmen. Der bereits 1845 von Asa Whitney eingebrachte Vorschlag einer transkontinentalen Eisenbahn wurde 1853 vom Kongreß genehmigt; allerdings verzögerte sich die Fertigstellung der Bahnlinie bis 1869. Ein Nebeneffekt der Bauarbeiten war, daß chinesische Arbeiter ins Land gerufen wurden, die ihrerseits den Grundstock für eine der größten ethnischen Minoritäten in Kalifornien legten. Die Zugverbindung zwischen Los Angeles (11 000 Einwohner) und San Francisco wurde erst 1876 fertiggestellt, und eine Anbindung der Stadt Los Angeles an das Schienennetz des Ostens der USA kam 1885 zustande. Bezeichnend für die lokale Wirtschaft war die Tatsache, daß bereits 1886 die erste Zugladung mit Orangen Los Angeles verließ; noch heute führt Kalifornien die Liste der größten amerikanischen Obst- und Gemüseproduzenten an.

Vom »Paris am Pazifik« zu »Citizen Kane«

Menschenmassen strömten nach Südkalifornien, weil dort ein mildes Klima lockte: Hotels, Kuranlagen und Sanatorien schossen in Pasadena oder Santa Monica wie Pilze aus dem Boden. 1887 lag die Bevölkerungszahl von Los Angeles bei 50 000; zur Jahrhundertwende war die Zahl auf 103 000 gestiegen. Die Lehmziegelbauten des Adobe Style mußten nach kurzer Zeit dem sogenannten Monterey Style weichen, der regionale Einflüsse mit der Architektur Neuenglands kombinierte, während nachfolgende Einwandererwellen aus dem Osten der Vereinigten Staaten immer neue

la présence permanente de l'une des plus importantes minorités ethniques en Californie. La voie de chemin de fer reliant Los Angeles (11 000 habitants) et San Francisco ne fut mise en service qu'en 1876, et Los Angeles ne fut raccordé au réseau de l'Est qu'en 1885. Grande date pour l'économie locale, le premier convoi d'oranges quitta Los Angeles en 1886 (la Californie reste encore aujourd'hui le premier producteur américain de fruits et de légumes). 1886 fut également l'année de la guerre des tarifs entre les compagnies de chemin de fer de Santa Fe et Southern Pacific. Le 6 mars 1887, le prix du billet de Kansas City à Los Angeles tombe à 1 $, et 120 000 personnes affluent dans les wagons de la Southern Pacific.

Du «Paris du Pacifique» au «Citizen Kane»

Les foules se précipitèrent en Californie du Sud, attirées par la promesse d'un climat agréable: hôtels, stations de villégiature et sanatoriums se multiplièrent à Pasadena et à Santa Monica. En 1887, la population de Los Angeles atteignit 50 000 habitants, et 103 000 à la fin du siècle. Les maisons en pisé laissèrent vite la place au style Monterey, qui associait la couleur locale au style Nouvelle Angleterre. Les vagues successives d'immigrants de l'Est importèrent d'autres modes, toujours un peu en retard par rapport à la côte atlantique. A un style italianisant succéda le néo-roman popularisé à l'Est par H.H. Richardson. Dès 1893, cependant, un remarquable bâtiment fut érigé dans le centre de Los Angeles, le Bradbury Building (George Herbert Wyman, architecte), considéré par certains, avec sa cour intérieure sous verrière, formule courante en Europe mais encore rare aux Etats-Unis, comme la plus intéressante réalisation architecturale de la ville. Au Nord, la région de San Francisco manifestait des ambitions architecturales plus affirmées. L'Université de Stanford à 45 km au sud de la ville se fit ainsi construire un vaste ensemble de bâtiments, le Quadrangle, commencé en 1888 par le cabinet d'architectes de Boston Shepley, Rutan & Coolidge et l'architecte paysager Frederick Law Olmsted. Cet exemple fut suivi, en 1896, par l'architecte Bernard Maybeck pour le campus de Berkeley de l'Université de Californie, sous le patronage de Phoebe Apperson Hearst, veuve du magnat

master plan for the city of San Francisco. Despite the with-
drawal of Mrs. Hearst from the proceedings, the competition went forward and received international attention,
resulting in the choice of Daniel Burnham in 1904, who set
out to make the city into the "Paris of the Pacific." The
catastrophic earthquake of 1906 razed much of the city,
making way for the sort of ambitious city planning that
Daniel Burnham had in mind, but his scheme was resisted,
and the city was rebuilt with no substantial changes. The
Panama-Pacific International Exposition of 1915 was a further occasion for San Francisco to express its architectural
ambitions. The city called on the celebrated New York firm
McKim, Mead & White to design the central courtyard of
the exposition, while Bernard Maybeck built the Palace of
Fine Arts. While clearly much more grandiose than anything
Los Angeles would attempt, these schemes and the architecture they gave rise to had none of the singular originality
of a structure like the Bradbury Building. The point was to
confirm the central role of San Francisco with an architecture directly inspired by the East Coast and Europe.

One of the initiatives of Phoebe Hearst at Berkeley had
been to create an architecture program there. One of the
first female graduates was Julia Morgan, who also studied,
like Bernard Maybeck, at the Ecole des Beaux-Arts in Paris.
Having established her office in Oakland near San Francisco, she designed the Los Angeles Examiner Building
(1915) in the so-called Mission style, inspired by the forms
of the remaining Spanish missions. She carried this attempt
to call on local inspiration to romantic heights in the Hearst
Castle at San Simeon (1919–42), half way between Los
Angeles and San Francisco. Here as in the case of the
Examiner Building, her client was William Randolph Hearst,
the son of George Hearst and owner of a publishing empire
including 18 newspapers, who inspired Orson Welles's 1941
film "Citizen Kane." The "Xanadu" of the film is of course
the "Castle," where the Mission style meets Roman baths
and the Italian Renaissance in a manner which certainly
brings to mind the extravagance of Hollywood. Fact and fiction, history and invention are entwined here in a uniquely
Californian way, which has a significance for much of what
has been built in the "Golden State" since then.

Moden mit sich brachten, allerdings einige Jahre hinter der
Zeit. Dem Italianate Style folgte die Neoromanik, die im
Osten von H.H. Richardson populär gemacht worden war.
Aber bereits 1893 wurde ein bemerkenswertes Gebäude in
der Innenstadt von Los Angeles errichtet: Das Bradbury
Building (George Herbert Wyman) gilt für viele als bedeu-
tendstes Bauwerk von Los Angeles. Sein von Oberlichtern
beleuchtetes Interieur war zwar nach europäischen
Gesichtspunkten nicht sonderlich ungewöhnlich, stellte
aber in den Vereinigten Staaten eine Seltenheit dar.

Im Gebiet von San Franciscon verfolgte man ehrgeizigere
architektonische Ziele, wie das Quadrangel der Stanford
University beweist, das 1888 etwa 45 Kilometer südlich der
Stadt unter Leitung der Bostoner Firma Shepley, Rutan &
Coolidge und des Landschaftsarchitekten Frederick Law
Olmsted entstand. Diesem Beispiel folgte der Architekt
Bernard Maybeck bei seinem Entwurf des Berkeley Campus der University of California, der nach 1896 dank der Förderung von Phoebe Apperson Hearst erbaut werden
konnte, der Witwe des Minenmagnaten und US-Senators
George Hearst. Auf Mrs. Hearsts Anregung hin organisierte
Maybeck einen Wettbewerb, der einen Bebauungsplan für
die Innenstadt von San Francisco zum Ziel hatte. Obwohl
sich Mrs. Hearst davon zurückzog, konnte der Wettbewerb
durchgeführt werden und erregte internationales Aufsehen.
1904 entschied sich die Jury schließlich für Daniel Burnham, der die Stadt nach seinen Vorstellungen in ein »Paris
am Pazifik« verwandeln wollte. Das katastrophale Erdbeben
von 1906 machte einen Großteil San Franciscos dem Erdbo-
den gleich. Dadurch entstand zwar genügend Raum für
Burnhams ehrgeizige Pläne, aber seine Entwürfe stießen
auf starken Widerstand, so daß die Stadt ohne grundle-
gende Veränderungen wiederaufgebaut wurde. Die internationale Panama-Pazifik-Ausstellung des Jahres 1915 bot San
Francisco eine weitere Gelegenheit zur Verwirklichung seiner architektonischen Ambitionen. Man beauftragte das
berühmte New Yorker Architekturbüro McKim, Mead &
White mit dem Entwurf des zentralen Innenhofes der Ausstellung und Bernard Maybeck mit dem Bau des Palace of
Fine Arts. Obwohl diese Pläne und die daraus entstehende
Architektur deutlich imposanter und pompöser waren als

des mines et sénateur, George Hearst. A l'instigation de celle-ci, Maybeck organisa un concours pour le plan directeur de la ville de San Francisco. Malgré le retrait prématuré du soutien de Mme Hearst, la compétition attira des participations du monde entier et aboutit, en 1904, au choix de Daniel Burnham, qui voulait faire de la ville le «Paris du Pacifique». Le catastrophique tremblement de terre de 1906 rasa la plus grande partie de la cité, laissant théoriquement la place aux ambitieux projets urbanistiques de Burnham. Mais il rencontra une forte résistance, et la ville fut reconstruite sans grandes modifications. L'Exposition Internationale Panama-Pacifique de 1915 fut une nouvelle occasion pour San Francisco d'afficher ses ambitions architecturales. On fit appel au célèbre cabinet new yorkais McKim, Mead & White pour concevoir le principal palais de l'exposition, tandis que Bernard Maybeck élevait celui des Beaux-Arts. Même si elles étaient plus grandioses que tout ce que Los Angeles tentait alors, ces réalisations ne présentaient pas l'originalité du Bradbury Building. Il semble que l'objectif ait été de faire impression et de confirmer la prééminence régionale de San Francisco à travers une architecture directement inspirée de celle de la Côte Est et de l'Europe. L'une des initiatives de Phoebe Hearst à Berkeley avait été de mettre sur pied un enseignement d'architecture. Une des premières femmes à être diplômée fut Julia Morgan qui, comme Bernard Maybeck, avait également étudié à l'Ecole des Beaux-Arts de Paris. Installée à Oakland, près de San Francisco, elle dessina le bâtiment du journal «Los Angeles Examiner» (1915) en style Mission, inspiré des quelques missions espagnoles subsistantes. Elle allait pousser cette recherche de racines locales jusqu'à un romantisme échevelé en édifiant le Hearst Castle à San Simeon (1919–42), à mi-distance de Los Angeles et de San Francisco. Comme pour le siège de l'«Examiner», il s'agissait là d'une commande de William Randolph Hearst, fils de George Hearst, propriétaire d'un empire de presse de 18 journaux, et inspirateur du film d'Orson Welles «Citizen Kane» (1941). Le «Xanadu» du film est ce «Castle», où le style Mission côtoie des thermes romains et la Renaissance italienne dans une extravagance très hollywoodienne. A San Simeon, la réalité et la fiction, la citation his-

Below: Bernard Maybeck, Palace of Fine Arts, San Francisco, 1915. Originally built for the Panama-Pacific Exhibition, restored in 1969, the building now houses a children's science museum.

Unten: Bernard Maybeck, Palace of Fine Arts, San Francisco, 1915. Das für die internationale Panama-Pazifik-Ausstellung errichtete und 1969 restaurierte Gebäude beherbergt heute ein Naturwissenschaftsmuseum für Kinder.

Ci-dessous: Bernard Maybeck, Palais des Beaux-Arts, San Francisco, 1915. Construit à l'origine pour l'exposition internationale Panama-Pacific, restauré en 1969, il abrite aujourd'hui un musée des sciences destiné aux enfants.

Frank Lloyd Wright, Millard House, Pasadena, 1923. The height of the neo-Mayan style.

Frank Lloyd Wright, Millard House, Pasadena, 1923. Der Höhepunkt des Neo-Mayan Style.

Frank Lloyd Wright, Millard House, Pasadena, 1923. Le style néo-maya à son apogée.

Southern California Lifestyles

The myth of California as the new American paradise certainly dates to the time of the rate war between the Santa Fe and Southern Pacific railroads, and the flood of new arrivals after 1887 included a number of talented architects from the East. Amongst them were Charles and Henry Greene, who established their practice in San Diego in 1894. Although they experimented with a number of styles, they are best known for works such as the Gamble House (Pasadena, 1908) which was inspired by the English Arts and Crafts movement, by Japanese architecture, and certainly by the favorable climate of Southern California. Their insistence on high standards of craftsmanship was blended with a pragmatic acceptance of mechanical production, and as such they had a strong influence on the evolution of the concept of the specifically Californian house.

Another arrival before the turn of the century was Irving Gill, who was born in Syracuse, New York and had worked with the firm of Adler and Sullivan before arriving in San Diego in 1893. Gill modified the Mission style in a way that foreshadowed the clean lines of the modern movement, and also dared to use concrete. Gill's Horatio West Court, (Santa Monica, 1919) was to have a direct influence on the work of Richard Neutra.

More than anyone else early in the century, Frank Lloyd Wright gave impetus to Southern California's interest in contemporary architecture. Between 1917 and 1925, he designed more than 40 projects for the region, and built seven houses. Wright rejected the Mission style in favor of a "local" influence which he found more significant, that of the Mayans. Just as Maybeck and Morgan had been encouraged by the Hearsts, Wright's muse was Aline Barnsdall. Described as an oil heiress and "parlor Bolshevik," she commissioned Wright to build Hollyhock House (1917–20) on her 36 acre Olive Hill estate, which today, under city ownership, serves as an art colony. This house remains a significant contribution to the history of architecture, because its strong neo-Mayan design represents Wright's effort to come to grips with modernity. As Anthony Alofsin has written, "by seeing primitivism as a source of artistic renewal, Wright was taking part in an

alle bisherigen Bauten der Stadt, fehlte ihnen dennoch die Einmaligkeit und Originalität des Bradbury Building. Anscheinend wollte man durch diese, direkt an den Vorbildern der Ostküste und Europas angelehnte Architektur den Betrachter beeindrucken und so die führende Rolle San Franciscos unterstreichen.

Phoebe Hearst hatte in Berkeley unter anderem auch den Aufbau eines Studienprogramms für Architektur angeregt. Zu den ersten Absolventinnen gehörte Julia Morgan, die ebenso wie Bernard Maybeck an der Ecole des Beaux-Arts in Paris studiert hatte. Nach der Gründung ihres eigenen Architekturbüros in Oakland bei San Francisco entwarf sie das Los Angeles Examiner Building (1915) im sogenannten Mission Style, der von den erhaltenen spanischen Missionen inspiriert war. Diesen Versuch der Rückorientierung auf regionale Einflüsse führte sie zu ungeahnten romantischen Höhen mit dem Bau des Hearst Castle in San Simeon (1919–42), auf halbem Wege zwischen Los Angeles und San Francisco. Ebenso wie beim Examiner Building hieß ihr Auftraggeber William Randolph Hearst, der Sohn von George Hearst und Besitzer eines Presseimperiums von insgesamt 18 Zeitungen, der Orson Welles als Vorbild zu seinem 1941 entstandenen Film »Citizen Kane« diente. Mit dem »Xanadu« des Films ist natürlich das »Castle« gemeint, in dem der Mission Style auf römische Bäder und italienische Renaissancearchitektur traf – was zu einer Kombination führte, die die ganze Extravaganz Hollywoods beinhaltet. Realität und Fiktion, Tradition und Phantasie sind in diesem Bauwerk miteinander verbunden – auf eine typisch kalifornische Art, die für viele der seitdem im »Golden State« entstandenen Bauten Vorbild ist.

Lebensstile in Südkalifornien

Der kalifornische Mythos vom neuen amerikanischen Paradies geht mit Sicherheit auf die Zeit des Preiskriegs zwischen der Santa Fe- und der Southern Pacific-Eisenbahngesellschaft zurück. Die Flut der nach 1887 ins Land strömenden Neuankömmlinge brachte auch eine Reihe talentierter Architekten aus dem Osten der USA mit sich, darunter Charles und Henry Greene, die 1894 in San Diego ihr Büro eröffneten. Obwohl sie mit einer Reihe von Stil-

torique et l'imagination débridée, sont inextricablement
entremêlées. On pourrait faire le même commentaire sur
beaucoup de ce qui a été construit depuis dans le «Golden
State».

Styles de vie sud-californiens

Le mythe de la Californie – nouveau paradis de l'Amérique
– remonte vraisemblablement à l'époque de la guerre des
tarifs entre les compagnies ferroviaires de Santa Fe et Southern Pacific. Parmi les innombrables nouveaux arrivants
accourus après 1887, se trouvaient un certain nombre
d'architectes de talent de la côte Est, dont Charles et Henry
Greene, établis à San Diego en 1894. Même s'ils se sont
illustrés dans plusieurs styles, ils sont surtout connus pour
des réalisations comme la Gamble House (Pasadena, 1908)
inspirée du mouvement britannique Arts and Crafts, de
l'architecture japonaise, et certainement par l'agréable climat californien. Leur souci de la qualité de la réalisation se
combinait à un recours tout pragmatique à la production
industrielle, et dans cet esprit, ils exercèrent une forte
influence sur l'évolution de la spécificité conceptuelle de la
maison californienne. Irving Gill arriva également sur la côte
Ouest à la fin du siècle. Né à Syracuse, dans l'Etat de New
York, il avait travaillé pour Adler et Sullivan avant de s'installer à San Diego, en 1893. Il fit évoluer le style Mission
d'une manière qui annonçait déjà les lignes épurées du
mouvement moderniste, et n'hésita pas à utiliser le béton.
Son Horatio West Court (Santa Monica, 1919) allait directement influencer Richard Neutra. Mais, au début du XXe
siècle, c'est Frank Lloyd Wright qui allait réellement faire
naître en Californie un certain intérêt pour l'architecture
contemporaine. De 1917 à 1925, il dessina plus de 40 projets pour la région, et y construisit sept maisons. Il rejeta le
style Mission au bénéfice d'une influence «locale» qu'il
jugeait plus significative, celles des Mayas. Exactement
comme Maybeck et Morgan avaient été encouragés par les
Hearst, Wright trouva son mécène en la personne d'Aline
Barnsdall. Héritière de puits de pétrole et «bolchevique de
salon», elle demanda à Wright de lui construire Hollyhock
House (1917–20) au milieu d'un domaine de 14,5 ha qu'elle
possédait sur Olive Hill, à Los Angeles. Cette demeure a

Rudolph Schindler, Schindler and Chase House, West Hollywood, 1922. A Japanese influence coupled with the new European vision of the modern.

Rudolph Schindler, Schindler and Chase House, West Hollywood, 1922. Japanischer Einfluß kombiniert mit der neuen europäischen Vision der Moderne.

Rudolph Schindler, Schindler and Chase House, West Hollywood, 1922. Influence japonaise et modernisme à l'européenne.

important preoccupation shared by modern artists in Europe, among them Pablo Picasso and Georges Braque. No longer did primitive have a pejorative meaning."[1] Wright's work on the Barnsdall Estate had another, more coincidental impact on architecture in Southern California. Born in Vienna in 1887, Rudolph Schindler came to the United States in 1914 and became an assistant of Wright. Since Wright was contractually obliged to spend a good part of his time overseeing the construction of the Imperial Hotel in Tokyo, Schindler was put in charge of Studio A, another structure on the estate.

Schindler was to remain in Southern California, where, together with his compatriot and friend Richard Neutra, he played a central role in the acceptance of modern architecture. They jointly designed a pergola and wading pool for Olive Hill in 1925. Schindler's own residence (Schindler and Chase House, West Hollywood, 1922) mixes a Japanese concept of indoor-outdoor space which is particularly well-adopted to the local climate, with a strong rectilinear modernity.

Strongly influenced by Adolf Loos, Neutra worked in the early 1920s for Erich Mendelsohn, author of the famous Einstein Tower (Potsdam, 1919–21), before coming to the United States in 1923, and working briefly for Wright in 1924. He and Schindler participated unsuccessfully in the 1926 League of Nations competition, but it was their meeting with Philip and Leah Lovell which was to form their reputations. In the mid-1920s, Schindler built three vacation houses for the Lovell's, the most famous of which is the Lovell Beach House (Newport Beach, 1925–26). Lifted up on ferro-concrete piers for reasons of privacy as well as the view from the balconies, this residence is the prototypical California beach house. Neutra and Schindler had a falling out over the next commission awarded by the Lovell's, but Neutra's Lovell "Health" House (Griffin Park, 1929), was to be the first steel-framed residence conceived in the International Style in the United States. Philip Lovell was a New York physician who advocated "natural" methods of healing and preventive health care, as well as frequent nude sunbathing and uninhibited sexual expression, ideas which he defended in his popular Los Angeles Times column "Care

Rudolph Schindler, Lovell Beach House, Newport Beach, 1925–26. The prototypical California beach house.

Rudolph Schindler, Lovell Beach House, Newport Beach, 1925–26. Das prototypische kalifornische Strandhaus.

Rudolph Schindler, Lovell Beach House, Newport Beach, 1925–26. Le prototype de la beach house (maison de plage) californienne.

richtungen experimentierten, sind sie vor allem für Arbeiten wie das Gamble House (Pasadena, 1908) bekannt, das von den Bauten der englischen Arts and Crafts-Bewegung, von japanischer Architektur und nicht zuletzt vom günstigen Klima Südkaliforniens inspiriert wurde. Die Greenes legten großen Wert auf qualitativ hochwertige Handwerksarbeiten und verbanden diese Haltung mit einer pragmatischen Akzeptanz mechanisierter Bauproduktion; auf diese Weise hatten sie großen Einfluß auf die Entwicklung des Konzepts des typisch kalifornischen Hauses.

Ebenfalls vor der Jahrhundertwende kam Irving Gill nach Kalifornien. Er war in Syracuse, New York, geboren und hatte in San Diego 1893 in der Firma von Adler und Sullivan gearbeitet. Gill veränderte den Mission Style dergestalt, daß in seinen Arbeiten bereits die klaren Linien der späteren Moderne zu erahnen sind; darüber hinaus wagte er sich an die Verwendung von Beton als Baumaterial. Gills Horatio West Court (Santa Monica, 1919) sollte einen direkten Einfluß auf die Arbeiten von Richard Neutra ausüben.

Aber niemand war zu Beginn des Jahrhunderts von größerem Einfluß auf Südkaliforniens Interesse an zeitgenössischer Architektur als Frank Lloyd Wright. Zwischen 1917 und 1925 entwarf Wright mehr als 40 Projekte für diese Region und erbaute sieben Häuser. Er lehnte den Mission Style ab und orientierte sich statt dessen an einem »regionalen« Einfluß, den er für wesentlich bedeutender hielt – der Kultur der Mayas. Was für Maybeck und Morgan die Hearsts, war für Wright seine Muse Aline Barnsdall. Diese Ölerbin und »Salon-Bolschewikin« beauftragte Wright mit dem Bau von Hollyhock House (1917–20) auf ihrem 14,5 Hektar großen Landsitz Olive Hill, heute Künstlerkolonie im Besitz der Stadt. Dieses Haus stellt einen bedeutenden Beitrag zur Geschichte der Architektur dar, da sein stark von der Maya-Kultur beeinflußtes Äußeres Wrights Bemühungen um eine Auseinandersetzung mit der Moderne widerspiegelt. Anthony Alofsin schrieb dazu: »Indem er den Primitivismus als Quelle künstlerischer Erneuerung ansah, befaßte sich Wright mit einer bedeutenden Strömung, an der sich auch moderne europäische Künstler wie Pablo Picasso und Georges Braque beteiligten. Dadurch verlor das Wort primitiv seine pejorative

été depuis transformée par la municipalité en centre artistique. Importante contribution à l'histoire de l'architecture, ses puissantes lignes néo-maya traduisent la volonté de l'architecte de se rapprocher de la modernité. Comme l'a écrit Anthony Alofsin, «en voyant dans le primitivisme une source de renouveau artistique, Wright participait à l'une des importantes préoccupations des artistes modernes européens, dont Pablo Picasso et Georges Braque. Le mot de primitif avait perdu son sens péjoratif».[1] Le travail de Wright sur la propriété Barnsdall eut un autre impact, plus de coïncidence cette fois, sur l'architecture de la région. Né à Vienne en 1887, Rudolph Schindler était arrivé aux Etats-Unis en 1914, et travaillait comme assistant de Wright. Comme celui-ci était obligé, par contrat, de passer une bonne partie de son temps sur le chantier de l'Imperial Hotel à Tokyo, Schindler fut chargé de dessiner le Studio A, un autre projet pour le domaine Barnsdall. Schindler s'installa définitivement en Californie du Sud, et, avec son compatriote et ami Richard Neutra, allait jouer un rôle central dans l'acceptation de l'architecture moderne. Les deutx hommes conçurent en commun une pergola et une retenue d'eau pour Olive Hill en 1925. La propre maison de Schindler (Schindler and Chase House, West Hollywood, 1922) associe le concept japonais d'espace intérieur/extérieur particulièrement bien adapté au climat local, à une rectilinéarité moderniste affirmée. Fortement influencé par Adolf Loos, Neutra avait travaillé dans les années 20 pour Erich Mendelsohn, l'auteur de la célèbre Tour Einstein (Potsdam, 1919–21), avant de s'installer aux Etats-Unis en 1923, où il collabora avec Wright en 1924. Schindler et lui participèrent sans succès au concours de 1926 pour le palais de la Société des Nations à Genève, mais ce fut la rencontre avec Philip et Leah Lovell qui allait leur donner l'occasion d'asseoir leur réputation. Au milieu des années 20, Schindler construisit trois résidences de vacances pour les Lovell, la plus célèbre étant Lovell Beach House (Newport Beach, 1925–26). Elevée sur pilotis de béton armé pour préserver l'intimité et améliorer la vue des balcons, elle est le prototype des maisons de plage de Californie. Neutra et Schindler se brouillèrent à l'occasion d'une nouvelle commande des Lovell. La Lovell Health House de Neutra (Griffin Park,

Richard Neutra, Lovell "Health" House, Griffin Park, 1929. An ample, geo-metrically defined interior, already far removed from the social ideas of the Bauhaus.

Richard Neutra, Lovell »Health« House, Griffin Park, 1929. Eine großzügige, geometrisch definierte Innenausstattung, die sich bereits weit von den sozialen Ideen des Bauhaus entfernt hat.

Richard Neutra, Lovell «Health» House, Griffin Park, 1929. Un intérieur ouvert et géométrique, déjà très éloigné des théories sociales du Bauhaus.

of the Body." The "Health" House was designed by Neutra with Lovell's philosophy in mind, and when the owner invited the readers of his column to visit the completed structure, 15 000 people responded. The ideas of Lovell, which symbolize the Southern California lifestyle, and Neutra's modern steel-frame design had a lasting impact.

The Golden Gate

The differences between San Francisco and Los Angeles are in a sense illustrated in the work of Frank Lloyd Wright. While he was later to design houses in Southern California, in San Francisco he proposed a twenty-story tower influenced by the Vienna Secessionists in an unbuilt project for The San Francisco Call (1913). By the 1920s skyscrapers of up to thirty stories began to reshape the city's skyline. San Francisco architect Timothy Pflueger contributed to the image of the city as a "Manhattan of the West" with his designs as presented in the drawings of Hugh Ferriss. At least in Ferriss's drawings, Pflueger's towers achieved a kind of crystalline geometry which undoubtedly carried the influence of the International Style. Timothy Pflueger acted as one of the consulting architects for the San Francisco-Oakland Bay Bridge (1934–36), the longest high-level steel bridge in the world. The even more symbolic Golden Gate Bridge (1933–37), with a clear span of 1 281 meters was until 1959 the longest in the world. San Francisco thus inaugurated, within a few months of each other, the two biggest bridges in the world, a fact which speaks eloquently of the city's ambitions, and of its geographical make-up as compared to Los Angeles. Recalling a tendency to adopt grand development schemes reaching back to the Burnham plan of the turn of the century, San Francisco remained enamored after the War of large-scale urban renewal as evidenced in master plans proposed by Skidmore, Owings & Merrill for the so-called Area E near the Embarcadero in 1957, or Kenzo Tange's massive Yerba Buena Center (1969). This latter scheme was fortunately never built, but the Yerba Buena district has recently completed a series of culturally-oriented buildings by Mario Botta or Fumihiko Maki which do a certain amount of justice to the ongoing aspirations of San Francisco.

Richard Neutra, Lovell "Health" House, Griffin Park, 1929. One of the first American examples of what would come to be called the International Style.

Richard Neutra, Lovell »Health« House, Griffin Park, 1929. Eines der ersten amerikanischen Beispiele für eine später als International Style bezeichnete Strömung.

Richard Neutra, Lovell «Health» House, Griffin Park, 1929. Un des premiers exemples américains de ce qui allait s'appeler le style international.

Bedeutung.«[1] Aber Wrights Arbeiten auf dem Barnsdall-Landsitz übten noch eine weitere, eher zufällige Wirkung auf die südkalifornische Architektur aus: Im Jahre 1914 kam der 1887 in Wien geborene Rudolph Schindler als Assistent Wrights in die Vereinigten Staaten. Da Wright vertraglich verpflichtet war, einen Großteil seiner Zeit mit der Beaufsichtigung der Bauarbeiten am Imperial Hotel in Tokio zu verbringen, übertrug er Schindler die Aufsicht über den Bau von Studio A, einem weiteren Gebäude auf dem Landsitz.

Schindler ließ sich schließlich in Südkalifornien nieder, wo er zusammen mit seinem Landsmann und Freund Richard Neutra zu einer Zentralfigur für die Einführung und Akzeptanz der modernen Architektur wurde. 1925 entwarfen sie eine Pergola und ein Watbecken für Olive Hill. Schindlers Wohnhaus (Schindler and Chase House, West Hollywood, 1922) kombiniert die japanische Auffassung der Durchdringung von Innen- und Außenraum – für das südkalifornische Klima besonders gut – mit einer strengen, rechtwinkligen Modernität.

Neutra, der stark von Adolf Loos beeinflußt wurde, arbeitete in den frühen 20er Jahren für Erich Mendelsohn, dem Schöpfer des berühmten Einsteinturms (Potsdam, 1919–21). Im Jahre 1923 kam er in die Vereinigten Staaten, wo er 1924 kurz für Wright tätig war. Schindler und Neutra nahmen 1926 erfolglos am Architekturwettbewerb zum Palais des Nations in Genf teil; erst ihre Begegnung mit Philip und Leah Lovell sollte ihnen zu Berühmtheit verhelfen. Mitte der 20er Jahre baute Schindler drei Ferienhäuser für die Lovells, am bekanntesten das Lovell Beach House (Newport Beach, 1925–26). Dieser Wohnsitz wurde auf Stahlbetonpfeilern errichtet, um den Bewohnern ungestörte Privatsphäre und eine besonders schöne Aussicht von den Balkonen zu bieten, und gilt als prototypisches kalifornisches Strandhaus. Zwar zerstritten sich Neutra und Schindler über den nächsten Auftrag der Lovells, aber Neutras Lovell »Health« House (Griffin Park, 1929) gilt als der erste Stahlskelettbau im International Style, der in den Vereinigten Staaten errichtet wurde. Philip Lovell war ein New Yorker Arzt, der sich für »natürliche« Heilmethoden, vorbeugende Gesundheitsfürsorge, häufiges Nacktbaden und freie Sexualität aussprach – Ideen, die er in seiner populären

1929) fut la première maison à structure d'acier conçue aux Etats-Unis dans le style international. Philip Lovell était un médecin new-yorkais qui s'était fait l'avocat de la prophylaxie et des thérapies «naturelles». Il recommandait les bains de soleil fréquents et une certaine liberté de comportement sexuel, idées qu'il défendait dans une rubrique très lue du «Los Angeles Times»: «Care of the Body» (Soins du corps). Sa Lovell «Health» House («Maison de santé») fut conçue par Neutra sur les bases de cette philosophie. Lorsque le propriétaire invita ses lecteurs à visiter la construction lors de son achèvement, 15 000 personnes se déplacèrent. Les idées de Lovell, qui symbolisent le style de vie de la Californie du Sud, et la structure en acier de Neutra exercèrent une influence durable.

Le Golden Gate

En un sens, toutes les différences entre San Francisco et Los Angeles sont illustrées par l'œuvre de Frank Lloyd Wright. Avant de construire des résidences privées à Los Angeles, il avait proposé, à San Francisco, pour le journal «San Francisco Call» (1913), une tour de vingt étages dans le style de la Sécession viennoise. Elle ne fut jamais construite. Au cours des années 20 cependant, des gratte-ciel de trente étages commencèrent à modifier le paysage urbain. L'architecte local Timothy Pflueger contribua à renforcer l'image de «Manhattan de l'Ouest» de San Francisco par des projets illustrés dans les dessins de Hugh Ferriss. Dans ceux-ci, les tours de Pflueger atteignaient à une sorte de géométrie cristalline qui traduisait déjà l'influence du style international. Timothy Pflueger était l'un des architectes consultants du pont de la baie d'Oakland-San Francisco (1934–36), le plus haut pont d'acier du monde. Plus symbolique encore, le Golden Gate Bridge (1933–37), avec sa portée de 1 281 m fut, jusqu'en 1959, le plus long au monde. San Francisco avait ainsi inauguré à quelques mois de distance les deux plus grands ouvrages d'art de la planète, ce qui manifestait clairement les ambitions de la cité et le caractère de son site, si différent de celui de Los Angeles. Fidèle à son goût pour les grands plans de développement urbain qui remonte au projet Burnham (voir plus haut), San Francisco se lança après guerre dans de vastes

Climate, geography and a conception of the urban environment have guided the development of San Francisco and its architecture in a very different direction than that of Los Angeles. Aspiring at first to resemble Paris, and then New York, San Francisco has taken its role as the "capital of the West" very seriously. Seen from Sausalito, across the still remarkable Golden Gate, it does form a unique urban image. With its dramatic hills and picturesque areas like Chinatown, San Francisco is one of the most attractive cities in the United States, but it is not the sort of place where improvisation or experimentation is really welcome.

Freeways, Movies, and Case Study Houses
Even if it is true that the most significant Los Angeles architecture, at least until a recent date, has been concentrated in private houses, other influences have played a significant role in forming the inventiveness of its contemporary builders. Los Angeles, too, like its northern rival, had grand urban schemes, such as Charles Robinson's 1909 plan which set down the guidelines for the wide boulevards, downtown blocks and open residential neighborhoods which still characterize the city. The promise of a better future and new industries such as the movies or armaments brought a continued influx of new immigrants to the area, with population increasing by 1.5 million between 1920 and 1930, and the automobile began to play a role symbolized by the opening of the Pasadena Freeway in 1939. Essentially a collection of small towns which gradually grew into the contemporary urban area, Los Angeles relied more and more heavily on cars both for work and leisure, and new, curving elevated freeways cut their wide paths across the city. Vast sections of the metropolis were blighted by these vehicular walls and the word "smog" was first used in 1942 to describe the already unbreathable air. Since the first movie was made there in 1911, Hollywood has come to symbolize Los Angeles for tourists and even for many residents. In 1994, 110 000 people earned their livelihood from film and television in the Los Angeles area. It can be said that the superficiality of the movies is part and parcel of the place some have called Tinseltown. This fact is important in understanding the architecture of a city

Kolumne »Care of the Body« (Pflege des Körpers) in der »Los Angeles Times« veröffentlichte. Das »Health« House wurde von Neutra im Sinne der Lovellschen Philosophie entworfen; und als der Eigentümer die Leser seiner Kolumne einlud, den fertiggestellten Bau zu besichtigen, folgten 15 000 seiner Aufforderung. Auf diese Weise übten Lovells Ideen und Neutras moderne Stahlskelettentwürfe einen dauerhaften Einfluß aus.

Die Golden Gate
Die Unterschiede zwischen San Francisco und Los Angeles werden in gewisser Weise durch die Arbeiten Frank Lloyd Wrights verkörpert. Während Wright in späteren Jahren Häuser in Südkalifornien entwarf, arbeitete er 1913 an einem (nicht realisierten) Projekt für die Zeitung »The San Francisco Call« – ein zwanzigstöckiges Hochhaus im Stil der Wiener Sezession. Zu Beginn der 20er Jahre veränderten bis zu dreißigstöckige Wolkenkratzer das Bild der Skyline von Grund auf. Der aus San Francisco stammende Architekt Timothy Pflueger trug mit seinen Entwürfen entscheidend zum Bild der Stadt als dem »Manhattan des Westens« bei. Zumindest in Zeichnungen von Hugh Ferriss besaßen Pfluegers Hochbauten eine kristalline Geometrie, die ohne Zweifel auf die Einflüsse des International Style zurückzuführen ist. Daneben war Pflueger als einer der beratenden Architekten am Bau der San Francisco-Oakland Bay Bridge (1934–36) beteiligt, der längsten stählernen Hängebrücke der Welt. Die noch symbolträchtigere Golden Gate Bridge (1933–37) war mit ihrer Spannweite von 1 281 Metern bis zum Jahr 1959 die längste Brücke der Welt. Innerhalb weniger Monate erlebte San Francisco also die Einweihung der beiden größten Brücken der Welt – eine Tatsache, die nicht nur den Ehrgeiz und die Ambitionen der Stadt verdeutlicht, sondern auch die im Vergleich zu Los Angeles völlig unterschiedlichen geographischen Voraussetzungen.

Da die Stadt seit Burnhams Plänen von der Idee großartiger stadtplanerischer Veränderungen fasziniert war, bemühte sich San Francisco auch nach dem Zweiten Weltkrieg um städtebauliche Entwicklungen in großem Maßstab. Dies führte zu den Bebauungsplänen, die 1957 von Skidmore, Owings & Merrill für das sogenannte Area E in

projets de rénovation urbaine, comme le montrent les plans proposés par Skidmore, Owings & Merrill pour la Zone E, près de l'Embarcadero, en 1957, ou le massif Yerba Buena Center de Kenzo Tange (1969). Ce dernier projet ne fut heureusement jamais édifié, mais le quartier s'est récemment doté de plusieurs bâtiments culturels signés Mario Botta et Fumihiko Maki, qui rendent une certaine justice aux aspirations de la cité à l'ordre urbanistique. Le climat, la géographie et une certaine conception de l'environnement urbain ont orienté le développement de San Francisco et de son architecture dans une direction très différente de celle de Los Angeles. Rêvant initialement de ressembler à Paris, puis à New York, San Francisco a pris très au sérieux son rôle de «capitale de l'Ouest». Vue de Sausalito, au delà du toujours superbe Golden Gate Bridge, la ville sait donner d'elle un visage exceptionnel. Avec ses collines spectaculaires et ses quartiers pittoresques, comme Chinatown, elle reste l'une des villes les plus attirantes des Etats-Unis. Elle n'en est pas pour autant très ouverte à l'improvisation, ou à n'importe quelle expérience.

Autoroutes, cinéma et Case Study Houses

S'il est exact qu'à Los Angeles les tentatives architecturales les plus intéressantes, du moins jusqu'à une date récente, concernent essentiellement des résidences privées, d'autres facteurs ont joué un rôle décisif dans la genèse de la créativité actuelle. De même que sa rivale du Nord, Los Angeles s'est dotée de grands schémas urbains, comme le plan de Charles Robinson (1909) qui traça les larges boulevards, les blocs d'immeubles du centre et les quartiers résidentiels aérés qui caractérisent encore la ville aujourd'hui. Entre 1920 et 1930, la promesse d'un avenir meilleur, et la présence de nouvelles industries comme le cinéma ou l'armement, attirèrent beaucoup de nouveaux immigrants, et la population s'accrût de 1,5 millions. L'automobile commença à marquer son territoire en 1939 avec l'ouverture du freeway de Pasadena. Constituée à l'origine d'une dispersion de petites communautés urbaines qui peu à peu se réunirent en une gigantesque conurbation, Los Angeles allait s'abandonner de plus en plus à l'automobile, aussi bien pour le travail que les loisirs. D'innombrables

Wurdeman and Becket, Pan Pacific Auditorium, Los Angeles, 1935. An outstanding example of the Streamline style.

Wurdeman and Becket, Pan Pacific Auditorium, Los Angeles, 1935. Ein herausragendes Beispiel für den Streamline Style.

Wurdeman et Becket, Pan Pacific Auditorium, Los Angeles, 1935. Un remarquable exemple du style Streamline.

which seems to have a growing tendency to confuse fact and fiction, film and reality. Amongst the more prophetic Hollywood productions, for example, the 1982 film "Blade Runner", directed by Ridley Scott and starring Harrison Ford, depicted a Los Angeles in 2093 whose sky is dark and filled with toxic rain. Filmed in part in the Bradbury Building, "Blade Runner's" apocalyptic design has had a direct influence on the architecture of contemporary groups like Morphosis. The line between the real city and its film versions is sometimes hard to draw. Craig Hodgetts, one of the more inventive Los Angeles architects has mused on the relationship between the creativity of Hollywood and contemporary architecture: "It's not the preciousness of materials or even character that's bankable now in Los Angeles – originality is held in higher esteem. What's seen as valuable is intellectual property, how even ordinary things are put together. Los Angeles is, after all, about making a piece of celluloid valuable."

Los Angeles is also a place where money talks and art is rarely appreciated. That said, architecture has had some high points since the time of Wright, Neutra and Schindler. Amongst these are several 1930s Streamline buildings like the Pan Pacific Auditorium (Los Angeles, Wurdeman and Becket, 1935) or the Shangri-La Apartments (Santa Monica, William Foster, 1940). The development of the city far outstripped the capacities of its "quality" architects, however, and this situation worsened with the large influx of workers for the wartime armaments industries implanted around Los Angeles. In 1943, John Entenza, editor of the magazine *Arts & Architecture* organized a competition under the title "Designs for Post-war Living." Foreseeing a need for large-scale housing construction, Entenza and Charles Eames wrote an essay in an issue of the magazine in 1944, calling for the conversion of war-time industrial technologies in the service of home building. The so-called Case Study House program was announced in the January 1945 issue of *Arts & Architecture*. Between that time and 1966, a total of 34 designs, intended as prototypical models of modern architecture for Southern California, were published in the magazine, and 23 were actually built. Amongst the eight original participants in the program were Eames, Eero Saarinen and

William Foster, Shangri-La Apartments, Santa Monica, 1940. Another Streamline monument which still operates as a hotel just above the palisades and the beach of Santa Monica.

William Foster, Shangri-La Apartments, Santa Monica, 1940. Ein weiteres Monument des Streamline Style, das noch heute als Hotel dient und direkt oberhalb des Strandes von Santa Monica liegt.

William Foster, Shangri-La Apartments, Santa Monica, 1940. Un autre monument du style Streamline, juste au-dessus de la falaise et de la plage de Santa Monica, est encore exploité comme hôtel.

der Nähe des Embarcadero ausgearbeitet wurden, wie auch zu Kenzo Tanges massivem Yerba Buena Center (1969). Letzteres wurde glücklicherweise nie verwirklicht; allerdings sind im Yerba Buena-Distrikt vor kurzem eine Reihe kulturell orientierter Gebäude nach Entwürfen von Mario Botta oder Fumihiko Maki fertiggestellt worden, die den nach wie vor hochgesteckten Zielen San Franciscos zumindest in Ansätzen gerecht werden.

Klima, Geographie und das Konzept einer urbanen Umgebung haben die Entwicklung San Franciscos und seiner Architektur seit jeher in eine ganz andere Richtung gelenkt als die von Los Angeles. Während letztere zunächst Paris und später New York nachstrebte, hat San Francisco seine Rolle als »Hauptstadt des Westens« immer sehr ernst genommen. Von Sausalito aus betrachtet, bietet sich dem Besucher – über die immer noch großartige Golden Gate hinweg – eine einzigartige Stadtansicht. Mit seinen reizvollen Hügeln und pittoresken Stadtvierteln wie Chinatown ist San Francisco eine der attraktivsten Städte der Vereinigten Staaten – aber es ist kein Ort, an dem Improvisation oder Experimentierfreude allzu gern gesehen sind.

Freeways, Filme und Fallstudienhäuser
Auch wenn es zutrifft, daß die bedeutendsten architektonischen Leistungen in Los Angeles – zumindest bis vor kurzem – im Bereich der Privathäuser anzutreffen sind, haben auch andere Einflüsse in der Entwicklung seiner heutigen innovativen Architekten eine wichtige Rolle gespielt. Ebenso wie seine Rivalin im Norden verfolgte auch Los Angeles hochgesteckte stadtplanerische Ziele – wie aus Charles Robinsons Plänen des Jahres 1909 deutlich hervorgeht, die die Grundlagen für die breiten Boulevards, die Blocks von Downtown Los Angeles und die offenen Wohnsiedlungen legten, die auch heute noch das Stadtbild bestimmen. Die Aussicht auf eine bessere Zukunft und neue Industrien wie Filmstudios und Rüstungsfabriken brachten einen ständigen Zustrom von Einwanderern in die Stadt, so daß die Bevölkerung zwischen 1920 und 1930 um 1,5 Millionen anwuchs. Das Automobil nahm einen immer bedeutenderen Platz in der urbanen Gesellschaft ein, was durch die Eröffnung des Pasadena Freeway 1939 verdeut-

nouvelles autoroutes surélevées sillonnèrent la ville, et de vastes sections de la métropole furent affectées par ces «murs» de voitures en mouvement. Dès 1942, on utilisa le terme de «smog» pour décrire un air devenu irrespirable. Depuis le premier film y fut réalisé en 1911, Hollywood en est venu à symboliser Los Angeles pour les touristes, et même beaucoup de ses habitants. En 1994, 110 000 personnes vivaient du cinéma et de la télévision dans la région de Los Angeles. On peut dire que le côté superficiel des films est indissolublement lié à ce lieu que certains ont baptisé «Tinseltown» (la ville des paillettes). Il faut en avoir conscience pour comprendre l'architecture d'une ville qui fait preuve d'une tendance croissante à confondre la réalité et la fiction, le cinéma et la vie. Parmi les productions les plus prophétiques d'Hollywood, par exemple, le film «Blade Runner», de Ridley Scott (1982), avec Harrison Ford, dépeignait un Los Angeles de 2093, au ciel menaçant, dégoulinant de pluies toxiques. Filmé en partie dans le Bradbury Building, ce film et son atmosphère apocalyptique ont exercé une influence directe sur des groupes d'architectes actuels comme Morphosis. La frontière entre la cité réelle et ses représentations filmées est parfois difficile à tracer. Craig Hodgetts, l'un des architectes contemporains les plus inventifs de Los Angeles, a réfléchi à la relation entre la créativité hollywoodienne et l'architecture contemporaine: «Ce n'est pas la préciosité des matériaux ni même le caractère qui paie actuellement à Los Angeles – c'est l'originalité qui est tenue en plus grande estime. Ce qui semble avoir du prix, c'est l'idée, la façon dont même les choses les plus ordinaires sont assemblées. Après tout, Los Angeles n'a-t-elle pas réussi à donner de la valeur à des morceaux de celluloïd?» Los Angeles est également un endroit où l'argent parle, et ou l'art n'est guère apprécié. Ceci dit, l'architecture y a connu quelques grandes réussites depuis l'époque de Wright, Neutra et Schindler. On peut compter parmi elles plusieurs immeubles du style Streamline comme le Pan Pacific Auditorium (Los Angeles, Wurdeman et Beckett, 1935), ou l'immeuble d'appartements Shangri-La (Santa Monica, William Foster, 1940). Le développement de la ville a cependant largement débordé les capacités de ses architectes «de qualité» et la situation a empiré avec

Charles and Ray Eames, Case Study House No. 8, Pacific Palisades, 1949. A "live-work" complex which has had considerable international influence.

Charles und Ray Eames, Case Study House Nr. 8, Pacific Palisades, 1949. Ein Arbeits- und Wohn-Komplex von internationaler Bedeutung.

Charles et Ray Eames, Case Study House N° 8, Pacific Palisades, 1949. Une maison pour vivre et travailler, qui a exercé une influence internationale considérable.

Richard Neutra. Reflecting the ad hoc nature of the procedure, the houses were numbered in no particular order. One of the most famous of the projects was Case Study House No. 8 by Charles and Ray Eames, situated in the Pacific Palisades area near a 50-meter cliff overlooking the ocean. Completed in 1949, it is considered one of the seminal California Modern residential complexes, with home and studio connected by a small garden. The house is known for its use of industrial materials such as the corrugated metal roof, covered by insulation board. Many of its components were ordered from parts catalogs, and Eames simplified the original plan by redesigning the home after the parts arrived on the site. The reputation of this house was undoubtedly enhanced by the wide distribution of chairs designed by Eames for Herman Miller, such as the famous Eames Lounge Chair (1956).

Located on a two-hectare plot purchased by the magazine, Case Study House No. 8 is next to House No. 9 designed by Eames with Saarinen for Entenza. This residence projects an even more radical simplicity than its neighbor, a theme which recurs in later program houses such as Case Study Houses No. 21 and No. 22 by Pierre Koenig. The spare lines and relatively empty interiors of these houses show that a Japanese influence continued to play its role in California architecture, as it had already in the Schindler and Chase House. As photographed by Julius Shulman, House No. 22 (Hollywood Hills, 1959), hanging over Los Angeles, is symbolic of the Case Study program's role in drawing attention to quality architecture in a city where indifferent houses were being churned out by the thousands. In Lakewood Park for example, the developer Louis Boyar created a community in 1950 designed for 17 000 houses, and built no fewer than 10 000 in the first two years.

Made up from the first of diverse communities, Los Angeles was and probably always will be the city of the automobile, where architecture usually has more to do with commerce than with any conception of quality. Although they are no longer in fashion, this was the city where restaurants in the shape of dogs, pigs and owls screamed out in the 1950s for attention from the roadside. But a par-

licht wurde. Los Angeles – ursprünglich eine Ansammlung von Kleinstädten, die zum heutigen Stadtgebiet zusammenwuchsen – wurde immer mehr vom Auto abhängig, und die neuen, geschwungenen und erhöhten Freeways schnitten breite Pfade quer durch die City. Riesige Teile der Metropole wurden von diesen Autolawinen vernichtet, und bereits 1942 benutzte man das Wort »Smog« für die kaum mehr zu atmende Luft.

Seit 1911 der erste Film dort gedreht wurde, hat sich Hollywood für die meisten Touristen und sogar für einige Einheimische zum Sinnbild von Los Angeles entwickelt. Im Jahre 1994 verdienten 110 000 Menschen im Großraum Los Angeles ihren Lebensunterhalt in der Film- und Fernsehindustrie. Man kann sagen, daß Oberflächlichkeit einen wesentlichen Bestandteil dieses Ortes ausmacht, den manche als »Tinseltown«, als Glitzerstadt, bezeichnen. Diese Tatsache ist von grundlegender Bedeutung für das Verständnis der Architektur einer Stadt, in der die Unterschiede zwischen Tatsache und Fiktion, Film und Realität immer mehr verwischen. Zu den in dieser Hinsicht prophetischen Produktionen gehört beispielsweise der 1982 von Ridley Scott gedrehte Film »Blade Runner« mit Harrison Ford in der Hauptrolle: Er zeigt ein Los Angeles des Jahres 2093, dessen Himmel dunkel und von saurem Regen verseucht ist. Der Film entstand teilweise im Bradbury Building und sein apokalyptisches Szenario hatte direkten Einfluß auf die Architektur zeitgenössischer Gruppen wie Morphosis. In manchen Fällen ist die Grenze zwischen der realen Stadt und den Filmversionen nur noch schwer zu ziehen. Craig Hodgetts, der zu den phantasievolleren Architekten in Los Angeles gehört, äußerte sich zum Verhältnis der Kreativität Hollywoods und der zeitgenössischen Architektur: »In Los Angeles zählen nicht der Wert der Materialien oder ihr Charakter – Originalität wird hier wesentlich höher angesehen. Geistiges Eigentum besitzt einen hohen Stellenwert, selbst wenn es sich dabei um eine neue Kombination alltäglicher Dinge handelt. Los Angeles ist schließlich dafür berühmt geworden, daß es ein Stück Zelluloid in bare Münze verwandeln kann.«

Los Angeles ist auch ein Ort, an dem das Geld regiert und Kunst wenig geschätzt wird. Dennoch hat die Architek-

l'afflux, pendant la guerre, de travailleurs pour les industries d'armement implantées autour de Los Angeles. C'est dans ce contexte que John Entenza, rédacteur en chef de la revue «Arts & Architecture», organisa en 1943 un concours intitulé «Projets pour la vie après la guerre». Prévoyant le besoin de grands ensembles d'habitation, Entenza et Charles Eames publièrent en 1944 dans la revue un article sur la reconversion de l'industrie militaire au service de la construction de logements. Le programme intitulé Case Study House (littéralement maison «étude de cas») fut annoncé dans le numéro de janvier 1945 d'«Arts & Architecture». De cette date à 1966, un total de 34 projets, qui se voulaient les prototypes d'une architecture moderne en Californie, furent publiés dans la revue, et 23 furent construits. Parmi les huit premiers participants figuraient Eames, Eero Saarinen et Richard Neutra. Le programme était souple, et les maisons furent numérotées un peu au hasard. L'un des projets les plus célèbres reste la Case Study House N° 8 de Charles et Ray Eames, située dans la zone de Pacific Palisades, au bord d'une falaise de cinquante mètres au-dessus de l'océan. Constituée d'une maison et d'un atelier reliés par un petit jardin, et achevée en 1949, elle est considérée comme l'une des réalisations essentielles de l'architecture moderne californienne. Elle est également célèbre pour l'emploi de matériaux industriels comme le toit en tôle ondulée, recouvert de panneaux isolants. Beaucoup de ses éléments furent commandés sur catalogues, et Eames simplifia le plan original en redessinant la maison après leur livraison. La notoriété de cette habitation doit aussi beaucoup à la forte présence des sièges dessinés par Eames pour Herman Miller (dont la fameuse Lounge Chair, 1956). Construite sur un terrain de deux hectares acquis par la revue, la Case Study House N° 8 se trouve non loin de la N° 9, dessinée par Eames et Eero Saarinen pour John Entenza. Elle affiche une simplicité encore plus radicale que sa voisine, thème récurrent des réalisations ultérieures du programme comme les Case Study Houses N° 21 et 22 de Pierre Koenig. Les lignes sobres et les intérieurs relativement vides montrent que l'influence japonaise continuait à exercer un rôle dans l'architecture californienne, comme, déjà, dans la maison

allel universe of expensive private houses in Malibu, Brentwood or the Hollywood Hills also exists where originality and good architecture sometimes meet. John Lautner, whose career spans 55 years, up to his death in 1994, is an example of the type of original architect that this environment has encouraged. Formed by Wright, in a tradition of organic architecture, he went on to build a series of drive-in restaurants that helped shape the face of the emerging car-culture city, but he later did more unexpected work. His Malin Residence (Chemosphere, Hollywood, 1960) a 20 meter octagon perched on a 4 meter concrete column, was a stunning if somewhat eccentric solution to the problem posed by the steep hillsides that are often the sites of private residences in Los Angeles.

Frank O. Gehry in the Cultural Wasteland
Despite California's wealth and willingness to experiment, the arts have been neglected more often than not. The Los Angeles County Museum of Art was founded in 1913 and did receive a major donation from none other than William Randolph Hearst, but only since the institution built its Wilshire Boulevard buildings (W.L. Pereira, 1965) and then renovated and enlarged them (Hardy Holtzman Pfeiffer, 1986), has it been in the same category as major museums of other large American cities. Even more surprising, although Los Angeles benefits today from a Museum of Contemporary Art whose able director Richard Koshalek actively promotes art and architecture in the city, its building, situated on Grand Avenue and designed by Arata Isozaki, was inaugurated only in 1987. Despite the late date of this construction, Isozaki's strong design represents an affirmation of the close connection which now exists between contemporary art and architecture, a connection which Wright had sought to establish long before with the Barnsdall house. It is also significant that an outside architect, in this case Japanese, was called on. Long after the big New York or Boston firms labored to make San Francisco the "Paris of the Pacific," occasional commissions have been given to noted architects from other regions, and these buildings, for example Louis Kahn's moving Jonas Salk Institute (La Jolla, 1959–65), have often had a

tur seit den Zeiten von Wright, Neutra und Schindler einige Höhepunkte erlebt. Dazu gehören in den 30er Jahren im Streamline Style entstandene Bauwerke wie das Pan Pacific Auditorium (Los Angeles, Wurdeman und Becket, 1935) oder die Shangri-La Apartments (Santa Monica, William Foster, 1940). Allerdings übertraf das Wachstum der Stadt bei weitem die Kapazitäten ihrer besten Architekten, und diese Entwicklung verschlimmerte sich noch durch den großen Zustrom von Arbeitskräften für die Kriegs- und Rüstungsindustrie, die rund um Los Angeles angesiedelt wurden. 1943 organisierte John Entenza, der Herausgeber von »Arts & Architecture«, einen Wettbewerb unter dem Titel »Designs for Post-war Living« (Entwürfe für das Leben nach dem Krieg). Da sie das Bedürfnis nach einem Wohnungsbau in großem Maßstab voraussahen, schrieben Entenza und Charles Eames 1944 einen Artikel für das Magazin, in dem sie die Umstellung der industriellen Technologie der Kriegszeit auf die Ansprüche des Hausbaus forderten. Das Programm für das sogenannte »Case Study House« (Fallstudienhaus) wurde 1945 in der Januar-Ausgabe von »Arts & Architecture« vorgestellt. Zwischen dieser Zeit und 1966 veröffentlichte die Zeitschrift insgesamt 34 Entwürfe als Prototypen moderner Architektur in Südkalifornien; 23 von ihnen wurden realisiert. Zu den ursprünglichen acht Teilnehmern an diesem Programm gehörten Eames, Eero Saarinen und Richard Neutra. Aufgrund der ad hoc durchgeführten Vorgehensweise numerierte man die Häuser in unregelmäßiger Reihenfolge. Zu den berühmtesten dieser Projekte gehörte das Case Study House Nr. 8 von Charles und Ray Eames, das im Stadtteil Pacific Palisades an einer 50 m hohen Klippe liegt und einen Ausblick über den Ozean bietet. Das 1949 fertiggestellte Haus zählte zu den zukunftsweisenden Wohnbauten der kalifornischen Moderne, wobei Haus und Atelier durch einen kleinen Garten miteinander verbunden sind. Dieses Haus ist berühmt für die Verwendung industrieller Materialien wie etwa des gewellten Metalldachs, das mit Dämmplatten abgedeckt wurde. Eames orderte einen Großteil der Bauelemente aus der Serienfertigung und überarbeitete seine Baupläne, wenn die Einzelteile am Bauplatz angekommen waren. Die

Schindler and Chase. La Case Study House N° 22 (Hollywood Hills, 1959), photographiée par Julius Shulman comme suspendue au-dessus de Los Angeles, est symbolique du rôle du programme des Case Studies qui était d'attirer l'attention sur la qualité de l'architecture, dans une ville qui produisait par milliers des maisons sans intérêt. A Lakewood Park, par exemple, le promoteur Louis Boyar créa un quartier prévu pour 17 000 maisons individuelles, et en construisit 10 000 au cours des deux premières années. Constituée au départ de communautés qu'il s'agissait de relier, Los Angeles a été et sera probablement toujours une cité de l'automobile, dans laquelle l'architecture obéit davantage au dieu Commerce qu'à la recherche de la qualité. C'est, par exemple la ville où dans les années 50 on construisait des restaurants en forme de chiens, de chouettes ou de porcs pour attirer l'attention des automobilistes. Mais on y trouve également tout un univers parallèle de riches résidences privées à Malibu, Brentwood ou dans les collines d'Hollywood, où architecture et originalité se retrouvent parfois. John Lautner, mort en 1994 et dont la carrière dura 55 ans, est un bon exemple de ces architectes originaux encouragés par la spécificité de l'environnement. Formé par Wright, dans la tradition de l'architecture organique, il construisit une série de restaurants drive-in qui contribuèrent à donner son visage à la culture locale de l'automobile, mais il réalisa aussi plus tard une œuvre surprenante: Malin Residence (Chemosphere, Hollywood, 1960). Il s'agit d'un octogone de 20 m de côté perché sur une colonne de béton de 4 mètres de haut. Il représente une solution surprenante, quoique plutôt excentrique, au problème posé par la forte dénivellation de ces collines qui sont souvent le site des résidences privées de Los Angeles.

Frank O. Gehry dans le désert culturel

En dépit de la richesse ambiante et de l'esprit d'ouverture aux expérimentations, les arts ont souvent été négligés en Californie. Le Los Angeles County Museum of Art a été fondé en 1913, et reçut à l'occasion une importante donation de William Randolph Hearst en personne. Mais ce

powerful influence on the evolution of local design. It should be recalled, by way of contrast, that for all of its more conservative solidity, San Francisco invested much earlier than its southern rival in modern art. The San Francisco Museum of Modern Art, which opened in 1935, gave its first solo exhibitions to Arshile Gorky (1941), Jackson Pollock (1945) and Mark Rothko (1946), and was one of the first American museums to recognize photography as an art form. With permanent holdings of 17 000 modern and contemporary art works, the SFMoMA has the best West Coast collection.

The 1980s with all their prosperity were clearly a time of cultural awakening in Los Angeles, as can be demonstrated in the area of architecture, but for a city with a population of 3.5 million people this would seem to be a case of too little, too late. Frank O. Gehry expresses this situation clearly with respect to his own emergence as an influential architect: "When I began to find my style there simply wasn't much of a support system for anyone trying to do something different . . . Designers were kind of isolated in my day, and I found my community among artists rather than architects. In L.A., I've long been considered strange and odd, a maverick. For years, no big corporation or major developer gave me a commission of any size. Disney Hall, which I won in close competition with James Stirling, Hans Hollein and Gottfried Boehm is the first big thing I've been given to do in my home town. In Los Angeles, despite all its freedom to experiment, the avant-garde remains peripheral to the mainstream of most of what's being built. I think artistic expression is the juice that fuels our collective souls, that innovation and responding to desperate social needs are not exclusive imperatives."

Born in 1929 in Toronto, Frank O. Gehry studied at the University of Southern California, Los Angeles (1949–51) and then at Harvard (1956–57). He created his own firm, Frank O. Gehry and Associates, Inc., in Los Angeles in 1962, but he was not to become well known outside of a relatively small circle until almost 20 years later. The significance of his contribution was recognized when he received the 1989 Pritzker Prize, and in his acceptance speech, he described some of the factors which explain his

Berühmtheit dieses Hauses wurde zweifellos noch verstärkt durch die weite Verbreitung der Stühle, die Eames für Herman Miller entwarf, wie etwa den berühmten Eames Lounge Chair (1956).

Case Study House Nr. 8 entstand auf einem zwei Hektar großen Grundstück, das die Zeitschrift zu diesem Zweck erworben hatte. Direkt daneben liegt das Haus Nr. 9, von Eames und Saarinen für Entenza entworfen. Dieses Wohnhaus ist von einer noch radikaleren Ökonomie als sein Nachbar – eine Schlichtheit, die sich in späteren Häusern des Programms wiederholte, wie etwa bei Case Study House Nr. 21 und Nr. 22, die von Pierre Koenig stammen. Die klare Linienführung und die relativ spärliche Innenausstattung dieser Häuser zeugen von dem ungebrochenen japanischen Einfluß in der Architektur Südkaliforniens, wie er bereits im Falle des Schindler and Chase House zu spüren war. Das von Julius Shulman fotografierte Haus Nr. 22 (Hollywood Hills, 1959), hoch über Los Angeles, kann als Symbol für die Rolle gelten, die das Case Study-Programm bei der Durchsetzung hochwertiger Architektur spielte in einer Stadt, in der wie am Fließband Tausende langweiliger Häuser produziert wurden. In Lakewood Park beispielsweise plante der Bauunternehmer Louis Boyar ab 1950 ein Stadtviertel mit 17 000 Häusern, von denen bereits in den ersten beiden Jahren 10 000 Stück fertiggestellt wurden.

Los Angeles – aus einem Konglomerat unterschiedlicher Gemeinden entstanden – wird wahrscheinlich immer eine Stadt des Automobils bleiben, in der Architektur im allgemeinen mehr mit Kommerz als mit Qualität zu tun hat. Obwohl sie heute etwas aus der Mode gekommen sind, buhlten hier seit den 50er Jahren Restaurants in Form von Hunden, Schweinen und Eulen um die Gunst der vorbeifahrenden Autopassagiere. Aber es existiert auch ein Paralleluniversum aus teuren Privatvillen in Malibu, Brentwood oder den Hollywood Hills. John Lautner, der bei seinem Tode 1994 auf eine 55jährige Berufslaufbahn zurückblicken konnte, ist ein gutes Beispiel für den Typus des innovativen Architekten, der durch eine solche Umgebung stimuliert wird. Von Wright beeinflußt und der Tradition einer organischen Architektur verhaftet, erbaute Lautner eine Reihe von Drive-in-Restaurants, die das Gesicht dieser sich ent-

n'est que depuis qu'il s'est installé dans de nouveaux bâtiments sur Wilshire Boulevard (W.L. Pereira, 1965), et les a rénovés et agrandis en 1986 (Hardy Holtzman Pfeiffer) qu'il peut prétendre faire partie des grands musées américains. Plus surprenant encore est le cas du Museum of Contemporary Art, dirigé par le brillant Richard Koshalek qui fait beaucoup pour l'art et l'architecture de sa ville, mais dont le bâtiment de Grand Avenue n'a été inauguré qu'en 1987. Ses formes franches dues à Arata Isozaki illustrent le rapport étroit qui existe actuellement entre l'art et l'architecture, lien que Wright avait cherché à établir il y a longtemps, dans sa Barnsdall House. Il est également significatif qu'un architecte étranger, en l'occurrence japonais, ait été appelé pour ce projet. Longtemps après que les grandes agences de New York ou de Boston se furent efforcées de faire de San Francisco le «Paris du Pacifique», la Californie du Sud a enfin passé des commandes à des architectes extérieurs célèbres, et leurs réalisations, comme par exemple l'émouvant Jonas Salk Institute de Louis Kahn (La Jolla, 1959–65), ont souvent exercé une puissante influence sur l'évolution architecturale locale. Par contraste, San Francisco, bien que plus conservatrice, a investi beaucoup plus tôt que sa rivale du sud dans l'art moderne. Le San Francisco Museum of Modern Art ouvert en 1935 a monté les premières expositions d'artistes comme Arshile Gorky (1941), Jackson Pollock (1945), et Mark Rothko (1946), et fut l'un des premiers musées américains à reconnaître la photographie comme expression artistique à part entière. Avec plus de 17 000 œuvres modernes et contemporaines, le SFMoMA possède la meilleure collection permanente de la Côte Ouest. La période de prospérité des années 80 a facilité l'éveil culturel de Los Angeles, en particulier architectural, mais pour une ville de 3,5 millions d'habitants, il semble encore que ce soit bien peu et bien tard. Frank O. Gehry explique les problèmes que lui a posés cette situation: «Lorsque j'ai commencé à trouver mon style, il n'y avait tout simplement aucun système capable d'aider quelqu'un qui tentait de faire quelque chose de différent... A mon époque, les architectes étaient un peu isolés, et je me retrouvais le plus souvent en compagnie d'artistes. J'ai longtemps été considéré

Frank O. Gehry, Gehry House, Santa Monica, 1978. In an ordinary residential neighborhood a radical deconstruction of bourgeois architecture.

Frank O. Gehry, Gehry House, Santa Monica, 1978. Die radikale Dekonstruktion bourgeoiser Architektur in einem ganz normalen Wohngebiet.

Frank O. Gehry, Gehry House, Santa Monica, 1978. Dans un quartier résidentiel banal, une déconstruction radicale de l'architecture bourgeoise.

style: "My artist friends, like Jasper Johns, Bob Rauschenberg, Ed Kienholz and Claes Oldenburg, were working with very inexpensive materials – broken wood and paper – and they were making beauty. These were not superficial details, they were direct, and raised the question in my mind of what beauty was. I chose to use the craft available, and to work with craftsmen and make a virtue out of their limitations. Painting had an immediacy that I craved for in architecture. I explored the process of new construction materials to try giving feeling and spirit to form. In trying to find the essence of my own expression, I fantasized that I was an artist standing before a white canvas deciding what the first move should be."

Drawn toward the experimental freedom of artists, Frank O. Gehry installed a 1968 exhibition for his friend the painter Billy Al Bengston at the Los Angeles County Museum of Art using raw plywood, corrugated metal and exposed wooden joists. These were the materials which he was to employ in his first widely published project, his own house in Santa Monica (1978). Situated on 22nd Street, a quiet and not particularly wealthy stretch of private houses, the Gehry residence, originally built in a style described as Dutch Colonial was dramatically transformed by its owner, who added large protruding surfaces of chain-link fence and paved his kitchen with asphalt. Although Gehry has since built in fashionable neighborhoods such as Brentwood, it is significant that this first incursion into the world of bourgeois "good taste" occurred in a very ordinary street, typical of many suburban areas, and distant, at least in style, from the hillsides and beach fronts where previous experimentation in Los Angeles architecture had been concentrated.

The Sky doesn't fall

In the early 1980s, Frank O. Gehry began to mark Los Angeles architecture in a profound way, albeit with relatively small structures. Much of this work was located in the neighboring beach front communities of Santa Monica and Venice, which have since become a fertile ground for other leading designers. The Norton House (1982–84), a three-story residence built on a narrow beach front lot facing the

Frank O Gehry, drawing for the Gehry House, Santa Monica, 1978.

Frank O. Gehry, Entwurfszeichnung zum Gehry House, Santa Monica, 1978.

Frank O. Gehry, dessin de la Gehry House, Santa Monica, 1978.

wickelnden Auto-Kulturmetropole mitformten. In späteren Jahren ging er zu ungewöhnlicheren Projekten über: Seine Malin Residence (Chemosphere, Hollywood, 1960) – ein 20 Meter großes Oktogon, das auf einem 4 Meter dicken Betonpfeiler thronte – war die verblüffende, wenn auch etwas exzentrische Lösung für das Bauen an steilen Abhängen, die in Los Angeles häufig als Baugrund für private Wohnsitze dienen müssen.

Frank O. Gehry im kulturellen Niemandsland

Trotz des Wohlstands und der Bereitschaft zum Experiment blieben die bildenden Künste in Kalifornien lange Jahre unbeachtet. Zwar erhielt das Los Angeles County Museum of Art nach seiner Gründung im Jahre 1913 eine großzügige Spende von niemand Geringerem als William Randolph Hearst, aber erst nachdem Gebäude am Wiltshire Boulevard erbaut (W.L. Pereira, 1965) und später renoviert und erweitert wurden (Hardy Holtzman Pfeiffer, 1986), kann sich diese Institution mit den wichtigsten Museen anderer amerikanischer Städte messen. Und obwohl sich Los Angeles heute eines Museum of Contemporary Art rühmen darf, dessen fähiger Direktor Richard Koshalek als aktiver Förderer der Kunst und der Architektur in der Stadt auftritt, stellt man verblüfft fest, daß dieses von Arata Isozaki entworfene und an der Grand Avenue errichtete Gebäude erst 1987 eröffnet wurde. Isozakis kraftvoller Entwurf stellt eine Bekräftigung der engen Verbindung dar, die zwischen zeitgenössischer Kunst und Architektur besteht – einer Verbindung, die Wright schon vor langen Jahren mit dem Bau des Barnsdall House angestrebt hatte. Es ist bezeichnend, daß für diesen Auftrag ein ortsfremder japanischer Architekt den Zuschlag erhielt. Selbst lange nach den Anstrengungen der großen New Yorker und Bostoner Architekturfirmen, San Francisco zum »Paris am Pazifik« zu machen, wurden vereinzelte Bauaufträge an bekannte Architekten aus anderen Teilen des Landes vergeben, und diese Gebäude, wie etwa Louis Kahns eindringliches Jonas Salk Institute (La Jolla, 1959–65), übten häufig einen starken Einfluß auf die Entwicklungen im Bereich der lokalen Architektur aus.

Im Vergleich dazu sollte daran erinnert werden, daß sich die Stadt San Francisco trotz ihrer konservativen Solidität

à L.A. comme étrange, curieux, non-conformiste. Pendant des années, aucune grande société ou promoteur important ne m'a passé la moindre commande. Le Disney Hall, remporté à la suite d'un concours auquel ont participé James Stirling, Hans Hollein et Gottfried Boehm, est le premier gros chantier que j'ai obtenu dans ma ville; à Los Angeles, malgré la liberté d'expérimentation, l'avant-garde reste à l'écart des grands chantiers. Je pense que l'expression artistique doit nourrir l'âme collective, et que l'innovation et la nécessité de répondre aux besoins sociaux les plus criants ne doivent pas s'exclure.» Né en 1929 à Toronto, Frank O. Gehry a fait ses études à l'University of Southern California, Los Angeles USC (1949–51), puis à Harvard (1956–57). Il crée son propre cabinet Frank O. Gehry and Associates, Inc., à Los Angeles en 1962, mais doit attendre 20 ans avant que sa notoriété ne dépasse un petit cercle de connaisseurs. L'importance de sa contribution est reconnue par l'attribution du Prix Pritzker en 1989. Dans son discours d'acceptation, il décrit ainsi quelques-uns des facteurs qui expliquent son style: «Mes amis artistes, comme Jasper Johns, Bob Rauschenberg, Ed Kienholz et Claes Oldenburg travaillaient avec des matériaux très bon marché – débris de bois, papier – et savaient en tirer de la beauté. Il n'y avait pas de détails superficiels, leur approche était directe, et ils m'amenèrent à me poser la question de la nature de la beauté. Je décidai de me servir de ce qui était disponible, de travailler avec des artisans, et de faire de leurs limites une vertu. J'avais envie de retrouver en architecture le caractère immédiat de la peinture. J'ai recherché de nouveaux matériaux de construction pour essayer de donner plus de sentiment et d'esprit à la forme. En tentant de trouver l'essence de ma propre expression, je m'imaginais en artiste devant une toile blanche, décidant du premier mouvement qu'il va faire.» Ainsi attiré par la liberté expérimentale des artistes, Frank O. Gehry imagina en 1968 la mise en scène d'une exposition pour son ami le peintre Billy Al Bengston, au Los Angeles County Museum of Art. Il se servit de contre-plaqué brut, de tôle ondulée et de grosses poutres. C'étaient les matériaux qu'il allait employer dans son premier projet si souvent publié, la maison qu'il se construisit à Santa Monica (1978). Située 22nd Street, au

Frank O. Gehry, Norton House, Venice, 1982–84. Just off the beach, forms inspired by the nearby lifeguard stations.

Frank O. Gehry, Norton House, Venice, 1982–84. Die nahegelegenen Rettungsschwimmerhäuschen am Strand dienten als Inspirationsquelle für das Design des Hauses.

Frank O. Gehry, Norton House, Venice, 1982–84. Donnant sur la plage, une maison aux formes inspirées par les postes de surveillance des sauveteurs.

Venice boardwalk reflects the chaotic architecture of its environment, and calls on such varied materials as concrete block, glazed tile, stucco and wooden logs. Its most notable feature is a freestanding study modeled on the lifeguard stations which dot the wide beaches of Venice and Santa Monica. Just a few meters from this house, California blondes, roller skaters, muscle builders, homeless people and T-shirt vendors jostle each other for attention, and the extraordinary impassable vista toward the Pacific opens. In this very particular and ephemeral environment, Gehry has created a house which responds in an original way, and breaks the usual molds of contemporary architecture.

Just a few blocks away, Rebecca's – a Mexican restaurant designed by Gehry in 1982–85 – represents another facet of the Southern California lifestyle. An existing building was "very simply renovated or used as found." Concrete floors, brick walls, stainless steel, copper, onyx and rough wooden beams and columns give a lively atmosphere completed by dangling crocodiles, fish lamps and an octopus chandelier designed by the architect and executed by stageset craftsmen. In recent years, restaurants, many of them situated in the Venice/Santa Monica area, have become a privileged form of expression for aspiring architects and designers, and Gehry was one of the leaders of that trend.

On Main Street, which leads from Santa Monica to Venice, there are two larger Gehry buildings. The first of these, the Edgemar Development (1984–88) incorporates part of the reclad facade of an existing dairy, and displays a remarkable variety of materials and forms. Five small structures, with three towers, clad in galvanized metal, gray stucco or chain link mesh form a sculptural ensemble. The connection of Gehry's work to art becomes even more evident in the nearby Chiat/Day-Main Street building (1975–91) where a central part of the facade is formed by an enormous pair of binoculars designed by Gehry's friends Claes Oldenburg and Coosje van Bruggen.

It may be that Frank O. Gehry's own sense of architecture as sculptural form reached its height with the Schnabel House (Brentwood, 1986–89). Copper, lead-coated copper panels or stucco cover a symphony of shapes which make

Frank O. Gehry, California Aerospace Museum, Los Angeles, 1982–84. An F-104 fighter plane hangs from the facade of this theater and museum complex.

Frank O. Gehry, California Aerospace Museum, Los Angeles, 1982–84. Ein F-104 Starfighter hängt an der Fassade dieses Theater- und Museumskomplexes.

Frank O. Gehry, California Aerospace Museum, Los Angeles, 1982–84. Un chasseur F-104 est suspendu en façade de ce complexe réunissant un musée et un auditorium.

wesentlich früher für moderne Kunst begeisterte als ihre weiter südlich gelegene Rivalin. Das 1935 eröffnete San Francisco Museum of Modern Art zeigte die ersten Einzelausstellungen von Arshile Gorky (1941), Jackson Pollock (1945) und Mark Rothko (1946) und gehörte zu den ersten amerikanischen Museen, die die Fotografie als Kunstform anerkannten. Mit einem permanenten Bestand von 17 000 modernen und zeitgenössischen Kunstwerken besitzt das SFMoMA die beste Sammlung an der Westküste.

Die 80er Jahre mit ihrem wirtschaftlichen Aufschwung bedeuteten für Los Angeles auch eine Zeit des kulturellen Erwachens, was sich vor allem im Bereich der Architektur zeigte. Aber für eine Stadt mit einer Bevölkerung von 3,5 Millionen war es zu wenig, und das zu spät. Frank O. Gehry beschrieb diese Situation treffend mit Bezug auf seine eigene Entwicklung: »Als ich meinen Stil zu finden begann, gab es einfach keinerlei Unterstützung für jemanden, der versuchte, etwas anderes zu machen... Zu meiner Zeit arbeitete man als Designer relativ isoliert, und ich fand meine Ansprechpartner eher bei den Künstlern als unter den Architekten. In L.A. galt ich lange als seltsam und verrückt, als Außenseiter. Jahrelang gab mir keine große Firma oder Baugesellschaft einen nennenswerten Auftrag. Die Disney Concert Hall, deren Ausschreibung ich in einem harten Wettbewerb gegen James Stirling, Hans Hollein und Gottfried Boehm gewann, ist der erste große Auftrag, den man mir in meiner Heimatstadt erteilte. In Los Angeles befindet sich die Avantgarde, trotz allem Mut zum Experiment, immer noch an der Peripherie der Architekturströmungen dieser Stadt. Ich bin der Ansicht, daß die künstlerische Ausdruckskraft der Stoff ist, der unsere kollektiven Seelen antreibt, und daß Innovation und ein Eingehen auf dringende soziale Bedürfnisse nicht als einander ausschließende Anforderungen aufgefaßt werden sollten.«

Der 1929 in Toronto geborene Frank O. Gehry gründete 1962 in Los Angeles seine eigene Firma, Frank O. Gehry and Associates, Inc., blieb aber beinahe 20 Jahre lang über einen relativ kleinen Kreis hinaus weitgehend unbekannt. Erst als Gehry 1989 den Pritzker-Preis erhielt, wurde er einem breiteren Publikum bekannt. In seiner Preisrede beschrieb er einige der Faktoren, die seinen Stil erklären:

milieu d'un alignement de maisons individuelles tranquilles et presque modestes, la résidence Gehry, construite à l'origine dans un style qualifié de «colonial hollandais», fut spectaculairement transformée par son propriétaire. Il lui ajouta de vastes protubérances en treillage métallique, et recouvrit d'asphalte le sol de sa cuisine. Bien qu'il ait depuis construit dans des quartiers élégants, comme Brentwood, il est significatif que sa première opération contre le «bon goût» bourgeois se soit faite dans une rue très ordinaire, typique d'innombrables banlieues, et éloignée, du moins dans le style, des collines et des plages sur lesquelles s'étaient concentrées jusqu'alors les expériences de l'architecture angélinienne.

Le ciel ne vous tombera pas sur la tête
C'est à partir du début des années 80, que Gehry commence à marquer profondément l'architecture de Los Angeles, bien qu'à travers des réalisations relativement modestes. L'essentiel de son travail se situe dans deux communes en bordure du Pacifique, Santa Monica et Venice, devenues depuis le terrain d'élection de quelques autres architectes célèbres. La Norton House (1982–84), résidence à trois niveaux construite à Venice sur un étroit terrain en front de mer, fait écho à l'architecture chaotique de son environnement, et se sert de matériaux très variés comme des blocs de béton, des carrelages vernissées, du crépi et des poutres en bois. Son élément le plus remarquable est un petit bureau indépendant qui rappelle les postes de guet des sauveteurs que l'on retrouve tout au long des plages de la région. La pièce bénéficie d'une vue extraordinaire sur le Pacifique et le front de mer où blondes Californiennes, patineurs à roulettes, culturistes, S.D.F. et vendeurs de T-shirts s'efforcent de se faire remarquer. Gehry a créé une maison en phase avec cet environnement éphémère très particulier et a, du même coup, brisé les règles courantes de l'architecture contemporaine. A quelques rues de là, Rebecca's, restaurant mexicain dessiné par Gehry en 1982–85, illustre une autre facette du style de vie californien. Le bâtiment existant a été «très simplement rénové, ou laissé comme tel». Sols en ciment, murs de brique, acier inoxydable, cuivre, onyx, poutres en

Frank O. Gehry, Chiat/Day-Main Street, Venice, 1975–91. The entrance to the garage of this building is below the enormous binoculars designed by Claes Oldenburg and Coosje van Bruggen.

Frank O. Gehry, Chiat/Day-Main Street, Venice, 1975–91. Die Einfahrt zur Garage dieses Gebäudes liegt unterhalb des gewaltigen, von Claes Oldenburg und Coosje van Bruggen entworfenen Fernglases.

Frank O. Gehry, Chiat/Day-Main Street, Venice, 1975–91. L'entrée du garage de cet immeuble de bureaux est située en dessous de ces énormes jumelles dessinées par Claes Oldenburg et Coosje van Bruggen.

up this remarkable house, part of which floats on a small artificial "lake." Far removed in its abrupt angles and compositional complexity from the radical simplicity sought in many of the Case Study Houses, the Schnabel House represents a high point of what a 1988 exhibition organized by Philip Johnson and Mark Wigley at the Museum of Modern Art in New York called "Deconstructivist Architecture." More than a superficial decorative scheme, the Schnabel House signals an effort to break with the Miesian dictum that "Form follows function."

Jealous of the freedom of artists, Gehry took a large step toward liberating architecture from its accepted ideas of the relationships between form, function and materials. This in itself is enough to make him an important figure, but he also has had a tremendous influence on younger designers, not as much through teaching as through a kind of emulation. As Craig Hodgetts has said, "Maybe the high level of Frank O. Gehry's executed work has made people see that the sky doesn't fall."

It is interesting to note, however, that a shift in Gehry's style seems to have occurred when he approached the design of the recently completed American Center in Paris (1988–93). Complex and heavy-handed, the building is clad in Parisian limestone which was the architect's homage to the city's architecture, but critics wondered why he had not chosen to create the sort of whimsical, inventive structure that he became famous for. "You know," says Frank O. Gehry, "this is the first big public building I have built. Maybe people aren't going to like it, and they will say that I do better little buildings. Life is tricky. You can't always win. I just did what I thought I should. I was having a good time. It was just as much struggle and fuss as anything I've done, but I think it is very French and very appropriate."[2] Could it be that California's architecture, like some of its wines, just doesn't travel well? Given the numerous particularities of life in Los Angeles, that might not be a surprising conclusion. Building in an earthquake prone, semi-tropical climate with an extraordinary ethnic diversity may not prepare architects well for Parisian classicism, or indeed for many other locations, but this remains to be more fully proven.

Indeed, the significance of what has happened in Los

»Meine Künstlerfreunde, wie Jasper Johns, Bob Rauschenberg, Ed Kienholz und Claes Oldenburg, arbeiteten mit sehr preiswerten Materialien – zerbrochenem Holz und Papier – und schufen daraus wahre Schönheit. Es gab keine oberflächlichen Details, sie waren direkt, und das brachte mich auf die Frage, was eigentlich Schönheit ausmacht. Ich entschied mich dafür, das zur Verfügung stehenden Handwerk zu benutzen, mit den Handwerkern zu arbeiten und aus ihren Beschränkungen eine Tugend zu machen. Die Malerei besaß eine Unmittelbarkeit, nach der ich mich in der Architektur immer gesehnt hatte. Ich erforschte den Herstellungsprozeß neuer Baumaterialien und bemühte mich, der Form Gefühl und Geist zu verleihen. Ich versuchte, die Essenz meiner eigenen Ausdruckskraft zu finden, indem ich mir vorstellte, ein Künstler zu sein, der vor einer weißen Leinwand steht und sich entscheiden muß, wie der erste Schritt aussehen soll.« Fasziniert von der experimentellen Freiheit der Künstler, schuf Frank O. Gehry 1968 im Los Angeles County Museum of Art eine Ausstellungshängung für seinen Freund, den Maler Billy Al Bengston, für die er nur rohes Sperrholz, Wellblech und freiliegende hölzerne Deckenbalken verwendete. Dies waren auch die Materialien, die er beim Bau seines ersten Projektes einsetzte, das einer größeren Öffentlichkeit bekannt wurde – seinem eigenen Wohnhaus in Santa Monica (1978). Gehrys Haus liegt an der 22nd Street, in einer ruhigen und nicht besonders wohlhabend wirkenden Reihe von Privathäusern. Es war im sogenannten Dutch Colonial Style erbaut worden, aber von seinem heutigen Besitzer von Grund auf umgestaltet: Gehry fügte große, auskragende Drahtgitterflächen hinzu und asphaltierte den Küchenfußboden. Obwohl Gehry inzwischen auch in vornehmen Wohnvierteln wie Brentwood tätig war, ist es bezeichnend, daß dieses erste Eindringen in die Welt des bürgerlichen »guten Geschmacks« in einer durchaus gewöhnlichen Straße stattfand, die als typisch für viele Vororte gelten kann.

Der Himmel stürzt nicht ein
Zu Beginn der 80er Jahre begann Frank O. Gehry, die Architektur von Los Angeles immer stärker zu beeinflussen, wenn auch mit relativ kleinen Projekten. Viele seiner Werke

Frank O. Gehry, Schnabel House, Brentwood, 1986–89. Perhaps the most significant and "sculptural" of Gehry's private houses.

Frank O. Gehry, Schnabel House, Brentwood, 1986–89. Wahrscheinlich das bedeutendste und »skulpturalste« der von Gehry entworfenen Privathäuser.

Frank O. Gehry, Schnabel House, Brentwood, 1986–89. Peut-être l'une des résidences privées les plus importantes et les plus «sculpturales» construites par Gehry.

bois à peine équarri et colonnes créent une atmosphère vivante, agrémentée de crocodiles suspendus, de lampes en forme de poisson, et d'un lustre-pieuvre dessiné par l'architecte et réalisé par des équipes d'artisans du spectacle. Ces dernières années, les restaurants – beaucoup d'entre eux dans le périmètre Santa Monica/Venice – sont devenus l'une des formes d'expression privilégiée des architectes et designers ambitieux, et Gehry s'est imposé comme l'un des représentants les plus éminents de cette tendance. Sur Main Street, qui mène de Santa Monica à Venice, se trouvent deux des plus importantes réalisations de Gehry. La première, Edgemar Development (1984–88), incorpore une partie de la façade d'une laiterie existante, et affiche une étonnante variété de matériaux et de formes. Cinq petites constructions, avec trois tours, un revêtement en métal galvanisé, du plâtre gris et du treillage forment un ensemble sculptural. La proximité entre l'art et l'œuvre de Gehry est encore plus marquée dans l'agence de publicité Chiat/Day (1975–91) sur Main Street, dont la façade est dotée en son centre d'une énorme paire de jumelles imaginée par ses amis, Claes Oldenburg et Coosje van Bruggen. C'est dans la Schnabel House (Brentwood, 1986–89) que l'intérêt de Gehry pour une architecture sculpturale atteint sans doute son sommet. Cuivre, panneaux de cuivre recouverts de plomb et crépi s'harmonisent curieusement dans cette remarquable maison, dont une partie flotte sur un «lac» artificiel. Avec ses angles vifs et sa composition complexe – très éloignée de la simplicité radicale recherchée par les Case Study Houses – la Schnabel House illustre brillamment ce qu'une exposition organisée en 1988 au MoMA de New York par Philip Johnson et Mark Wigley avait appelé «l'architecture déconstructiviste». Plus qu'un propos décoratif superficiel, elle marque un effort de rupture avec le diktat de Mies van de Rohe, «la forme suit la fonction». Séduit par la liberté des artistes, Gehry a aidé l'architecture à se libérer des idées toutes faites sur les rapports entre forme, fonction, et matériaux. Ne serait-ce, qu'à ce titre, il fera date dans l'histoire de l'architecture, et cela d'autant plus qu'il a exercé une formidable influence sur les jeunes architectes, moins par son enseignement que par une sorte d'esprit d'émulation. Comme l'a dit Craig Hod-

Angeles architecture since the early 1980s has only recently been grasped. Other figures than Gehry, who remain less well known, explored the new directions. Brian Murphy used corrugated fiberglass and asphalt shingles on facades more than 15 years ago because they were cheap and unexpected, just as Frederick Fisher made a virtue of employing common bathroom tiles and concrete block. As Joseph Giovannini has written, "unlike New Yorkers, who excavated the architectural past for styles and precedents, the young and irreverent Los Angeles avant-garde looked to movies, sports cars, Nintendo games and the ordinary street-side vernacular for inspiration...The buildings were hardly meant to be timeless. The basic notion was not to remake the city in the image of a utopian ideal, but to take parts of what UCLA classicist and architectural theorist Ann Bergren called 'the most deconstructed city in the world' as cues for buildings that do not add up to balanced wholes. If discontinuity is the urban reality in Los Angeles, then it is realistic to design buildings as pieces."[3]

The SCI-Arc Dynasty
Although USC and UCLA have good architecture programs, one school has stood out over the past years as a crucible for new thinking. The Southern California Institute of Architecture, now located on Beethoven Street near Santa Monica, was founded in 1972 by a group which rejected traditional approaches. Amongst them was of course Frank Gehry, but his influence has given way to that of Michael Rotondi, former partner with Thom Mayne in Morphosis and now principal of RoTo. According to Rotondi, the idea of SCI-Arc is "to produce architects who are truly artists and thus inherently subversive." Amongst the faculty of SCI-Arc, Mayne, Rotondi and Eric Owen Moss stand out as some of the most inventive architects of the post-Gehry generation.

Whereas the quest of Gehry has centered on formal concerns related to materials, color or design, the SCI-Arc builders have gone further in thinking out the reasons for the existence of new architectural directions. The critic Charles Jencks has written this summary of their view: "Dead Tech, that is, High-Tech after the Bomb, or ecolo-

befinden sich in den Strandgemeinden Santa Monica und Venice, die seitdem zu einem fruchtbaren Boden für andere führende Designer wurden. Das Norton House (1982–84), dreigeschossig, auf einem schmalen Gelände am Strand von Venice, reflektiert die chaotische Architektur der Umgebung und entstand aus solch unterschiedlichen Materialien wie Betonblöcken, glasierten Fliesen, Putz und Holzbalken. Das auffälligste Kennzeichen des Hauses ist jedoch ein freistehendes Arbeitszimmer, das an die Rettungsschwimmerhäuschen erinnert, die die weiten Strände von Venice und Santa Monica zieren.

Nur wenige Häuserblöcke entfernt repräsentiert Rebecca's, ein von Gehry 1982–85 entworfenes mexikanisches Restaurant, eine andere Facette des südkalifornischen Lifestyle. Das bereits vorhandene Gebäude wurde »nur minimal renoviert oder wie vorgefunden verwendet«. Betondecken, Ziegelsteinmauern, Edelstahl, Kupfer, Onyx sowie schwere Holzbalken und -träger zaubern eine eigene Atmosphäre, die von der Decke herabhängende Krokodile, fischähnliche Lampen und ein vom Architekten entworfener (und von Bühnenbildnern angefertigter) Kronleuchter in Form eines Kraken abrunden. In den vergangenen Jahren entwickelten sich gerade Restaurants, insbesondere im Bereich von Venice/Santa Monica zu einer bevorzugten Ausdrucksform aufstrebender Architekten und Designer – ein Trend, den Gehry an vorderster Front anführte.

Auf der Main Street, die von Santa Monica nach Venice führt, befinden sich zwei größere Bauwerke Gehrys. Das Edgemar Development (1984–88) umfaßt einen Teil der neuverkleideten Fassade einer bereits existierenden Molkerei und zeigt eine beachtliche Material- und Formenvielfalt. Fünf kleine Gebäude mit drei Türmen, die mit Zinkblech, grauem Putz oder Drahtgittern verkleidet sind, bilden eine skulpturale Einheit. Beim nahegelegenen Chiat/Day-Main Street Building (1975–91) wird Gehrys Bezug zur Kunst noch deutlicher: Ein von Gehrys Freunden Claes Oldenburg und Coosje van Bruggen entworfenes, riesiges Fernglas beherrscht die Fassade.

Möglicherweise erreichte Frank O. Gehrys Verständnis der Architektur als skulpturale Form ihren Höhepunkt mit dem Schnabel House (Brentwood 1986–89). Kupfer, mit

Left and below: Frank O. Gehry, American Center, Paris, France, 1988–93. A large, almost ungainly building clad with local limestone.

Links und unten: Frank O. Gehry, American Center, Paris, Frankreich, 1988–93. Ein großes, fast plumpes Gebäude mit einer Verkleidung aus Kalkstein.

A gauche et ci-dessous: Frank O. Gehry, American Center, Paris, France, 1988–93. Un vaste bâtiment, presque laid, recouvert de pierre calcaire.

getts: «Le haut niveau de qualité de l'œuvre de Frank Gehry a peut-être fait comprendre à beaucoup que le ciel n'allait pas leur tomber sur la tête». Le projet pour l'American Center à Paris, récemment achevé (1988–93), semble indiquer une intéressante évolution du style de Gehry. Complexe et plutôt lourd, le bâtiment est plaqué de pierre calcaire en hommage à la capitale. Beaucoup de critiques se sont demandés pour quelle raison Gehry avait ainsi renoncé au type de réalisations inventives et baroques qui l'avaient rendu célèbre. «Vous savez», répond-il, «c'est le premier bâtiment pour le grand public que je construis. Les gens ne vont peut-être pas l'aimer, et diront que je réussis mieux les petites constructions. La vie est pleine de pièges. On ne peut pas toujours gagner. J'ai juste fait ce que je pensais devoir faire. Je me suis bien amusé. Il y a eu autant de bagarres et d'histoires ici que pour tout ce que j'ai fait jusqu'à présent, mais je pense que c'est très français et très bien adapté au problème.»[2] L'architecture de Californie, comme certains de ses vins, voyagerait-elle mal? Etant données les nombreuses particularités de la vie à Los Angeles, cela n'aurait rien de surprenant. Construire dans une zone sismique, sous un climat semi-tropical, et dans le cadre d'une extraordinaire diversité ethnique n'est peut-être pas la meilleure préparation au classicisme parisien (entre autres), mais ceci reste encore à prouver. En fait, la signification de ce qui s'est produit dans l'architecture angélinienne depuis le début des années 80 n'a été saisie que très récemment. D'autres architectes moins connus que Gehry ont exploré ces mêmes nouvelles directions. Brian Murphy revêtait déjà ses façades de panneaux de fibre de verre ondulés et de carreaux d'asphalte, il y a plus de quinze ans, parce que ces matériaux étaient bon marché et inattendus; de même, Frederick Fisher mettait un point d'honneur à utiliser des carrelages de salle de bain ordinaires et des parpaings. Comme l'a écrit Joseph Giovannini: «A la différence des New-Yorkais qui explorèrent le passé de l'architecture pour y trouver à la fois des styles et des modèles, la jeune et irrévérencieuse avant-garde de Los Angeles a plutôt recherché son inspiration dans les films, les voitures de sport, les jeux Nintendo, et l'environnement quotidien de la rue... Ses constructions ne se voulaient cer-

Pages 40/41: Morphosis, Kate Mantilini Restaurant, Beverly Hills, 1986. "Dead Tech" chic on Wilshire Boulevard.

Seite 40/41: Morphosis, Kate Mantilini Restaurant, Beverley Hills, 1986. »Dead Tech« Chic auf dem Wilshire Boulevard.

Pages 40/41: Morphosis, Kate Mantilini Restaurant, Beverly Hills, 1986. «Dead Tech» chic sur Wilshire Boulevard.

gical catastrophe, signified a new, sophisticated attitude towards modernism coming out of SCI-Arc, the avant-garde school of architecture that Mayne's partner Michael Rotondi took over in the 1980s. Whereas modernists had a faith in industrial progress, signified by the white sobriety of the International Style, the post-modernists of SCI-Arc had a bitter-sweet attitude towards technology. They knew it brought pollution, knew that progress in one place was paid for by regress in another, but nevertheless still loved industrial culture enough to remain committed to the modernist impulse of dramatizing technology."[4]

Formed in 1979 by Mayne and Rotondi, Morphosis has been one of the most influential California architectural practices, again, usually through small-scale projects like their 72 Market Street restaurant (Venice, 1982–85), or the more visible Kate Mantilini restaurant on Wilshire Boulevard in Beverly Hills, whose interior design revolves around a curious sculptural steel object. Mayne calls this sculpture a "useless object" and declares "our interest had nothing to do with the restaurant function, but rather with creating a public space which would reverberate, between the individual and the automobile." Intensely intellectual, with a meandering style of expression, Thom Mayne explains his approach to architecture: "The business of architecture serves clients. You go out there and you find out what clients need today – what are they interested in today. Real architecture is the antithesis of that. Your interests are more private and personal over an extended period of time and require an independence which is akin to leadership. It is up to you to define the issues. I am not interested in fashion or even in the look of the work. I am interested in starting ideas that take you someplace, and in the process, in the methodological process. You have to build to get feedback. Some people start with the visual or physiognomic characteristics. They work towards manifesting that vision. I don't work that way. I work with concepts that build to something. I don't know where I am going. Materials are chosen very late. It has to do with lines and directions and forces which have nothing to do with appearance. It is not easy to deal with clients because most of them are not at all interested in the investigation. The solution is a

Blei ummantelte Kupferplatten und Putz bedecken eine Symphonie der Formen, die teilweise auf einem kleinen künstlichen »See« schwimmt. Mit ihren abrupten Winkeln und der kompositorischen Komplexität weit entfernt von der radikalen Schlichtheit, die viele der Case Study Houses auszeichnet, repräsentiert das Schnabel House den Höhepunkt dessen, was während einer von Philip Johnson und Mark Wigley 1988 organisierten Ausstellung im Museum of Modern Art in New York als »dekonstruktivistische Architektur« beschrieben wurde. Über das äußerliche dekorative Schema hinausgehend signalisiert das Schnabel House den Bruch mit Mies van der Rohes Maxime »Die Form folgt der Funktion«.

Eifersüchtig auf die Freiheit der Künstler, unternahm Gehry einen großen Schritt zur Befreiung der Architektur von ihren anerkannten Vorstellungen in bezug auf das Verhältnis zwischen Form, Funktion und Material. Gehry hat auch einen enormen Einfluß auf jüngere Designer. Dieser Einfluß kam weniger durch seine Lehren zustande als vielmehr durch den Effekt des Nacheiferns – oder wie Craig Hodgetts es formulierte: »Vielleicht hat das hohe Niveau von Frank O. Gehrys verwirklichten Arbeiten anderen Menschen gezeigt, daß der Himmel nicht einstürzt.«

Interessanterweise scheint sich Gehrys Stil verändert zu haben, als er sich mit dem Entwurf für das kürzlich fertiggestellte American Center in Paris (1988–93) beschäftigte. Das komplexe, massive Gebäude ist mit Kalkstein verkleidet – eine Hommage des Architekten an die Architektur der Stadt. Allerdings fragten sich einige Kritiker, warum er sich nicht für die Art eigenwilliger, erfindungsreicher Konstruktion entschieden hatte, für die er berühmt geworden ist. Gehry antwortete darauf: »Dies war mein erster Auftrag für ein großes, öffentliches Gebäude. Vielleicht werden die Leute es nicht mögen und sagen, daß ich kleinere Bauten besser beherrsche. Aber das Leben ist nicht immer einfach. Man kann nicht immer gewinnen. Ich habe das getan, was ich dachte, tun zu müssen, und habe mich dabei wohlgefühlt. Es war nicht mehr und nicht weniger kompliziert und chaotisch als bei allen meinen Bauten, aber ich halte das Gebäude für sehr französisch und durchaus passend.«[2] Wäre es denkbar, daß sich kalifornische Architektur, nicht

tainement pas éternelles. L'idée n'était pas de refaire la ville selon un schéma utopique idéal, mais d'utiliser des éléments de ce que la théoricienne de l'architecture Ann Bergren appelait 'la ville la plus déconstruite du monde', comme des répliques à des constructions qui n'ont pas à s'intégrer dans un ensemble équilibré. Si la discontinuité est la réalité urbaine de Los Angeles, alors il est réaliste de concevoir le bâti comme un agrégat de pièces disparates.»[3]

La dynastie SCI-Arc

Bien que les universités d'USC et UCLA possèdent de bons programmes d'enseignement de l'architecture, c'est une autre école, qui, depuis quelques années, représente le creuset de la nouvelle pensée: le Southern California Institute of Architecture (SCI-Arc), installé dans Beethoven Street près de Santa Monica. Il a été fondé en 1972 par un groupe qui rejetait les approches traditionnelles. Parmi ses membres se trouvait bien sûr Frank O. Gehry, mais son influence a été supplantée par celle de Michael Rotondi, ancien associé de Thom Mayne dans Morphosis, et actuellement responsable de RoTo. Selon Rotondi, l'idée de SCI-Arc est «de former des architectes qui soient des artistes authentiques et donc subversifs». Enseignants à SCI-Arc, Mayne, Rotondi et Eric Owen Moss figurent parmi les architectes les plus inventifs de la génération de l'après-Gehry. Alors que la recherche de celui-ci se centrait sur des préoccupations formelles liées aux matériaux, aux couleurs et au dessin, les architectes du SCI-Arc sont allés plus loin, et ont réfléchi aux raisons mêmes de l'existence de nouvelles tendances architecturales. Le critique Charles Jencks a résumé ainsi leur position: «Le Dead Tech, c'est-à-dire le high-tech d'après la Bombe ou la catastrophe écologique, exprimait les positions – nouvelles et sophistiquées par rapport au modernisme – de SCI-Arc, l'école d'architecture d'avant-garde dont Michael Rotondi, l'associé de Mayne, prit la tête dans les années 80. Alors que les modernistes restaient confiants dans le progrès industriel, exprimé par la sobriété épurée du style international, les post-modernistes de SCI-Arc éprouvaient des sentiments beaucoup plus mêlés face à la technologie. Ils savaient qu'elle apportait la pollution, savaient que le progrès dans une direction était

RoTo Architects, Qwfk House (model), New Jersey, 1989–95. An extremely complex design which continued to evolve during construction.

RoTo Architects, Qwfk House (Modell), New Jersey, 1989–95. Ein extrem komplexes Design, das während der Bauarbeiten weiterentwickelt wurde.

RoTo Architects, Qwfk House (maquette), New Jersey, 1989–95. Un plan d'une extrême complexité qui a continué à évoluer pendant la construction.

process of getting to a further or deeper analysis of the problem. People react to architecture in stylistic terms, but making architecture has to do with the invention of something that contains its own power and beauty – its own authenticity. Laying a few things on top of each other isn't enough. Out of that has to come some sort of invention. The process of actually making follows the invention. It is that first part which is more difficult. I start with complete blackness."[5]

Michael Rotondi certainly shares his former partner's obsession with "the poetics of making," with an architecture which evolves in patterns related to the uncertainties of contemporary life. Perhaps taking a cue from Gehry's improvisational approach, Rotondi has gone even further, modifying working drawings for a house he is building on a daily basis. As he said: "The objective was to produce a project over a long period of time like a city develops – starting, stopping, remembering and forgetting ..."

A third SCI-Arc faculty member of interest is Eric Owen Moss. Born in Los Angeles in 1943, educated at UCLA, he opened his own office in Culver City in 1976, and a peculiarity of his work is that most of it is situated in that area of the city. Through his affiliation with a developer based in Culver City, located mid-way between downtown Los Angeles and Santa Monica, Moss has had the opportunity to build complexes that incrementally connect together, such as the Paramount Laundry-Lindblade Tower-Gary Group Complex, completed between 1987 and 1990. More recent rehabilitation of these large warehouse-type structures originally built for the movie industry include The Box and IRS buildings, located nearby. Making very inventive use of common materials such as sewer pipes serving as columns or bolts bent in a U shape to form florescent light fixtures, Moss has managed to create an impetus for forward-looking advertising or recording companies to install themselves in an area which was all but abandoned a few years ago. The architect Philip Johnson has dubbed him "the jeweler of junk." Like Mayne, Moss projects an intensely intellectual approach to his designs, relating them to his understanding of the state of the world in an interesting manner. As Moss says, "T.S. Eliot wrote about 'the still

gut transportieren läßt? Die Bautätigkeit in einem erdbebengefährdeten Gebiet mit mediterranem Klima und einer außerordentlichen ethnischen Vielfalt bereitet die Architekten anscheinend nicht gerade auf den Pariser Klassizismus oder auch auf viele andere Orte vor.

Tatsächlich hat man die Bedeutung der Veränderungen in der Architektur Los Angeles' zu Beginn der 80er Jahre erst vor kurzem erkannt. Neben Gehry beschritten auch weniger bekannte Architekten neue Wege. Brian Murphy verwendete bereits vor 15 Jahren Fiberglaswellplatten und Asphaltziegel für seine Fassaden, da es sich dabei um preiswerte und unerwartete Materialien handelte, und Frederick Fisher machte aus der Verwendung von herkömmlichen Badezimmerfliesen und Betonblöcken eine Tugend. Joseph Giovannini beschrieb dieses Phänomen so: »Im Gegensatz zu den New Yorker Architekten, die architektonische Stilrichtungen und Vorlieben aus längst vergangenen Zeiten ausgruben, ließen sich die jungen, respektlosen Avantgarde-Architekten aus Los Angeles von Filmen, Sportwagen, Nintendo-Spielen und dem ganz alltäglichen Straßenbild inspirieren... Ihre Gebäude waren keineswegs für die Ewigkeit gebaut. Es ging ihnen nicht darum, das Bild Los Angeles' im Sinne eines utopischen Ideals zu verändern, sondern bestimmte Teile einer Stadt zu nehmen, die die UCLA-Architekturtheoretikerin Ann Bergren als 'die de-konstruierteste Stadt der Welt' bezeichnete, und diese Teile als Anhaltspunkte für Gebäude zu verwenden, die sich nicht zu einem ausgewogenen Ganzen zusammenfügen lassen. Wenn in Los Angeles Zusammenhangslosigkeit die urbane Wirklichkeit darstellt, dann ist es nur realistisch, Gebäude als Teile zu entwerfen.«[3]

Die SCI-Arc Dynastie
Obwohl die USC und die UCLA gute Architekturbereiche besitzen, hat sich in den vergangenen Jahre eine andere Schule als Schmelztiegel einer neuen Denkweise hervorgetan: das Southern California Institute of Architecture, Sci-Arc, das sich heute an der Beethoven Street in der Nähe von Santa Monica befindet, wurde 1972 von einer Gruppe von Architekten gegründet, die traditionelle Ansätze ablehnten. Darunter befand sich natürlich auch Frank O. Gehry,

payé par des reculs dans d'autres, mais étaient encore suffisamment attachés à la culture industrielle pour rester sensibles à l'impulsion moderniste du spectacle de la technologie.»[4] Créé en 1979 par Mayne et Rotondi, Morphosis a été l'une des agences d'architecture les plus influentes de Californie, mais là encore, la plupart du temps à travers des projets à petite échelle, comme le restaurant du 72 Market Street (Venice, 1982–85), ou le très remarqué Kate Mantilini Restaurant, de Wilshire Boulevard (Beverly Hills) dont l'architecture intérieure s'organise autour d'une curieuse sculpture-objet en acier. Mayne parle d'elle comme d'un objet «sans utilité» et déclare: «Nous ne nous intéressons pas à la fonction restaurant, mais plutôt à la création d'un espace public qui renverrait des échos entre l'individu et l'automobile.» Intensément intellectuel, passant facilement d'un sujet à un autre, Thom Mayne explique ainsi son approche de l'architecture: «L'architecture commerciale sert des clients. On va chercher ce dont les clients ont besoin aujourd'hui, ce qui les intéresse aujourd'hui. Selon moi, la véritable architecture est l'antithèse de tout cela. Sur le long terme, vos intérêts sont plus personnels et demandent une indépendance de pensée qui vous donne l'autorité de choisir. C'est à vous, en tant qu'architecte, qu'il revient de définir les enjeux. Je ne m'intéresse pas à la mode ou même à ce à quoi ressemble l'œuvre. Ce qui m'intéresse, c'est de lancer des idées qui conduisent quelque part, et, ce faisant, à des processus méthodologiques. Il faut construire pour recevoir un feedback, un retour. Certains commencent par les caractéristiques visuelles ou physionomiques de l'architecture. Ils travaillent pour donner forme à cette vision. Ce n'est pas mon cas. Je travaille avec des concepts qui mènent à la construction de quelque chose. Je ne sais pas où je vais. Les matériaux sont choisis très tard. C'est une démarche en relation avec des lignes, des directions et des forces qui n'ont pas de rapport avec l'apparence. Il n'est pas facile d'avoir une relation avec des clients parce que la plupart d'entre eux ne sont pas du tout intéressés par les recherches. La solution est dans un processus qui permet d'aller plus loin ou plus profond dans l'analyse. Les gens réagissent à l'architecture en termes stylistiques, mais l'architecture consiste à inven-

point of the turning world.' Lao Tse wrote about 'the square with no corners.' You can't have a square with no corners, can you? If a building represents fixity, then it represents a particular condition or an understanding at a particular point in time. But if the architecture itself could include oppositions, so that the building itself as an aspiration was about movement or the movement of ideas, then it might be more durable. It would embody something that would move notwithstanding the fact that it represents something which physiologically is fixed."[6] This theoretical stance is given form in an architecture which conserves reminiscences of its own design process (Lawson-Westen House, Los Angeles, 1993). Morphosis has engaged in its own exploration of the "archeology" of the present in projects like the Crawford House (Montecito, 1987–92), whose plan seems to be inscribed in a partially buried circle, a relic of some past or future civilization, like that portrayed in the movie "Blade Runner."

Stranger than Paradise

No fewer than 22 million tourists came to L.A. in 1994. Four of America's top ten leisure attractions are located in the Los Angeles basin. This is certainly one of the reasons that if greater Los Angeles were a country, its $ 380 billion of purchasing power would make it a bigger economy than South Korea.[7] More than an economic factor, the movie industry is symbolic of the city itself, and of the ways in which its influence reaches out across the world. For some Angelenos, it is simply referred to as "The Industry." Los Angeles architecture could not help but take this into account. Despite his cerebral approach, Thom Mayne for one defines his work by making reference to film, albeit of the more intellectual variety: "Jim Jarmusch made the film 'Stranger than Paradise,' from nothing. Today, buildings are as ephemeral as film. The most solid aspect of my work is what has been published. The buildings are gone in ten years. Buildings are not that permanent anymore. There has got to be room in architecture for the Jim Jarmusches, not just the Spielbergs."[8] As Joseph Giovannini writes, "From the 1960s on, painting came out of the frame and sculpture off the pedestal, eventually migrating into the

dessen Einfluß den Weg für Michael Rotondi bereitete, dem ehemaligen Partner von Thom Mayne bei Morphosis und heutigem Leiter von RoTo. Nach Rotondi bestand die Idee von Sci-Arc darin, »Architekten hervorzubringen, die wahre Künstler sind und daher inhärent subversiv.« Unter den Talenten von Sci-Arc gehören Mayne, Rotondi und Eric Owen Moss zu den erfindungsreichsten Architekten der Generation nach Gehry.

Während sich Gehrys Streben auf formale Belange bezüglich Material, Farbe oder Design konzentrierten, gingen die SCI-Arc-Architekten einen Schritt weiter und versuchten, Gründe für die Existenz neuer architektonischer Richtungen zu erforschen. Der Kritiker Charles Jencks faßte ihre Thesen so zusammen: »Tote Technik, d.h. High-Tech nach der Bombe oder ökologischen Katastrophe, kündigte eine neue intellektuelle Haltung zum Modernismus an, die aus der Schmiede von SCI-Arc stammte, der avantgardistischen Architekturschule, die Maynes Partner Michael Rotondi in den 80er Jahren übernommen hatte. Während die Modernisten auf den technischen Fortschritt vertrauten, was sich im nüchternen Weiß des International Style äußerte, vertraten die Postmodernisten von SCI-Arc eine bittersüße Einstellung gegenüber der Technologie. Sie wußten, daß die Technologie zur Umweltverschmutzung führte, und daß Fortschritt in einem Bereich mit rückläufiger Entwicklung in einem anderen Bereich bezahlt wird. Dennoch hingen sie so sehr an der industriell geprägten Kultur, daß sie sich dem modernistischen Impuls zur Dramatisierung von Technologie weiterhin verpflichtet fühlten.«[4]

Das 1979 von Mayne und Rotondi gegründete Architekturbüro Morphosis zählte zu den einflußreichsten Kaliforniens, auch hier wieder aufgrund kleinerer Projekte wie das 72 Market Street Restaurant (Venice, 1982–85) oder das bekanntere Kate Mantilini Restaurant am Wilshire Boulevard in Beverly Hills, dessen Innenausstattung rund um eine seltsame Stahlskulptur konzipiert wurde. Mayne nennt diese Skulptur ein »nutzloses Objekt« und verkündet: »Unser Interesse galt nicht der Gestaltung eines Restaurants, sondern der Schaffung eines öffentlichen Raumes, in dem eine Wechselwirkung zwischen Individuum und Automobil stattfindet.« Thom Mayne erklärt seine Einstellung

ter quelque chose qui contient sa propre force, sa propre beauté, sa propre authenticité. Additionner quelques trucs les uns au-dessus des autres ne suffit pas. Une certaine invention doit ressortir de tout cela. Le processus de la mise en œuvre suit l'invention. Cette première partie est la plus difficile. Je commence dans le noir total.»[5] Michael Rotondi partage certainement l'obsession de son ancien associé pour «la poétique de la mise en œuvre». Son architecture se développe à partir de maquettes complexes qui ne sont pas sans rapport conceptuel avec les incertitudes de la vie contemporaine. S'inspirant peut-être de l'approche improvisatrice de Gehry, Rotondi est encore allé plus loin, modifiant, par exemple, chaque jour les plans d'une maison en cours de construction: «L'objectif était de produire un projet sur une période de temps étalée, de même qu'une ville se développe...» commencer, s'arrêter, se souvenir, oublier...„ Troisième célébrité du groupe SCI-Arc, Eric Owen Moss naît à Los Angeles en 1943, étudie à UCLA et, en 1976, ouvre son agence à Culver City où se trouve l'essentiel de ses réalisations. Grâce à des accords avec un promoteur de Culver City (à mi-chemin entre le centre de L.A. et Santa Monica), il a eu l'opportunité de rénover divers bâtiments qui, peu à peu, ont constitué un ensemble, comme le Paramount Laundry-Lindblade Tower-Gary Group Complex (1987–90). Il a également réhabilité de vastes entrepôts, conçus à l'origine pour l'industrie du cinéma, dont les bâtiments The Box et IRS, situés non loin, sur National Boulevard. Il utilise avec beaucoup d'inventivité des matériaux courants, comme des tuyaux d'égouts qui lui servent de colonnes, ou des boulons mis en U pour créer des luminaires au néon. Moss a réussi à donner envie à des sociétés de disques ou des agences de publicité de s'installer dans un quartier encore pratiquement abandonné il y a peu. L'architecte Philip Johnson l'a surnommé «le joaillier de la ferraille». Comme Mayne, Moss pratique une approche très intellectualisée, qu'il relie à son analyse de l'état du monde. Comme il le déclare: «T.S. Eliot a parlé 'du point fixe au monde changeant', Lao-tseu 'du carré sans coins'. Peut-on avoir un carré sans coin? Si un bâtiment représente la fixité, alors il représente une situation ou une analyse particulière à une époque donnée. Mais si l'archi-

Franklin Israel, Art Pavilion, Beverly Hills, 1991. Designed to exhibit a substantial art collection, a form inspired by a great ark.

Franklin Israel, Art Pavilion, Beverly Hills, 1991. Eine große Arche war die Inspirationsquelle für dieses Gebäude, das als Ausstellungsfläche für eine umfangreiche Kunstsammlung konzipiert wurde.

Franklin Israel, Art Pavilion, Beverly Hills, 1991. Forme inspirée par une grande arche pour abriter une importante collection d'œuvres d'art.

open landscape. Architects in Los Angeles were designing buildings that could be interpreted as site-specific urban sculpture. A small, but slowly widening circle of architects was practicing in the fertile blur between architecture and the arts, generating nonconformist buildings that defied the laws of featureless design blended into common denominators. For some, the blur extended to movies. 'The ice-breaker is somewhere in the entertainment industry – more than architectural theorists and historians,' Craig Hodgetts says, citing the powerful production designs for MTV, which established a precedent for stimulating design. Visual futurist Syd Mead, who created the look of 'Blade Runner,' devised intergalactic megastructures, far more powerful than walk-through sets because of their overwhelming scale."[9]

Beyond simply making reference to film in a theoretical sense, Franklin Israel, who was born in New York in 1945, and came to California to teach, actually worked in 1978 and 1979 as an art director for Paramount Films. As he said, "I arrived in Los Angeles in 1977, eager to reach a synthesis between my architectural education and the cinematic intrigues of Hollywood." Working subsequently for film industry clients like the director Robert Altman, Israel applied his knowledge of film, designing a studio for Propaganda Films, Bright and Associates with a sequence of spaces which he likens to the "sequential reality" of movies. Although his work has now evolved to a more complex approach, Israel's avowed affinity for film reveals his opinion that the very particular circumstances of architecture in Southern California can lead to interesting new solutions. Not only movies, but the very fact that the earth can tremble at any moment in this area lead to a need to deal with rapidly evolving situations, and as Franklin Israel says, "what one can learn from practicing in Los Angeles may contribute greatly to an understanding of how to build in any dynamic environment today."

The Shining City
Not everyone is of like mind about the beneficial impact of the heterogeneous Los Angeles environment on contemporary architecture. Richard Meier, for one, who was

Franklin Israel, Fine Arts Building, University of California, Riverside (model), 1994. A large-scale project for one of the more promising young California architects.

Franklin Israel, Fine Arts Building, University of California, Riverside (Modell), 1994. Ein Großprojekt für einen vielversprechenden jungen kalifornischen Architekten.

Franklin Israel, Fine Arts Building, University of California, Riverside (maquette), 1994. Projet à grande échelle de l'un des plus prometteurs des jeunes architectes californiens.

zur Architektur auf seine sehr intellektuelle und zugleich verschlungene Ausdrucksweise: »Das Geschäft der Architektur besteht darin, Kunden zu bedienen. Man geht hinaus, um herauszufinden, was die Kunden heute benötigen – wofür sie sich heutzutage interessieren. Wahre Architektur ist das genaue Gegenteil davon. Hierbei handelt es sich um ein eher privates und persönliches Interesse, das über einen längeren Zeitraum andauert und eine Unabhängigkeit erfordert, die an Führerschaft grenzt. Die Themen kann jeder selbst bestimmen. Ich interessiere mich nicht für Modeerscheinungen und das Erscheinungsbild der Arbeit. Ich interessiere mich dafür, Ideen anzuregen, die uns weiterbringen, und für den Vorgang, den methodischen Vorgang. Man muß bauen, um eine Rückmeldung zu erhalten. Manche beginnen mit den sichtbaren oder äußeren Charakteristika. Sie arbeiten daran, diese Vision zu manifestieren. Aber das ist nicht meine Vorgehensweise. Ich arbeite mit Konzepten, die sich zu irgendetwas zusammenfügen, wobei ich nicht weiß, in welche Richtung es gehen wird. Die Materialien wähle ich erst sehr spät aus. Es geht um Linien und Ausrichtungen und Kräfte, die nichts mit dem äußeren Erscheinungsbild zu tun haben. Der Umgang mit den Kunden ist nicht immer leicht, da die meisten nicht an einer solchen Erkundung interessiert sind. Die Lösung besteht darin, das Problem in einem fortlaufenden Prozeß immer genauer oder tiefer zu analysieren. Viele Menschen reagieren auf Architektur in stilistischen Begriffen, aber das Schaffen von Architektur handelt von der Erfindung eines Objektes, das seine eigene Kraft und Schönheit besitzt – seine eigene Authentizität. Es reicht nicht, einfach irgendwelche Dinge übereinanderzustapeln; statt dessen muß sich daraus eine Art Erfindungsgabe entwickeln. Der Prozeß des tatsächlichen Bauens folgt der Erfindung. Und dieser Teil ist erheblich schwieriger. Ich beginne mit einer völligen Leere.«[5]

Rotondi teilt die Begeisterung seines ehemaligen Partners für »die Poesie des Schaffens« und bringt sie in einer Architektur aus Mustern zum Ausdruck, welche mit der Ungewißheit des heutigen Lebens zusammenhängen. Möglicherweise ausgehend von Gehrys improvisatorischem Ansatz ging Rotondi noch einen Schritt weiter, indem er die

tecture elle-même pouvait intégrer des oppositions, de telle façon que le bâtiment lui-même, en tant qu'aspiration, intègre le mouvement ou le mouvement des idées, il pourrait alors devenir plus durable. Il représenterait quelque chose qui bouge, et cela malgré son immobilité physique.»[6] Cette position théorique génère une architecture qui conserve les traces de son processus de création (Lawson-Westen House, Los Angeles, 1993). Morphosis s'est lancé dans sa propre exploration de «l'archéologie» du présent dans des projets comme la Crawford House (Montecito, 1987–92), dont le plan s'inscrit dans un cercle en partie enterré, relique de quelque civilisation future ou passée, comme celle de «Blade Runner».

Stranger than Paradise
Quelque 22 millions de touristes ont visité L.A. en 1994. Quatre des principales attractions américaines de loisirs sont situées dans le bassin de Los Angeles. C'est l'une des raisons pour lesquelles le Grand Los Angeles, s'il était indépendant, représenterait, avec ses 380 milliards de $ de pouvoir d'achat, une économie plus puissante que la Corée du Sud tout entière.[7] Plus qu'une simple branche économique, l'industrie du cinéma est le symbole même de cette ville et l'un des vecteurs de son influence internationale. Un certain nombre d'Angéliniens en parlent comme de «l'Industrie». L'architecture ne pouvait pas y rester indifférente. Avec son intellectualisme habituel, Thom Mayne définit son travail par référence au cinéma: «Jim Jarmusch a réalisé le film 'Stranger than Paradise' à partir de rien. Aujourd'hui, le bâti est aussi éphémère qu'un film. L'aspect le plus solide de mon travail est sa publication. Les bâtiments disparaissent en dix ans. Ils ne sont plus permanents. En architecture, il faut de la place pour les Jim Jarmusch, pas seulement les Spielberg.»[8] Comme le dit Joseph Giovannini: «A partir des années 60, la peinture est sortie du cadre, et la sculpture a abandonné le socle, pour émigrer vers des espaces ouverts. Les architectes de Los Angeles dessinaient des immeubles qui pouvaient être vus comme des sculptures urbaines spécifiques à leur site. Un cercle d'architectes, réduit mais s'élargissant peu à peu, explorait le terrain vierge entre l'architecture et les arts, et imagina

Arata Isozaki, Museum of Contemporary Art, Los Angeles, 1986. A defining monument in the heart of downtown L.A. from one of Japan's foremost architects.

Arata Isozaki, Museum of Contemporary Art, Los Angeles, 1986. Ein charakteristisches Monument im Herzen von Los Angeles, entworfen von einem der führenden japanischen Architekten.

Arata Isozaki, Museum of Contemporary Art, Los Angeles, 1986. Au cœur de Los Angeles, un monument déterminant signé par l'un des plus grands architectes japonais.

Richard Meier, Getty Center, Brentwood (model), 1985–97. By far the largest cultural project in the world, to be completed by the end of the 1990s.

Richard Meier, Getty Center, Brentwood (Modell), 1985–97. Dieses bei weitem größte Kulturprojekt der Welt soll gegen Ende der 90er Jahre fertiggestellt werden.

Richard Meier, Getty Centre, Brentwood (maquette), 1985–97. De loin le plus important projet culturel du monde, il sera achevé à la fin de cette décennie.

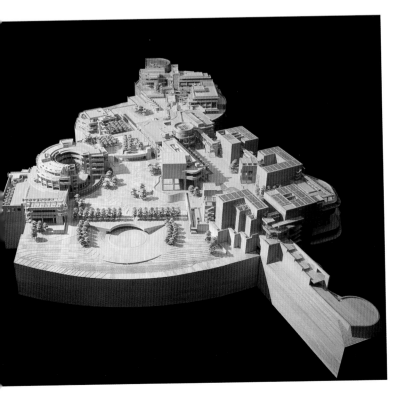

selected to build the massive new Getty Center on a Brentwood hilltop in 1984, openly opted for a classical solidity emphasized by an unusual rough cleft travertine cladding. When asked about architects who compare buildings to a Jim Jarmusch movie, he says bluntly, "I think that they have been in Los Angeles too long." The billion dollar Getty Center, which should open at the end of the decade will consist of six low-lying buildings with a total area of 88 200 m², and according to the architect, will resemble "an Italian hill town." To others it looks like a monastery or a fortress sitting above the Santa Monica Freeway, more a defensive structure than an inviting one. Again responding very directly when asked if he had not found some sort of inspiration in the contemporary situation of Los Angeles, Richard Meier replies, "we're bringing the rest of the world to Los Angeles." Meier is of course a New York based architect, but his clients are decidedly Californian. Their decision to build a sort of ideal city for culture, reflects not only the great wealth of the Getty Trust, but also the point of view that Los Angeles, now one of the great cities of the burgeoning Pacific Rim, the most powerful economic region in the world, should have monuments and cultural institutions which reflect its importance. Or at least this was the point of view of the 1980s. Successive catastrophes from the riots of 1992 to the Los Angeles earthquake of early 1994, coupled with an economic downturn did much to undermine confidence. A popular joke in this city of eternal spring is that there are after all four seasons in Los Angeles, and they are called Earthquake, Flood, Fire, and Drought.

The dream of the shining, ideal city reflected in the Getty Center project seems closer in its ambitions to the attitude of San Francisco than to that of Los Angeles. Indeed, San Francisco has just completed what was known for 40 years as the city's most troubled redevelopment area. The 40 hectare Yerba Buena zone includes a two hectare urban park created by MGA/Romaldo Giurgola; a theater by the New York architect James Stewart Polshek; the Yerba Buena Center, a silver, boat-shaped kunsthalle designed by 1993 Pritzker Prize winner Fumihiko Maki; and the San Francisco Museum of Modern Art, an 18 500 m² brick block-

Fumihiko Maki, Yerba Buena Center, San Francisco, 1993. A silver-skinned ship from this refined master of Japanese architecture.

Fumihiko Maki, Yerba Buena Center, San Francisco, 1993. Ein silbern verkleidetes Schiff, geschaffen von dem subtilen Meister japanischer Architektur.

Fumihiko Maki, Yerba Buena Center, San Francisco, 1993. Un vaste navire argenté, par l'un des grands maîtres raffinés de l'architecture japonaise.

Baupläne eines Hauses, das er errichtet, täglich überarbeitet. Er selbst beschreibt es mit den folgenden Worten: »Das Ziel war die Errichtung eines Projekts, das über einen langen Zeitraum entwickelt wurde – so wie sich eine Stadt entwickelt: man beginnt, dann folgt eine Unterbrechung, vieles wird überdacht und manches verworfen, vergessen...«

Ein drittes bedeutendes Fakultätsmitglied der SCI-Arc ist Eric Owen Moss. Er wurde 1943 in Los Angeles geboren, studierte an der UCLA und eröffnete 1976 sein eigenes Architekturbüro in Culver City. Die meisten seiner Arbeiten befinden sich in diesem Gebiet der Stadt. Aufgrund seiner Verbindung zu einem Stadtplaner in Culver City (zwischen der Innenstadt von Los Angeles und Santa Monica) hatte Moss Gelegenheit zum Bau großer Komplexe, die zunehmend aneinander anschließen, wie etwa der zwischen 1987 und 1990 fertiggestellte Paramount Laundry-Lindblade Tower-Gary Group Complex. Zu den jüngsten Sanierungsarbeiten dieses ursprünglich für die Filmindustrie errichteten, lagerhausähnlichen Komplexes zählen das nahegelegene The Box und das IRS Building. Moss gab fortschrittlich orientierten Werbeagenturen oder Plattenfirmen durch die einfallsreiche Verwendung von herkömmlichen Materialien – z.B. Abwasserrohre, die als Säulen dienen, oder U-förmig gebogene Bolzen als Leuchtstoffröhrenhalter – den Anstoß, sich in einer noch vor wenigen Jahren nahezu ausgestorbenen Gegend niederzulassen. Der Architekt Philip Johnson taufte ihn den »Juwelier des Schrotts«. Genau wie Mayne zeigt Moss eine ausgesprochen intellektuelle Haltung zu seinen Entwürfen und verknüpft sie auf interessante Weise mit seinen Vorstellungen über den Zustand der Welt: »T.S. Eliot schrieb über den 'Ruhepunkt der sich drehenden Welt'. Lao Tse schrieb über 'das Quadrat ohne Ecken'. Aber es gibt kein Quadrat ohne Ecken, oder? Wenn ein Gebäude die Beständigkeit repräsentiert, dann steht es für einen bestimmten Zustand oder ein Verständnis zu einem ganz bestimmten Zeitpunkt. Aber wenn die Architektur an sich Gegensätze beinhalten könnte, so daß das Gebäude das Streben nach Bewegung oder die Bewegung von Ideen symbolisiert, dann wäre die Architektur möglicherweise von dauerhafterer Natur. Sie würde etwas verkörpern, das sich bewegt – ungeachtet der Tatsache, daß sie etwas

des constructions non conformistes qui défiaient les lois d'une architecture monotone engluée dans ses dénominateurs communs. Pour certains, ce flou s'étendait jusqu'au cinéma. 'Ce qui a brisé les tabous doit davantage être recherché du côté de l'industrie du divertissement que chez les théoriciens et les historiens de l'architecture' a pu écrire Craig Hodgetts, tout en citant les stimulantes productions de MTV. Le créateur futuriste Syd Mead, qui a imaginé le décor de «Blade Runner», a aussi rêvé de mégastructures intergalactiques à l'échelle écrasante beaucoup plus impressionnantes que n'importe quel décor.»[9] Franklin Israel, né à New York en 1945, et venu en Californie pour enseigner, ne s'intéresse pas simplement au cinéma d'un point de vue théorique: il a réellement travaillé comme directeur artistique pour la Paramount, en 1978 et 1979. «Je suis arrivé à Los Angeles en 1977, en recherchant une synthèse entre ma formation d'architecte et les arcanes cinématographiques d'Hollywood. »Intervenant par la suite pour des clients du monde du cinéma, comme Robert Altman, Israel a appliqué sa connaissance de la profession, en dessinant un studio pour Propaganda Films, Bright and Associates, qui présentait une succession d'espaces comparés à «la réalité séquentielle» d'un film. Bien que son travail ait aujourd'hui évolué vers une approche plus complexe, son affinité revendiquée avec le cinéma montre que les circonstances très particulières de la pratique architecturale en Californie du Sud peuvent conduire à d'intéressantes solutions nouvelles. Le cinéma, mais aussi la menace permanente des tremblements de terre, poussent vers une nécessaire prise en compte de la rapidité d'évolution des situations. Pour citer une fois encore Franklin Israel: »Avoir travaillé à Los Angeles aide beaucoup à comprendre comment construire aujourd'hui dans un environnement dynamique.«

La Cité idéale
Tout le monde n'est pas convaincu que l'influence de l'hétérogénéité de l'environnement angélinien a eu une influence positive sur l'architecture contemporaine. Richard Meier, par exemple, sélectionné pour édifier l'énorme nouveau Getty Center au sommet d'une colline de Brentwood

house by the Swiss architect Mario Botta. Although Maki's building projects a lightness and subtlety typical of this important Japanese architect, the Yerba Buena complex as a whole reflects the fact that where bridges or skyscrapers were once a mark of a city's importance, the right thing to do these days is to promote culture. Mario Botta does make a case for the notion that contemporary upheavals can be dealt with by cultural monuments and an architecture of permanence, rather than the ephemeral expressions favored in Los Angeles. As he says, "in today's city, the museum plays a role analogous to that of the cathedral of yesterday. A place of common encounter and confrontation. A place we require in order to challenge the hopes and contradictions of our time... In fact, it might be possible to interpret the museum as a space dedicated to witnessing and searching for a new religiosity, which promotes and enriches those spiritual values that we so strongly need." Although Frank O. Gehry did participate in the consultation organized by the trustees of the San Francisco Museum of Modern Art before they selected Botta, it is interesting to note that none of the new Yerba Buena buildings were designed by California architects. San Franciscans still seem eager to build a "Paris of the Pacific" long after they began their quest.

The Changing of the Guard
A carefully designed metallic armature resembling a billboard hangs over a simple rectangular structure in Marina del Rey. In small letters, the word "Brix" identifies this building as a restaurant. Elsewhere, in Joshua Tree, to the east of Los Angeles, a sculptural assembly of brightly colored pavilions stands out against the rocky desert environment. More solid, yet just as incongruous, a huge brick faced structure rises up in the Brentwood campus of UCLA, its upper reaches a tangle of ominous pipes, steel frames and smoke stacks. Each of these buildings, in a different way, represents a new generation of California architects. The first, the Brix Restaurant (1991) is by the young group called Central Office of Architecture, whose three principals, Ron Golan, Eric A. Kahn and Russell N. Thomsen graduated from the California Polytechnic State University

repräsentiert, das physiologisch feststehend ist.«[6] Diese theoretische Haltung manifestiert sich in einer Architektur, die Erinnerungen an ihren eigenen Entstehungsprozeß enthält (Lawson-Westen House, Los Angeles 1993). Morphosis hat sich um eine Erforschung der »Archäologie« der Gegenwart bemüht, beispielsweise mit solchen Projekten wie dem Crawford House (Montecito 1987–92), dessen Pläne in einem teilweise vergrabenen Kreis eingraviert zu sein scheinen, Relikt einer vergangenen oder zukünftigen Zivilisation – vergleichbar der in dem Film »Blade Runner« dargestellten.

Stranger than Paradise
1994 kamen über 22 Millionen Touristen nach Los Angeles, in dessen Einzugsgebiet vier von Amerikas beliebtesten Freizeitattraktionen liegen. Dies ist sicherlich einer der Gründe dafür, daß Los Angeles (wäre es ein unabhängiger Staat) mit seiner Kaufkraft von 380 Milliarden Dollar eine bedeutendere Wirtschaftsmacht darstellen würde als beispielsweise Südkorea.[7] Aber von noch größerer Bedeutung als alle wirtschaftlichen Faktoren ist die Filmindustrie: Sie symbolisiert die Stadt selbst und deren Einfluß auf die ganze Welt. Einige Angelenos bezeichnen sie einfach als »Die Industrie«. Der Architektur von Los Angeles blieb nichts anderes übrig, als dem Rechnung zu tragen. Ungeachtet seines rein intellektuellen Ansatzes verglich Thom Mayne seine Arbeit mit einem Film (wenn auch einem eher intellektuellen): »Jim Jarmusch drehte den Film 'Stranger than Paradise' sozusagen aus dem Nichts. Heutzutage sind Bauwerke genauso vergänglich wie Filme. Daher ist der beständigste Aspekt meiner Arbeit der Teil, der veröffentlicht wurde. Die Gebäude werden in zehn Jahren verschwunden sein; sie sind nicht mehr so 'langlebig' wie früher. In der Architektur sollte daher mehr Raum geschaffen werden für Leute wie Jim Jarmusch, und nicht nur für die Spielbergs.«[8] Joseph Giovannini schrieb: »Seit den 60er Jahren kamen die Gemälde aus ihren Rahmen und die Skulpturen stiegen von ihren Sockeln, um schließlich in die offene Landschaft überzusiedeln. Architekten in Los Angeles entwarfen Gebäude, die als geländespezifische, urbane Skulpturen interpretiert werden konnten. Ein kleiner, aber

pour un solide classicisme, souligné par un curieux revêtement en travertin brut. Lorsqu'on lui demande ce qu'il pense des architectes qui comparent leurs constructions à des films de Jim Jarmusch, il répond sèchement «qu'ils ont vécu trop longtemps à Los Angeles». Le Getty Center, un investissement de 1 billion de $, et qui devrait être inauguré à la fin de cette décennie, sera composé de six bâtiments bas couvrant une surface totale de 88 200 m². Selon l'architecte, il ressemblera à «un village italien dans les collines». D'autres évoquent plutôt, pour cet édifice plus défensif qu'accueillant, un monastère ou une forteresse perchée au-dessus de l'autoroute de Santa Monica. Répondant très directement à ceux qui lui demandent s'il n'a pas trouvé en partie son inspiration dans la situation actuelle de Los Angeles, Richard Meier réplique «nous faisons venir le reste du monde à Los Angeles». Meier est de New York, mais ses clients sont décidément californiens. Leur décision de construire une sorte de cité idéale de la culture reflète non seulement l'immense richesse de la Fondation Getty, mais aussi l'idée que Los Angeles, l'une des grandes métropoles d'une région Pacifique en pleine expansion qui est aussi la plus forte concentration économique du monde, se doit de posséder des monuments et des institutions culturels qui reflètent son importance. C'était du moins l'idée qui prévalait dans les années 80. Les catastrophes successives des émeutes de 1992, et le tremblement de terre du début de 1994, couplées à la récession économique ont beaucoup fait pour miner cette confiance en soi. On entend souvent dire, dans cette cité de l'éternel printemps, qu'existent néanmoins quatre saisons qui ont pour nom tremblement de terre, inondation, incendie et sécheresse. Ce rêve d'une brillante cité idéale reflété par le projet du Getty Center semble plus proche des ambitions de San Francisco que de celles de L.A... En fait, San Francisco vient juste de mettre la dernière main à ce qui était, depuis quarante ans la plus problématique de ses opérations de rénovation urbaine. Cette zone de 40 hectares, Yerba Buena, comprend un parc urbain de deux hectares, créé par MGA/Romaldo Giurgola, un théâtre, par l'architecte new-yorkais James Stewart Polshek, le Yerba Buena Centre, un centre d'expositions artistiques en forme de

Central Office of Architecture, Brix Restaurant, Venice, 1991. From a young group of architects, a sophisticated take-off on typical Los Angeles billboards.

Central Office of Architecture, Brix Restaurant, Venice, 1991. Das junge Architektenteam entwarf dieses Restaurant in Anspielung auf typische Los Angeles Reklametafeln.

Central Office of Architecture, Brix Restaurant, Venice, 1991. Par un jeune groupe d'architectes, une utilisation détournée des célèbres enseignes de Los Angeles.

in San Luis Obispo in 1981. Almost minimalist in its expression their restaurant engages in a sublimation of the roadside imagery which is deeply rooted in the California psyche. The spareness of their means is an indication of a new, less extravagant mood, following the excesses of the 1980s. The sculptural appearance of Josh Schweitzer's Monument at Joshua Tree is a reminder that California continues to play a role in a redefinition of the relationship between art and architecture. Finally, the UCLA Chiller Plant/Facilities Complex on the Brentwood campus is a container for gas turbines, boilers, chillers and exhaust stacks, plus miles of pipes, ducts and raceways. The work of the San Francisco firm Holt Hinshaw Pfau Jones, and especially of Wes Jones who has now formed Jones Partners-Architecture, this plant is intended to call into question the esthetic and intellectual place of technology in everyday life. In the earthquake zone of Los Angeles, it questions the supposed ability of technology to dominate nature. Solid, even massive, one might say that it has a curious San Francisco air to it. What is interesting about the investigation of Wes Jones is that he is exploring "the continuing possibilities of mechanically influenced architecture in the post-mechanical future." He has clearly thought about the implications of the new universe of electronics, for architecture. As he says, "the dominance of the mechanical metaphor as a way of viewing the world is waning. In place of mechanical analogy and interpretation, an explosion of electronic imagery – a mediated reality is asserting itself." But rather than trying to embrace the undefinable limits of "cyberspace," Jones declares, "the electronic will give the mechanical life, maybe even consciousness, while the mechanical will continue to give the electronic substance, will free it too have effect and act in the substantial world." Thus the consciously mechanical metaphor of the UCLA plant.[10]

These less well-known architects seem prepared to trace new directions for architecture in California at a time when the founding father of the current schools, Frank O. Gehry is still very active. Others, including the SCI-Arc trio of Mayne, Moss and Rotondi have worked mainly on small, local buildings, but their notoriety assures that they will

sich langsam vergrößernder Kreis von Architekten arbeitete im fruchtbaren Grenzgebiet zwischen Architektur und Kunst und brachte nonkonformistische Gebäude hervor, die gegen das ungeschriebene Gesetz eines Designs ohne herausragende Kennzeichen ankämpften, dem gemeinsamen Nenner vieler Entwürfe. Für einige Architekten erstreckte sich dieses Grenzgebiet bis in die Welt des Films. 'Irgendetwas im Bereich der Unterhaltungsindustrie hat das Eis gebrochen – jedenfalls in bedeutenderem Maße als Architekturtheorien und Historiker', verkündet Craig Hodgetts und bezieht sich dabei auf die einflußreichen Produktionsentwürfe für MTV, die einen Vorreiter für stimulierendes Design bildeten. Syd Mead, ein offensichtlicher Futurist, der den Look von 'Blade Runner' schuf, erfand intergalaktische Megastrukturen, die aufgrund ihres überwältigenden Maßstabs erheblich einflußreicher sind als Bühnenbilder.«[9]

Franklin Israel, der 1945 in New York geboren wurde, ging über den rein theoretischen Bezug zum Film hinaus und war zwischen 1978 und 1979 für die Paramount Filmgesellschaft als künstlerischer Leiter tätig: »Als ich 1977 nach Los Angeles kam, strebte ich nach einer Synthese zwischen meinem architektonischen Wissen und dem kinematographischen Intrigenspiel Hollywoods.«

Während seiner anschließenden Arbeit mit dem Regisseur Robert Altman und anderen Kunden aus der Filmindustrie setzte Israel seine Kenntnisse ein und entwarf ein Studio für Propaganda Films, Bright and Associates mit einer Folge von Räumen, die er mit der »Sequenzen-Realität« des Films verglich. Obwohl Israels Arbeiten sich heute durch eine komplexere Haltung auszeichnen, hält er mit seiner erklärten Liebe zum Film an der Ansicht fest, daß die besonderen Umstände und Bedingungen der Architektur in Südkalifornien neue, interessante Lösungen hervorbringen können.

Nicht nur die Filmindustrie, auch die Tatsache, daß die Erde hier jeden Moment erbeben kann, bedingen die Notwendigkeit, sich mit rapide wechselnden Situationen auseinanderzusetzen. Franklin Israel formulierte es so: »Das, was man durch die Arbeit in Los Angeles lernen kann, trägt zum Verständnis einer modernen Bauweise bei, die sich auf jede dynamische Umgebung anwenden läßt.«

navire argenté, typique de la légèreté et de la subtilité de cet important architecte japonais qu'est le lauréat du Prix Pritzker 1993, Fumihiko Maki, et le San Francisco Museum of Modern Art, blockhaus de brique de 18 500 m^2, dû à l'architecte suisse Mario Botta. Yerba Buena confirme une fois encore que si naguère les ponts ou les gratte-ciel symbolisaient l'importance d'une ville, ce qui compte aujourd'hui pour une cité est la mise en avant de sa culture. Mario Botta affirme à sa façon que les bouleversements contemporains peuvent être traités par des monuments culturels et une architecture toute de permanence, plutôt que par les expressions éphémères qui ont la faveur de Los Angeles. Il déclare ainsi: «Dans la vie d'aujourd'hui, le musée joue un rôle analogue à celui des cathédrales d'hier. Un lieu de rencontre et de confrontation. Un lieu dont nous avons besoin pour répondre aux espoirs et aux contradictions de notre temps... Il est peut-être possible d'interpréter le musée comme un espace consacré au témoignage et à la recherche d'une nouvelle religiosité, qui défend et enrichit ces valeurs spirituelles dont nous ressentons si fortement le besoin.» Même si Frank O. Gehry a participé à la consultation organisée par le conseil d'administration du San Francisco Museum of Modern Art qui sélectionna Botta, il est intéressant de noter qu'aucun des nouveaux bâtiments de Yerba Buena n'a été confié à des architectes californiens. Après tant d'années, San Francisco semble toujours chercher à construire son «Paris de l'Ouest».

La relève de la garde

A Marina del Rey, une armature métallique qui ressemble à un panneau d'affichage dessiné avec soin est suspendue au-dessus d'une construction rectangulaire simple. Le mot «Brix» inscrit en petits caractères indique qu'il s'agit d'un restaurant. Plus loin, à Joshua Tree, à l'Est de Los Angeles, un assemblage sculptural de pavillons de couleurs vives s'élève dans un environnement désertique et minéral. Plus massive, mais tout aussi étonnante, une énorme construction en brique se dresse sur le campus de Brentwood de UCLA, et se termine par un enchevêtrement de tuyaux, de poutrelles d'acier et de cheminées. Chacun de ces bâtiments, à sa façon, signale l'existence d'une nouvelle géné-

Pages 54/55: Holt Hinshaw Pfau Jones, UCLA Energy Services Facility, Los Angeles, 1994. The attempt of the designer Wes Jones to come to grips with the forms of industry.

Seite 54/55: Holt Hinshaw Pfau Jones, UCLA Energy Services Facility, Los Angeles, 1994. Der Versuch des Designers Wes Jones, sich mit der Formensprache der Industrie auseinanderzusetzen.

Pages 54/55: Holt Hinshaw Pfau Jones, UCLA Energy Services Facility (centrale thermique), Los Angeles, 1994. Une tentative de Wes Jones de se mesurer aux formes industrielles.

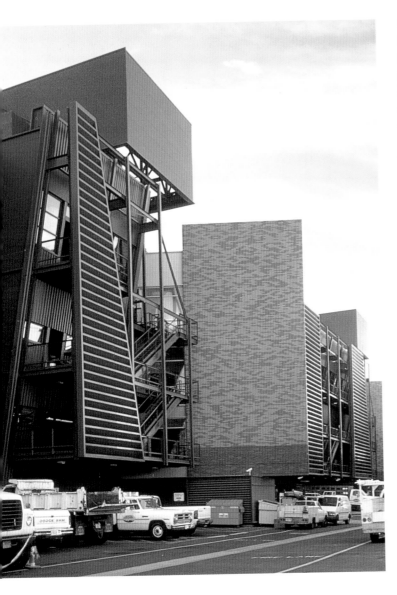

continue to form architectural thinking. Complex, intellectual, often given to the use of curious materials, these architects may never be able to seduce the corporate or government clients who usually give larger-scale work to less inventive architects. Moss has nonetheless proven the commercial viability of his warehouse transformations in Culver City, and Mayne is set to build schools in California.

It is difficult to tell if the circumstances will permit California architects to be as inventive in the years to come as they were in the 1980s. Thom Mayne feels that the period of maximum creativity is already a thing of the past. Like Gehry, he seems bitter about the fundamental lack of recognition which the considerable achievements of local architects have received. In an ephemeral environment which is driven more than anything else by money, the quality of the built environment is not a priority, and the number of persons who are able to identify an interesting contemporary structure is limited. The recession which dealt a strong blow to the California economy dried up sources of financing for innovative buildings. Yet, this is a culture of experimentation, which at least on a small scale is willing to try anything. The mild climate in Southern California in particular encourages the use of unusual materials, and the example of Frank Gehry has permitted numerous others to create works which occupy a newly defined space between art and architecture. That in itself is a considerable accomplishment.

[1] Anthony Alofsin, *Frank Lloyd Wright and Modernism,* Frank Lloyd Wright, Architect, The Museum of Modern Art, New York, 1994.
[2] Interview of Frank Gehry, Frank O. Gehry & Associates, 1520-B Cloverfield Boulevard, Santa Monica, May 16, 1994.
[3] *L. A. Architects: They Did It Their Way,* Joseph Giovannini, Los Angeles Times Magazine, May 15, 1994.
[4] Heteropolis, Los Angeles, *The Riots and the Strange Beauty of Hetero-Architecture,* Charles Jencks 1993.
[5] Interview of Thom Mayne, Morphosis Architects, 2041 Colorado Avenue, Santa Monica, May 12, 1994.
[6] Interview of Eric Owen Moss, 8557 Higuera Street, Culver City, May 14, 1994.
[7] The Economist, February 4, 1995.
[8] Interview of Thom Mayne, Santa Monica, May 12, 1994.
[9] *L. A. Architects: They Did It Their Way,* Joseph Giovannini, Los Angeles Times Magazine, May 15, 1994.
[10] Wes Jones, *The Mech in Tecture,* Any, n°10, January 1995.

Die strahlende Stadt

Nicht jeder ist von den positiven Einflüssen der heterogenen Umgebung Los Angeles' auf die zeitgenössische Architektur überzeugt. Richard Meier beispielsweise, der 1984
zum Architekten für das neue, monumentale Getty Center
auf einem Hügel in Brentwood ernannt wurde, entschied
sich dabei für eine klassisch-massive Bauweise, die durch
die ungewöhnliche Verkleidung aus rauhem gespaltenen
Travertin noch betont wird. Als man ihn nach seiner Meinung zu den Architekten befragte, die ihre Gebäude mit Fil-
men von Jim Jarmusch verglichen, antwortete er unver-
blümt: »Ich glaube, daß sie schon zu lange in Los Angeles
sind«. Das eine Milliarde Dollar teure Getty Center, das
gegen Ende des Jahrhunderts fertig sein soll, besteht aus
sechs niedrigen Gebäuden; es besitzt eine Gesamtfläche
von 88 200 m² und wird nach Aussage des Architekten
einem »italienischen Bergdorf« ähneln. Andere beschreiben
es als Kloster oder Burganlage, die hoch über dem Santa
Monica Freeway aufragt – eher eine Verteidigungsanlage
als ein einladendes Kulturzentrum. Auf die Frage, ob die
gegenwärtige Situation in Los Angeles ihn nicht doch inspiriert hätte, antwortete Richard Meier erneut sehr direkt:
»Wir bringen den Rest der Welt nach Los Angeles«. Meiers
Architekturbüro befindet sich natürlich in New York, aber
seine Klienten sind entschieden Kalifornier. Ihr Wunsch
nach einer Art Idealstadt der Kultur spiegelt nicht nur den
Reichtum des Getty Trust wider, sondern auch die Ansicht,
daß Los Angeles – als eine der großen Städte am florieren-
den Pacific Rim in einer der wirtschaftlich mächtigsten
Regionen der Welt – über Monumente und kulturelle Ein-
richtungen verfügen sollte, die diese Bedeutung reflektie-
ren. Zumindest vertrat man diese Ansicht während der 80er
Jahre. Aber verschiedene aufeinanderfolgende Katastro-
phen (von den Unruhen 1992 bis hin zum Erdbeben in Los
Angeles Anfang 1994) in Kombination mit einem Konjunk-
turrückgang untergruben dieses Selbstvertrauen. Einem
beliebten Scherz zufolge gibt es in dieser Stadt des ewigen
Frühlings sehr wohl vier Jahreszeiten: Erdbeben, Flut,
Feuer und Dürre. Der Traum von der strahlenden Idealstadt,
der sich in dem Getty Center-Projekt widerspiegelt, scheint
San Francisco näher zu stehen als Los Angeles. Tatsächlich

ration d'architectes californiens. Le premier, le restaurant
Brix (1991) est signé par un jeune groupe, le Central Office
of Architecture, dont les principaux associés, Ron Golan,
Eric A. Kahn et Russell N. Thomsen ont été diplômés de la
California Polytechnic State University à San Luis Obispo en
1981. D'expression presque minimaliste, leur restaurant
représente une sublimation de l'imagerie du bord de route,
si profondément enracinée dans la conscience californienne. L'économie des moyens mis en œuvre signale une
attitude nouvelle, moins extravagante, qui succède aux
excès des années 80. L'apparence sculpturale de la réalisation de Josh Schweitzer à Joshua Tree rappelle que la Californie reste très présente dans la redéfinition de la relation
entre l'art et l'architecture. La centrale thermique de UCLA
sur le campus de Brentwood réunit des turbines à gaz, des
chaudières, une centrale de réfrigération, et des kilomètres
de tuyaux et de conduites d'eau. Œuvre de l'agence de San
Francisco Holt Hinshaw Pfau Jones, et spécialement de
Wes Jones qui vient d'ouvrir Jones Partners-Architecture,
elle est censée interpeller la place esthétique et intellectuelle de la technologie dans la vie quotidienne. Dans une
région menacée par les tremblements de terre, elle remet
en question la capacité supposée de la technologie à domi-
ner la nature. Avec son volume plein, et même massif, on
peut dire qu'elle fait curieusement penser à San Francisco.
L'intérêt de l'investigation de Wes Jones est qu'il explore
«les possibilités permanentes d'une architecture influencée
par la mécanique dans un avenir post-mécanique». Il a
réfléchi aux implications architecturales du nouvel univers
électronique: «La domination de la métaphore mécanique
comme façon de concevoir le monde s'évanouit. Une
explosion d'imagerie électronique, une réalité médiatisée
«vient remplacer les analogies et interprétations méca-
niques.» Mais, déclare Jones, plutôt que d'essayer
d'embrasser les limites indéfinissables du «cyber space»,
«l'électronique insufflera la vie, voire même peut-être la
conscience, dans la mécanique, tandis que la mécanique
continuera à fournier à l'électronique sa substance, et lui
donnera les moyens d'agir et d'intervenir dans le monde
concret.» D'ou la métaphore délibérément mécaniste de
l'usine d'UCLA.[10] Ces architectes moins connus semblent

feierte San Francisco gerade die Fertigstellung eines umstrittenen Sanierungsgebiets, das die Stadt 40 Jahre lang beschäftigt hatte. Zu diesem 40 Hektar großen Yerba Buena-Distrikt gehören ein zwei Hektar großer städtischer Park von MGA/Romaldo Giurgola, ein von dem New Yorker Architekten James Stewart Polshek erbautes Theater, das Yerba Buena Center (eine silberfarbene, schiffsähnliche Kunsthalle, die Fumihiko Maki, Gewinner des Pritzker-Preises 1993, entworfen hatte) sowie das San Francisco Museum of Modern Art, ein massives, 18 500 m² großes Bauwerk mit Ziegelverblendung, des Schweizer Architekten Mario Botta. Obwohl Makis Gebäude eine für diesen japanischen Architekten typische Leichtigkeit und Raffinesse vermittelt, reflektiert der Yerba Buena-Komplex die Tatsache, daß, wo früher Brücken oder Wolkenkratzer die Bedeutung einer Stadt dokumentierten, das Gebot der heutigen Zeit die Förderung der Kultur ist. Mario Botta legt Wert auf die Feststellung, daß zeitgenössische soziale Umbrüche eher durch Kulturmonumente und eine Architektur der Beständigkeit kompensiert werden können als durch die vergänglichen Ausdrucksformen, die man in Los Angeles so schätzt und daß »in der heutigen Stadt ein Museum die gleiche Bedeutung hat wie die Kirche in den vergangenen Jahrhunderten. Es ist ein Ort der Begegnung und der Konfrontation. Ein Ort, den wir benötigen, um die Hoffnungen und Widersprüche unserer Zeit zu hinterfragen... Tatsächlich könnte man das Museum als einen Raum interpretieren, der der Bestätigung und der Suche nach einer neuen Religiösität gewidmet ist, welche die spirituellen Werte, derer wir so dringend bedürfen, fördert und verstärkt.« Obwohl Frank O. Gehry an der Gesprächsrunde teilnahm, die die Treuhänder des San Francisco Museum of Modern Art organisiert hatten, bevor sie sich für Botta entschieden, wurde interessanterweise kein einziges der neuen Yerba Buena-Gebäude von einem kalifornischen Architekten entworfen. Die Bewohner von San Francisco scheinen (nach all den Jahren) immer noch ein »Paris am Pazifik« bauen zu wollen.

prêts à ouvrir de nouvelles voies à l'architecture californienne, alors que le père fondateur des écoles actuelles, Frank O. Gehry, reste toujours très actif. Les autres, comme le trio SCI-Arc de Mayne, Moss et Rotondi, travaillent essentiellement sur de petites commandes d'intérêt local, mais leur notoriété laisse entrevoir qu'il vont poursuivre leur contribution à la formation de la pensée architecturale. Complexes, intellectuels, souvent disposés à recourir à de curieux matériaux, ces architectes ne seront peut-être jamais en mesure de séduire la clientèle des grandes entreprises ou de l'administration, qui généralement confient leurs grandes commandes à des agences moins inventives. Moss a néanmoins prouvé la viabilité commerciale de ses transformations d'entrepôts à Culver City, et Mayne s'apprête à construire des écoles. Il est difficile de dire si les circonstances permettront aux architectes californiens d'être aussi créatifs au cours des années à venir qu'ils l'ont été dans les années 80. Thom Mayne pense que la période de créativité maximum appartient déjà au passé. Comme Gehry, il ressent amèrement le manque fondamental de reconnaissance des authentiques réussites des architectes locaux. Sous le règne de l'éphémère, avec une créativité essentiellement soumise à l'argent, la qualité de l'environnement construit n'est pas une priorité, et le nombre de personnes capables de discerner une construction contemporaine intéressante est limité. La récession qui a durement frappé l'économie californienne a asséché les sources de financement ouvertes à une architecture innovante. Et cependant, on trouve ici une culture de l'expérimentation qui, au moins à petite échelle, est prête à tout. L'agréable climat de la Californie du Sud encourage le recours à des matériaux inhabituels, et l'exemple de Frank O. Gehry a permis à beaucoup de ses confrères de créer des œuvres qui occupent un nouvel espace entre l'art et l'architecture. En elle-même, la réussite n'est pas mince.

Die Wachablösung

In Marina del Rey hängt ein sorgfältig gestaltetes Metallgebilde, das an eine Reklametafel erinnert, über einem schlichten, rechtwinkligen Gebäude, das durch das Wort »Brix« in kleinen Buchstaben als Restaurant identifiziert ist. In Joshua Tree, östlich von Los Angeles, befindet sich eine skulpturenartige Ansammlung von leuchtendbunten Pavillons vor dem Hintergrund eines felsigen Wüstengebiets. Auf dem Brentwood Campus von UCLA erhebt sich eine solidere, dennoch genauso widersprüchlich erscheinende, gewaltige Ziegelsteinkonstruktion mit einem Gewirr von ominösen Röhren, Stahlgerüsten und Schornsteinen. Jedes dieser Gebäude repräsentiert auf seine Weise eine neue Generation kalifornischer Architekten. Das Brix Restaurant (1991) stammt von der jungen Gruppe Central Office of Architecture, deren drei Leiter, Ron Golan, Eric A. Kahn und Russell N. Thomsen, 1981 ihr Studium an der California Polytechnic State University in San Luis Obispo abschlossen. Ihr Restaurant – in seiner Ausdruckskraft nahezu minimalistisch – stellt die Sublimierung eines typischen Straßenbildes dar, das tief in der kalifornischen Psyche verankert ist. Die bewußte Beschränkung der Mittel ist ein Zeichen für eine neue, weniger extravagante Einstellung nach den Exzessen der 80er Jahre. Das skulpturale Erscheinungsbild von Josh Schweitzers Monument in Joshua Tree erinnert daran, daß Kalifornien nach wie vor eine wichtige Rolle beim Überdenken des Verhältnisses zwischen Kunst und Architektur spielt. Bei dem UCLA Chiller Plant/Facilities Complex auf dem Brentwood Campus schließlich handelt es sich um eine Hülle für Gasturbinen, Dampfkessel, Kühlaggregate und Abluftvorrichtungen sowie Kilometer von Röhren, Leitungen und Kabelschächten. Diese Heizanlage – ein Werk der Firma Holt Hinshaw Pfau Jones in San Francisco und insbesondere von Wes Jones (der vor kurzem das Büro Jones Partners-Architecture gründete) – soll den ästhetischen und intellektuellen Stellenwert der Technologie im alltäglichen Leben in Frage stellen. Wes Jones erforscht hiermit »die fortgesetzten Möglichkeiten mechanisch beeinflußter Architektur in einer post-mechanischen Zukunft«. Die Auswirkungen des neuen Universums der Elektronik auf die Architektur hat er sorgfältig durchdacht: »Die Vorherrschaft der mechanischen Metapher im Weltbild nimmt immer mehr ab. Statt mechanischer Analogien und Interpretationen erfolgt eine Explosion elektronischer Metaphorik – eine als Bindeglied fungierende Realität setzt sich durch.« Aber anstatt sich auf die undefinierbaren Grenzen des »Cyberspace« einzulassen, erklärt Jones: »Die Elektronik wird der Mechanik Leben, vielleicht sogar Bewußtsein verleihen, während das Mechanische der Elektronik nach wie vor Substanz gibt, sie befreien wird, und ihr somit ermöglicht, in der substantiellen Welt Einfluß zu nehmen«. So erklärt sich die bewußt mechanische Metapher der UCLA-Heizanlage.[10]

Es ist schwer zu beurteilen, ob die Umstände den kalifornischen Architekten gestatten werden, in den kommenden Jahren genauso innovativ zu arbeiten wie in den Achtzigern. Thom Mayne ist davon überzeugt, daß die Zeit maximaler Kreativität vorüber ist. Wie Gehry scheint er verbittert darüber, daß die beachtlichen Ergebnisse, die lokale Architekten erzielten, nicht anerkannt werden. In einer kurzlebigen Umgebung, die mehr als alles andere vom Geld beherrscht ist, spielt die Qualität des gebauten Umfeldes keine große Rolle, und die Zahl derer, die ein interessantes zeitgenössisches Gebäude identifizieren können, ist begrenzt. Die Rezession, die Kaliforniens Wirtschaft schwer traf, ließ zahlreiche Quellen zur Finanzierung innovativer Bauten versiegen. Dennoch ist dies eine Kultur der Experimente, die zumindest im kleinen Rahmen zu allem bereit ist. Insbesondere das milde Klima Südkaliforniens ermutigt zur Verwendung ungewöhnlicher Materialien, und Frank O. Gehrys Beispiel hat es zahlreichen anderen Architekten ermöglicht, Bauwerke zu schaffen, die einen neudefinierten Raum zwischen Kunst und Architektur einnehmen. Dies ist an sich schon eine beachtliche Errungenschaft.

Asymptote

Lise Anne Couture

Hani Rashid

Steel Cloud, West Coast Gateway, Los Angeles, 1988 (project).

Steel Cloud, West Coast Gateway, Los Angeles, 1988 (Projekt).

Steel Cloud, West Coast Gateway, Los Angeles, 1988 (projet).

Established in 1987 by Lise Anne Couture and Hani Rashid, Asymptote has been involved in a wide variety of competitions and projects, many of which have remained theoretical. Best known for their 1988 prize winning commission for the Los Angeles West Coast Gateway they have also submitted proposals for the recent Yokohama International Port Terminal, Berlin Spreebogen, Groningen National Court House, and Alexandria Library competitions. They have also participated in exhibitions, such as the "Urban Revisions" show first seen at the Museum of Contemporary Art in Los Angeles in May 1994, or displays of entries for the Spreebogen or Alexandria competitions. Their Steel Cloud project for Los Angeles, one of 200 entries for the 1988 competition was an effort to "give physical form to the information city and the technologically globalized nature of contemporary life." Though based in New York, their West Coast Gateway, which Couture hopes will yet be built, represents a significant episode in recent California architecture.

Das 1987 von Lise Anne Couture und Hani Rashid gegründete Architekturbüro Asymptote war an einer Reihe von Wettbewerben und Projekten beteiligt. Durch ihren preisgekrönten Beitrag zur Ausschreibung für die Los Angeles West Coast Gateway (1988) wurden die beiden international bekannt. Darüber hinaus nahmen sie an den Wettbewerben um den Yokohama International Port Terminal, das Berliner Spreebogenprojekt, den Nationalen Gerichtshof in Groningen und die Alexandria Library teil sowie an verschiedenen Ausstellungen – darunter die »Urban Revisions«-Show im Museum of Contemporary Art in Los Angeles (Mai 1994). Ihr Steel Cloud-Projekt in Los Angeles – einer von 200 Wettbewerbsbeiträgen (1988) – entstand in dem Bemühen, »der Informationsstadt und dem technologisch globalisierten Charakter des heutigen Lebens eine physische Form zu verleihen«. Obwohl sich ihr Büro in New York befindet, repräsentiert ihr West Coast Gateway eine wichtige Episode in der jüngsten Geschichte kalifornischer Architektur.

Créée en 1987 par Lise Anne Couture et Hani Rashid, Asymptote a participé à de multiples concours et projets, dont beaucoup n'ont pas dépassé le stade théorique. Les deux associés ont récemment pris part aux concours du terminal portuaire de Yokohama, du Spreebogen à Berlin, du palais de justice de Groningue et de la bibliothèque d'Alexandrie. Ils ont également participé à des expositions comme «Urban Revisions», mise en place pour la première fois au Museum of Contemporary Art de Los Angeles en mai 1994, ou à celle du concours du Spreebogen et de la bibliothèque d'Alexandrie. Leur projet du «Steel Cloud» (à Los Angeles), l'une des 200 participations au concours de 1988, voulait «donner une forme physique à la cité de l'information et à la nature technologique et globalisante de la vie contemporaine». Bien que basés à New York, ils ont fait avec «West Coast Gateway» l'une des propositions marquantes de l'architecture californienne récente. Lise Anne Couture espère encore qu'elle sera construite.

Steel Cloud, West Coast Gateway, Los Angeles 1988 (project)

The 1988 Los Angeles Gateway Competition organized by Nick Patsaouras drew some 200 entries. The winning design was submitted by the young New York architects Lise Anne Couture and Hani Rashid. Their 500 meter linear structure was intended to cross an eight lane freeway with an "episodic architecture inspired by optical machinery, simulators, surveillance technologies and telecommunication systems." A highly symbolic architectural gesture, the "Steel Cloud" was conceived as a clear signal that Los Angeles has replaced New York as the "Ellis Island of the 1990s." Metaphorically it is a deconstruction of the Statue of Liberty, or perhaps of Tatlin's Monument to the Third International, and although it was portrayed in the media as a folly, this project, which includes numerous screens to project information or movies, represents the recuperation of a dead space over a sunken freeway. Intended as a privately financed project, the Steel Cloud, long delayed, may still one day be built.

Über 200 Architekten beteiligten sich 1988 an der von Nick Patsaouras organisierten Los Angeles Gateway-Ausschreibung, aus der Lise Anne Couture und Hani Rashid als Gewinner hervorgingen. Ihre 500 Meter lange, lineare Konstruktion sollte eine achtspurige Schnellstraße als »episodische Architektur« überspannen, die »von optischen Geräten, Simulatoren, Überwachungsanlagen und Telekommunikationssystemen inspiriert ist«. In ihrer Funktion als stark symbolhafte Architektur wurde die »Steel Cloud« als ein deutliches Zeichen dafür aufgefaßt, daß Los Angeles die Stadt New York als das »Ellis Island der 90er Jahre« ersetzt hat. Im metaphorischen Sinne stellt dieses Bauvorhaben eine Dekonstruktion der Freiheitsstatue oder Tatlins Denkmal der Dritten Internationale dar. Dieses Projekt, das zahlreiche Bildschirme für Informationen oder Spielfilme und Leinwände umfaßt, strebt die Rückeroberung des toten Raumes oberhalb einer tiefergelegten Schnellstraße an. Das ursprünglich privat zu finanzierende Bauvorhaben wird möglicherweise eines Tages doch noch ausgeführt.

200 architectes ont participé au concours «Los Angeles Gateway» organisé en 1988 par Nick Patsaouras. Le projet retenu fut celui de la jeune agence new-yorkaise de Lise Anne Couture et Hani Rashid. «Architecture épisodique inspirée par les machines optiques, simulateurs, technologies de surveillance et systèmes de télécommunication», leur bâtiment de 500 mètres de long devrait passer par-dessus une autoroute à huit voies. Geste architectural hautement symbolique, le «Steel Cloud» était censé proclamer que Los Angeles était devenue l'«Ellis Island des années 90», à la place de New York. Métaphoriquement, il s'agit d'une déconstruction de la statue de la Liberté, ou peut-être du monument à la Troisième Internationale de Tatline. Présenté dans les médias comme une folie ce projet, qui comportait de nombreux écrans pour projeter des informations ou des films, récupérait un espace mort au-dessus d'une autoroute. Le «Steel Cloud» devrait être financé par des capitaux privés. Il sera peut-être enfin construit un jour.

Pages 60/61: The "Steel Cloud " is described by its designers as an effort to "unearth the dichotomy of the actual and the simulated, the violent and the picturesque." In reality it represents an entirely new version of the pedestrian bridge, in a city where it is very difficult to go on foot.

Seite 60/61: Die »Steel Cloud« wird von ihren Designern als der Versuch beschrieben, »die Dichotomie des Realen und des Simulierten, des Gewalttätigen und des Pittoresken ans Licht zu bringen«. Tatsächlich repräsentiert dieses Bauwerk eine völlig neue Version einer Fußgängerbrücke in einer Stadt, in der es sehr schwierig ist, sich zu Fuß zu bewegen.

Pages 60/61: «Steel Cloud» (Nuage d'acier) est décrit par ses concepteurs comme une tentative de «révéler la dichotomie entre le réel et le simulé, le violent et le pittoresque». En fait, il représente aussi une conception entièrement neuve de la passerelle pour piétons, dans une ville où il est difficile de se déplacer à pied.

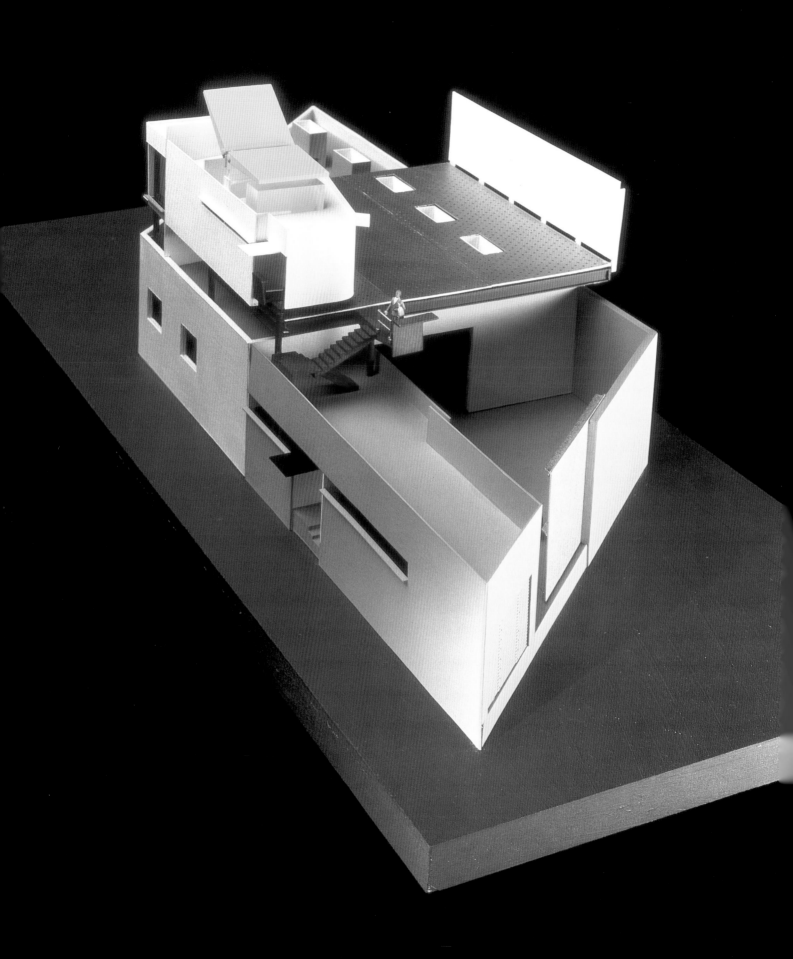

Central Office of Architecture

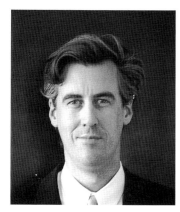

Russell N. Thomsen

Eric A. Khan

Ron Golan

Central Office of Architecture was created in 1986 by Russell N. Thomsen, Eric A. Kahn and Ron Golan, who all received their B. Arch. degrees from the California Polytechnic State University, San Luis Obispo in 1981. Aside from teaching at the Southern California Institute of Architecture (SCI-Arc) their projects include residences in Laguna Beach and Pacific Palisades, a 1990 design of prototypical concrete and steel public restrooms for the City of Los Angeles, the Hawkes Photo Studio (1993) and the Brix Restaurant, originally designed in 1990. Their current work includes the Janczak Residence and the MAK Center for Art and Architecture in Los Angeles. They have also written extensively about the condition of architecture and the city.

Page 62: Hawkes Photo Studio/Penthouse, 1993 (model).

Seite 62: Hawkes Photo Studio/Penthouse, 1993 (Modell).

Page 62: Hawkes Photo Studio/Penthouse, 1993 (maquette).

Central Office of Architecture wurde 1986 von Russell N. Thomsen, Eric A. Kahn und Ron Golan gegründet, die alle drei 1981 ihren Bachelor of Architecture an der California Polytechnic State University, San Luis Obispo, erhielten. Neben ihrer Lehrtätigkeit am Southern California Institute of Architecture (SCI-Arc) sind sie an verschiedenen Projekten beteiligt, darunter zwei Residenzen in Laguna Beach und Pacific Palisades, ein 1990 entworfener Prototyp für öffentliche Toilettenbauten aus Stahl und Beton (im Auftrag der Stadt Los Angeles), das Hawkes Photo Studio (1993) und das Brix Restaurant, dessen Entwurf aus dem Jahre 1990 stammt. Zu ihren derzeitigen Arbeiten gehören die Janczak Residence und das MAK Center for Art and Architecture in Los Angeles. Darüber hinaus haben sie diverse Abhandlungen zur Situation der Architektur und der Stadt verfaßt.

Cette agence a été créée en 1986 par Russell N. Thomsen, Eric A. Kahn et Ron Golan, tous diplômés en architecture (B.Arch.) de la California State University, San Luis Obispo, en 1981. Enseignants au Southern California Institute of Architecture (SCI-Arc), ils comptent parmi leurs projets des maisons d'habitation à Laguna Beach et Pacific Palisades, un prototype de toilettes publiques en béton et acier pour la ville de Los Angeles, le studio de photo Hawkes (1993), et le restaurant Brix, dont le projet remonte à 1990. Parmi leurs travaux actuels: Janczak Residence et le MAK Center for Art and Architecture à Los Angeles. Ils ont par ailleurs beaucoup écrit sur la situation de l'architecture et sur la ville.

Brix Restaurant, Venice
1991

One of the principals of this young group is a graduate of the Southern California Institute of Architecture (Ron Golan), and another worked with Morphosis (Eric Kahn), so it may not be surprising that they dealt with the main feature of this 120 m² drive-through health food restaurant, an enormous, empty sign, like a "found object." The enigmatic simplicity of this sign, which contained only the title of the restaurant in small letters was conceived as a counterpoint to the "highly chaotic commercial fabric" of a lot located near a large intersection. Amplifying the small structure behind it, the sign is also intended to attract the attention of passersby, who are more likely to be in cars than on foot. In a different style, this type of idea had already been a focus for Frank O. Gehry's Santa Monica Place. Exemplifying an almost minimalist style which seems to be the successor of the deconstructivist fantasies of the late 1980s, this building is evidence that a new generation is staking out its place behind SCI-Arc founders like Mayne or Rotondi.

Da Ron Golan am Southern California Institute of Architecture studiert hat, und Eric Kahn bereits mit Morphosis zusammenarbeitete, verwundert es nicht, daß sie das Hauptkennzeichen dieses 120 m² großen Drive-in-Vollwertrestaurants – ein gewaltiges, leeres Schild – wie ein »objet trouvé« behandelten. Die geheimnisvolle Schlichtheit dieses Zeichens, das nur den Namen des Restaurants in kleinen Buchstaben enthält, gilt als Kontrapunkt zu der »hochchaotischen kommerziellen Struktur« des Baugeländes, das in der Nähe einer großen Straßenkreuzung liegt. Das Zeichen vergrößert den dahinterliegenden Bau und zieht die Aufmerksamkeit der Passanten auf sich. Wenn auch in anderem Stil, so hatte diese Idee schon bei Frank O. Gehrys Santa Monica Place Verwendung gefunden. Als beispielhaftes Exemplar eines nahezu minimalistischen Stils, der offensichtlich die dekonstruktivistischen Phantasien der späten 80er Jahre ablöst, beweist dieses Gebäude, daß eine neue Generation ihren Platz hinter den Begründern von SCI-Arc, wie Mayne und Rotondi, beansprucht.

L'une des grandes originalités de ce restaurant diététique de 120 m², une énorme enseigne vide, sorte «d'objet trouvé», étonne moins lorsque l'on sait que l'un des associés de ce groupe d'architectes est diplômé du Southern California Institute of Architecture (Ron Golan), et qu'un autre a travaillé avec Morphosis (Eric Kahn). La simplicité énigmatique de cette enseigne, qui ne contient que le nom du restaurant en petits caractères, vient en contrepoint du «tissu commercial hautement chaotique» de cette parcelle de terrain proche d'un grand carrefour. Amplifiant la petite taille du bâtiment, elle a également pour objet d'attirer l'attention des passants, plutôt automobilistes que piétons. Dans un style différent, Frank O. Gehry avait déjà utilisé ce type d'idée pour le Santa Monica Place. Exemple de style minimaliste qui semble succéder aux fantaisies déconstructivistes de la fin des années 80, ce bâtiment montre qu'une nouvelle génération apparaît derrière les fondateurs de SCI-Arc comme Mayne ou Rotondi.

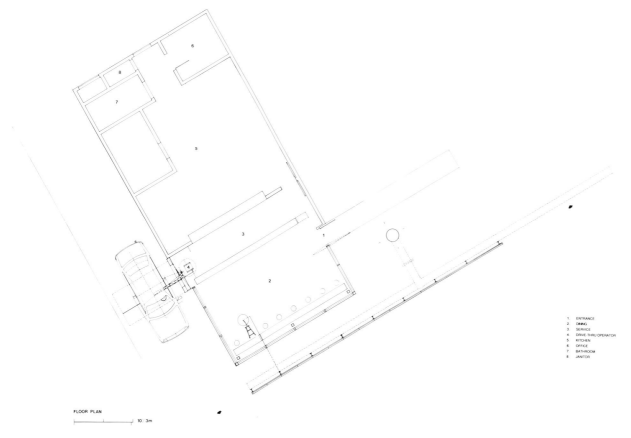

1. ENTRANCE
2. DINING
3. SERVICE
4. DRIVE-THRU OPERATOR
5. KITCHEN
6. OFFICE
7. BATHROOM
8. JANITOR

FLOOR PLAN
10 3m

Pages 64/65: Plans and photographs reveal the extremely simple design of the Brix Restaurant. The meticulous detailing and construction of the giant billboard is a direct reference to the numerous similar signs visible all over Los Angeles, their strong supports designed to resist earthquakes. Normally such billboards hold enormous, blatantly commercial signs, a use which is entirely reversed by Central Office of Architecture.

Seite 64/65: Die Baupläne und Abbildungen verdeutlichen das extrem einfache Design des Brix Restaurant. Die akribische Gestaltung der riesigen Reklametafel ist eine direkte Anspielung auf die zahllosen, über ganz Los Angeles verstreuten Tafeln mit ihren starken Trägern, die selbst Erdbeben standhalten sollen. Normalerweise tragen diese Reklameständer riesige, aufdringliche Werbetafeln, aber dieser Verwendungszweck wurde vom Central Office of Architecture in sein Gegenteil verkehrt.

Pages 64/65: Plans et photographies montrent la grande simplicité de conception du Brix Restaurant. Le soin apporté aux détails de construction du panneau géant est en référence directe aux panneaux omniprésents à Los Angeles, dont les poteaux de soutien sont conçus pour résister aux tremblements de terre. Normalement, ils supportent de gigantesques enseignes commerciales, usage inversé dans ce cas par le Central Office of Architecture.

Cigolle & Coleman

Mark Cigolle
Kim Coleman

This husband and wife team has engaged in an unusual form of collaboration in that both members are involved in design, and that they have acted as general contractor in building their design work. They have been particularly involved in the design of "live-work" houses, such as the Canyon House (Santa Monica, 1987–90 design 1990–92 completed), and the unbuilt Mills Musingo House (Los Angeles, 1985–87). They formed their partnership in 1982. Kim Coleman (BA Smith College, M. Arch. University of Virginia) worked as a general contractor in Washington, D.C. before obtaining her graduate degree. Mark Cigolle (BA Princeton, M. Arch. Princeton) worked in the offices of Michael Graves, I.M. Pei, Richard Meier and Peter Eisenman before starting his own firm in New York. They both teach at the University of Southern California, and have worked extensively on exploring the impact of the computer on the design process.

Dieses Ehepaar-Team hat eine ungewöhnliche Form der Zusammenarbeit entwickelt: Beide betätigen sich als Designer wie auch als Bauunternehmer bei der Errichtung ihrer Gebäude. Zu ihren Werken zählen insbesondere der Entwurf von Wohn- und Arbeitshäusern, wie etwa das Canyon House (Santa Monica, 1987–90 entworfen, 1990–92 fertiggestellt) und das bisher nicht gebaute Mills Musingo House (Los Angeles, 1985–87). Ihr gemeinsames Architekturbüro gründeten sie 1982. Kim Coleman (Bachelor of Arts, Smith College/Master of Architecture, University of Virginia) war als Bauunternehmerin in Washington, D.C. tätig, bevor sie ihren Hochschulabschluß erwarb. Mark Cigolle (Bachelor of Arts, Princeton/Master of Architecture, Princeton) arbeitete für Michael Graves, I.M. Pei, Richard Meier und Peter Eisenman, bevor er seine eigene Firma in New York gründete. Beide lehren an der University of Southern California und haben sich intensiv mit dem Einfluß des Computers auf den Entwurfsprozeß beschäftigt.

Ce couple marié pratique une forme peu courante de collaboration puisqu'il crée ses projets et les réalise en tant que maître d'œuvre. Ils se sont consacrés en particulier à la création de maisons à double fonction – travail et vie familiale – comme la Canyon House (Santa Monica, conçue en 1987–90, réalisée en 1990–92), et la Mills Musingo House (Los Angeles, 1985–87), non encore construite. Ils travaillent ensemble depuis 1982. Kim Coleman (BA Smith College, M. Arch. University of Virginia) a travaillé comme maître d'œuvre à Washington, D.C., avant de passer ses diplômes de fin d'études. Mark Cigolle (BA Princeton, M. Arch. Princeton) a collaboré avec Michael Graves, I.M. Pei, Richard Meier et Peter Eisenman avant d'ouvrir sa propre agence à New York. Ils enseignent tous deux à l'University of Southern California, et s'intéressent l'influence de l'ordinateur sur la conception.

Canyon House, Santa Monica Canyon, 1990–92, entrance.

Canyon House, Santa Monica Canyon, 1990–92, Eingang.

Canyon House, Santa Monica Canyon, 1990–92, entrée.

Canyon House, Santa Monica Canyon 1990–92

Located on a steeply sloped site, this studio workplace-house was designed by the architects for their own use. Though in a somewhat different style, this structure recalls the local tradition established by the Eames House and Studio where professional and domestic activities were combined. Here, the living areas are located on the two floors below the studio, facing the canyon and a back garden, but the architects insist that certain spaces, such as the study at the top of the tower are of indeterminate function, and indeed this notion of "in-between" space could also be applied to some of the large bays opening out onto the terraces, where the limit between inside and outside is not clearly established. The 14 meter high tower is rotated out from the rest of the composition to the west and the sea. Despite the use of an industrial vocabulary (freight containers, exposed metal frames etc.) the structure is livable and attractive.

Dieses Atelier-Wohnhaus, das auf einem steil abfallenden Gelände liegt, haben die Architekten für sich selbst geplant. Trotz seiner unterschiedlichen stilistischen Gestaltung erinnert das Gebäude an die örtliche Tradition des Eames House and Studio, in dem berufliche und häusliche Tätigkeiten miteinander kombiniert wurden. Im Canyon House befinden sich die Wohnräume in den beiden Etagen unterhalb des Ateliers mit Blick auf den Canyon bzw. auf einen Hintergarten. Aber die Architekten bestehen darauf, daß bestimmte Räume, wie etwa das Atelier in der Turmspitze, nicht auf eine spezielle Funktion festgelegt sind. Diese Idee der »Zwischen«-Räume gilt auch für einige der großen Alkoven, die sich zu den Terrassen hin öffnen, so daß der Übergang von Innen- und Außenbereichen nicht klar definiert ist. Der 14 Meter hohe Turm orientiert sich nach Westen zum Meer hin. Trotz der Formensprache von Industriebauten (Frachtcontainer, freiliegende Metallrahmen etc.) besticht das Gebäude durch sein attraktives und wohnliches Design.

Implantée sur un site très en pente, cette maison-atelier a été conçue par les architectes pour leur usage personnel. Bien que dans un style assez différent, elle rappelle la tradition locale lancée par la Eames House and Studio, où se mêlaient déjà activités professionnelles et vie domestique. Ici, la zone d'habitation se répartit sur deux niveaux en dessous de l'atelier, face au canyon et à un jardin arrière, mais les architectes insistent sur l'absence de fonction définie de certains espaces, comme le studio au sommet de la tour. Il est vrai que cette notion d'espace indéfini pourrait aussi s'appliquer aux grandes baies des terrasses, où la limite entre l'intérieur et l'extérieur n'est pas clairement tracée. La tour de 14 m de haut pivote vers l'ouest et la mer, par rapport au reste de la composition. Les matériaux industriels (conteneurs, cadres métalliques apparents) n'empêchent pas cette maison d'être vivable et séduisante.

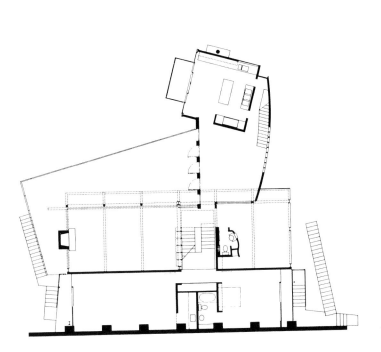

Middle level plan

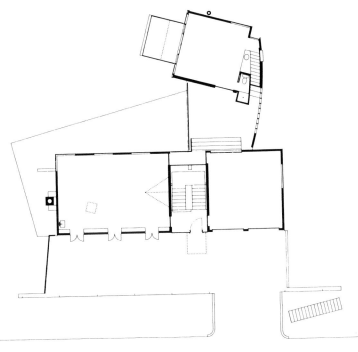

Upper level plan

Pages 68/69: The rotation of the two essential elements of this house serves both practical and symbolic purposes. The lower, office entrance section is aligned with the street whereas the rotation of the tower signals a different (private) use and accommodates the available views.

Seite 68/69: Die beiden Hauptbereiche haben sowohl eine praktische als auch eine symbolische Funktion. Der untere Gebäudeteil orientiert sich am Straßenverlauf, während der winklig dazu angelegte Turm einen privaten Verwendungs- zweck signalisiert.

Pages 68/69: La rotation des deux composantes essentielles de cette maison obéit à des objectifs pratiques et symboliques. Le niveau bas – l'entrée des bureaux – est aligné sur la rue, tandis que le pivotement de la tour signale un usage différent – privé – et permet de profiter de la vue.

Steven **Ehrlich**

Steven Ehrlich

49 years old, Steven Ehrlich has used his experience of working in North and West Africa and Japan to create a personal style intended to blend Los Angeles tradition and architectural innovation. His homes have often included courtyards which bring nature into his architecture, creating an environment which he sees as a "cleansing from the outside world." In the 1990s he has branched out into larger projects, with the 1991 Shatto Recreation Center which · *Newsweek* called a "graceful example of defensive architecture," and the Sony Music Entertainment Campus (Santa Monica, 1992), a 9 500 m² complex blending indoor and outdoor space.

Der 49jährige Steven Ehrlich machte sich seine langjährige Berufserfahrung in Nord- und Westafrika sowie in Japan zunutze und entwickelte einen persönlichen Stil, bei dem die Tradition der Stadt Los Angeles und architektonische Innovation miteinander verschmelzen. Seine Häuser besitzen häufig einen Innenhof, durch den die Natur in die Architektur einbezogen wird. Damit schafft Ehrlich eine Umgebung, die er als »Ort der spirituellen Reinigung von der Außenwelt« bezeichnet. Seit Beginn der 90er Jahre beschäftigt sich Ehrlich mit größeren Projekten wie etwa dem Shatto Recreation Center (1991), das »Newsweek« ein »anmutiges Beispiel defensiver Architektur« nannte, und dem Sony Music Entertainment Campus (Santa Monica, 1992), einem 9 500 m² großen Komplex, der Außen- und Innenräume miteinander verbindet.

A 49 ans, Steven Ehrlich a su tirer parti de ses expériences professionnelles en Afrique du Nord et de l'Ouest et au Japon pour se créer un style personnel qui associe tradition angélinienne et innovation architecturale. Ses maisons comportent souvent des patios qui laissent pénétrer la nature et créent un environnement qui «purifie du monde extérieur». Dans les années 90, il s'est lancé dans des projets plus importants, comme le Shatto Recreation Center (1991) qualifié par «Newsweek» «d'exemple gracieux d'architecture défensive», et le Sony Music Entertainment Campus (Santa Monica, 1992), ensemble de 9 500 m² mêlant espaces intérieurs et extérieurs.

Ehrman-Coombs Residence, Santa Monica, 1989–91, interior view.

Ehrman-Coombs Residence, Santa Monica, 1989–91, Innenansicht.

Ehrman-Coombs Residence, Santa Monica, 1989–91, vue intérieure.

Ehrman-Coombs Residence, Santa Monica 1989–91

Located on the beach in Santa Monica, with its back facing the Pacific Coast Highway and the eroded palisades, this visually arresting 325 m² house was built on a narrow lot. Local zoning restrictions required that it be no more than 5.2 meters wide and 13.7 meters high. Within this unusual configuration, Steven Ehrlich placed a 5.5 meter high living room. Slightly elevated above beach level for privacy, this room features a 4.8 meter high sectional glass door which rolls up completely to the ceiling, offering a spectacular view of the wide ocean horizon, and dissolving the border between interior and exterior. The apparently closed shape of the house, which gives it a good deal of privacy despite the very animated beach just opposite, is thus skillfully blended with an interior that is very bright and open. Ehrlich's use of slabs and balconies for this house has led it to be compared to the work of Neutra and Schindler, the Austrian pioneers of modernist California houses.

Dieses am Strand von Santa Monica gelegene, eindrucksvolle, 325 m² umfassende Gebäude, dessen Rückseite auf den Pacific Coast Highway und die erodierten Palisaden zeigt, steht auf einem sehr schmalen Platz. Da die örtlichen Bauauflagen eine mehr als 5,2 Meter breite und 13,7 Meter hohe Bebauung untersagten, schuf Steven Ehrlich innerhalb dieses ungewöhnlichen Geländes ein Wohnzimmer von 5,5 Metern Höhe. Aufgrund seiner Lage etwas oberhalb des Strandniveaus bietet dieser Raum den Bewohnern dennoch genügend Privatsphäre; er besitzt eine 4,8 Meter hohe, gefächerte Glastür, die bis zur Decke hochgerollt werden kann und eine spektakuläre Aussicht auf die Weite des Pazifiks gewährt, wodurch die Grenze zwischen Innen und Außen verschwimmt. Die schmale Form des Hauses, die trotz des stark frequentierten Strandes noch genügend Privatsphäre bietet, kombinierte der Architekt sorgfältig mit einer Innenausstattung, die sehr hell und offen wirkt. Wegen seiner Betonsockel und Balkone wurde das Haus mit den Arbeiten von Neutra und Schindler verglichen, den österreichischen Pionieren modernistischer kalifornischer Häuser.

Située sur la plage de Santa Monica, appuyée contre la Pacific Coast Highway et les palissades érodées, cette fascinante maison de 325 m² a été construite sur une étroite parcelle de terrain. La réglementation locale lui interdisait d'avoir plus de 5,2 m de large et 13,7 m de haut, et malgré ces contraintes inhabituelles, Steven Ehrlich a réussi à y placer une salle de séjour de 5,5 m de hauteur sous plafond. Légèrement surélevée par rapport à la plage, pour des raisons d'intimité, cette pièce possède une porte de verre de 4,8 m de haut en plusieurs sections qui se relèvent contre le plafond, offrant une vue spectaculaire sur l'océan, et faisant disparaître les limites entre intérieur et extérieur. La forme apparemment fermée de l'ensemble assure l'intimité nécessaire malgré la présence d'une plage très fréquentée et délimite un espace intérieur ouvert et lumineux. L'utilisation des dalles et des balcons rappelle le travail de Neutra et Schindler, les pionniers autrichiens des maisons californiennes modernistes.

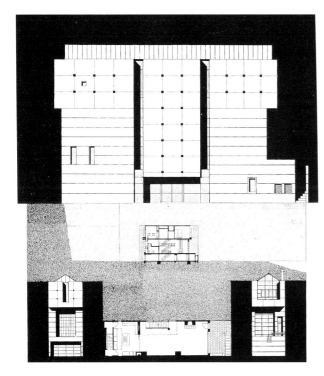

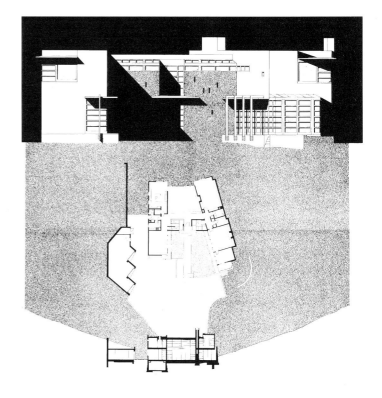

Pages 74/75: With its back close to the Pacific Coast Highway, the Ehrman-Coombs Residence reserves its large open bay to the side of the Santa Monica beach. Photography cannot capture the majestic, wide-open vista afforded by the seaside in this location, but the very large opening devised by Steven Ehrlich is a grand gesture to the remarkable view, which manages to retain the privacy of the clients.

Seite 74/75: Während die Rückseite der Ehrman-Coombs Residence unmittelbar auf den Pacific Coast Highway blickt, öffnet sich die Front zum Strand von Santa Monica. Abbildungen können das weitläufige Panorama, das die Strandlage dieses Geländes bietet, nicht annähernd wiedergeben, aber die sehr große, bis zur Decke reichende Glasfront dokumentiert Steven Ehrlichs Referenz an die spektakuläre Aussicht, ohne dabei die Privatsphäre der Bewohner zu beeinträchtigen.

Pages 74/75: Pratiquement adossée au grand axe routier de la Pacific Coast Highway, la Ehrman-Coombs Residence s'ouvre largement du côté de la plage de Santa Monica. La photographie ne peut rendre la majesté de l'immense paysage qui se déploie à cet endroit, mais la très grande ouverture imaginée par Steven Ehrlich permet d'embrasser une vue remarquable tout en préservant l'intimité des habitants.

Pages 72/73: The Ehrman-Coombs Residence is located just below William Foster's 1940 Streamline Shangri-La Apartments. Its very peculiar configuration is an active response to the lot size and zoning requirements, but despite a typically heterogeneous architectural environment, it stands on its own very successfully.

Seite 72/73: Die Ehrman-Coombs Residence liegt genau unterhalb von William Fosters Shangri-La Apartments, die 1940 im Streamline Style errichtet wurden. Die ganz spezielle Konstruktionsweise dieses Gebäudes ergab sich als Reaktion auf die Größe des Baugeländes und die Bestimmungen des Flächennutzungsplans. Trotz einer für das Gebiet typischen heterogenen architektonischen Umgebung kommt das Haus sehr gut zur Geltung.

Pages 72/73: Ehrman-Coombs Residence est située juste en dessous de l'immeuble d'appartements de style streamline de William Foster, le Shangri-La (1940). Sa configuration très particulière répond à la forme du terrain et à la réglementation locale.

Schulman Residence, Brentwood 1989–92

Ehrlich's reference to early California modernism is even clearer in this house, located in the fashionable Brentwood area of Los Angeles. Poured-in-place concrete walls, wood and stucco alternate to give a rich variety of surfaces within a limited range of colors. Two wings of the house are set at angles determined by the proximity of canyon walls, with the central living room located between them. These wings are connected by a bridge, at the second story, reached by two stairways located in the entrance. The floor area of this large house is close to 800 m². The generous presence of nature and the use of wood, together with the configuration dictated by topography show how modernist principles are adapted by the architect to the very particular conditions of design and construction in Southern California.

Bei diesem Haus in Los Angeles' vornehmem Viertel Brentwood kommt Ehrlichs Anspielung auf den frühen kalifornischen Modernismus noch deutlicher zum Ausdruck. Gußbetonwände, Holz und Stuckputz wechseln sich ab und bilden eine vielfältig strukturierte Oberfläche innerhalb eines begrenzten Farbspektrums. Vorgegeben durch die Lage am Canyon wurden zwei Flügel des Hauses angewinkelt und über eine Brücke im zweiten Geschoß miteinander verbunden, das über zwei Treppen im Eingangsbereich erreichbar ist. Zwischen den Flügeln liegt der Hauptwohnraum. Die Grundfläche dieses Hauses beträgt etwa 800 m². Üppige Natur und großzügige Verwendung von Holz in Kombination mit der von der Topographie bestimmten Lage des Geländes demonstrieren, wie der Architekt modernistische Prinzipien den sehr speziellen Anforderungen an Design und Bauweise in Südkalifornien angepaßt hat.

La référence d'Ehrlich aux débuts du modernisme californien est encore plus claire dans cette maison, située à Brentwood, élégant quartier de Los Angeles. Murs en béton coulé, bois et crépi alternent pour offrir une riche variété de surfaces dans une gamme réduite de couleurs. Les deux ailes de la maison sont disposées selon des angles déterminés par la proximité des parois du canyon. La salle de séjour est en position centrale. Les ailes sont réunies au second niveau par un pont, relié à l'entrée par deux escaliers. La surface au sol mesure près de 800 m². La présence généreuse de la nature et le recours au bois, ainsi que la configuration dictée par la topographie, montrent la manière dont les principes modernistes sont adaptés par l'architecte aux conditions très particulières de conception et de construction de la Californie du Sud.

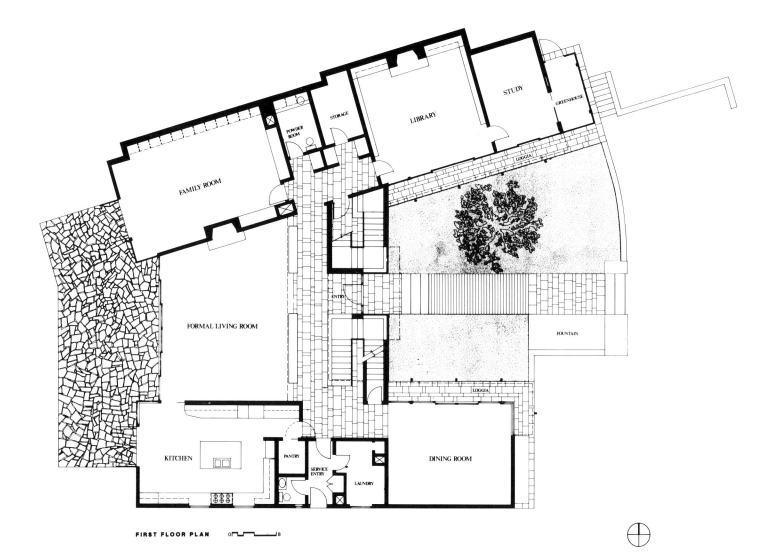

FIRST FLOOR PLAN 0 ⌐_⌐_⌐ 8

Pages 76-79: Photographs and plans highlight the capacity of the architect to employ an historic allusion to early Southern California modernism as practiced by Schindler or Neutra in a very contemporary mode. As in the case of the Ehrman-Coombs Residence, the layout of the house is an almost natural outgrowth of the constraints of the site.

Seite 76-79: Die Abbildungen und Baupläne unterstreichen die Fähigkeit des Architekten, historische Anspielungen auf einen frühen südkalifornischen Modernismus (wie ihn Schindler oder Neutra vertraten) in zeitgenössischer Art in das Gebäude einfließen zu lassen. Genau wie bei der Ehrman-Coombs Residence entstand auch der Entwurf dieses Gebäudes als Reaktion auf die Gegebenheiten des Geländes.

Pages 76-79: Les plans et les photographies soulignent le talent de l'architecte qui a traité de façon très contemporaine cette allusion historique aux premiers pas du modernisme dans le sud de la Californie qu'illustrèrent Schindler et Neutra. Comme pour la Ehrman-Coombs Residence, la conception de la maison en fait presque un prolongement naturel des contraintes du site.

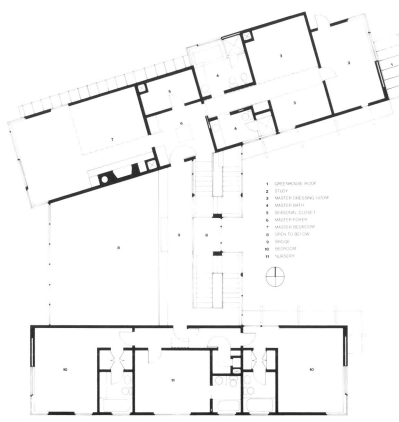

1 GREENHOUSE ROOF
2 STUDY
3 MASTER DRESSING ROOM
4 MASTER BATH
5 SEASONAL CLOSET
6 MASTER FOYER
7 MASTER BEDROOM
8 OPEN TO BELOW
9 BRIDGE
10 BEDROOM
11 NURSERY

SECOND FLOOR PLAN

Pages 80/81: Despite the apparent solidity of the house, there is a constant dialogue between interior and exterior. This recalls the early and frequent associations between the conception of Japanese architecture, where the distinction between interior and exterior is less obvious than in the West, and the architecture of Southern California. Naturally the local climate makes such opening all the more feasible.

Seite 80/81: Trotz der offensichtlich massiven Struktur des Hauses besteht hier ein beständiger Dialog zwischen Außen- und Innenbereichen, der an die frühen und zahlreichen Beziehungen zwischen japanischer Architektur (bei der die Trennung zwischen Außen- und Innenbereichen weniger deutlich ist als in der westlichen Welt) und der Architektur Südkaliforniens erinnert. Natürlich unterstützt das örtliche Klima eine solche Öffnung in erheblichem Maße.

Pages 80/81: La solidité évidente de la maison n'empêche pas un dialogue constant entre l'intérieur et l'extérieur. C'est un rappel des liens précoces et fréquents entre la conception japonaise de l'architecture (avec une distinction entre le dedans et le dehors moins marquée qu'en Occident) et celle de la Californie du Sud. Le climat local facilite évidemment ce type d'ouverture.

Hempstead Residence, Venice
1990–93

Although the preoccupation of California architects with spaces between interior and exterior can be linked to the traditions of Japan, it is above all related to the very mild climate of the Los Angeles area. Thus in this house, located in the beach community of Venice, "the pool, patio and surrounding stone walls appear as extensions of the living room," according to the architect. This openness is contrasted with the surrounding walls which give privacy in the chaotic semi-urban environment of Venice. Although the basic forms of the house remain faithful to the modernist penchants of Steven Ehrlich, here, the warm, organic colors and stucco finish seem to recall the intimate relationship of Southern California with the Hispanic traditions brought from Mexico very early in the recorded history of the area. The floor space of this house is 220 m².

Obwohl die intensive Beschäftigung der kalifornischen Architekten mit Räumen zwischen dem Innen- und dem Außenbereich auf den Einfluß der japanischen Tradition zurückgeführt werden kann, ist diese architektonische Gestaltung in erster Linie durch das sehr milde Klima im Gebiet von Los Angeles bestimmt. Bei diesem Haus »scheinen der Pool, die Terrasse und die umliegenden Steinmauern wie eine Erweiterung des Wohnzimmers«, wie es der Architekt formuliert. Diese Offenheit steht im Kontrast zu den umgebenden Wänden, die den Bewohnern in der chaotischen semi-urbanen Umgebung von Venice ein wenig Privatsphäre sichern. Obwohl die Grundformen des Hauses nach wie vor mit Steven Ehrlichs Vorliebe für den Modernismus korrespondieren, erinnern die warmen, erdigen Farben und der Stuckputz an die enge Beziehung zwischen Südkalifornien und der von Mexiko ausgehenden hispanischen Tradition, die seit jeher ihren Einfluß ausübte. Die Grundfläche der Hempstead Residence beträgt 220 m².

Si l'intérêt porté par les architectes californiens aux espaces et aux limites entre l'intérieur et l'extérieur peut se rattacher aux traditions japonaises, il est avant tout dicté par la douceur du climat. Ainsi, dans cette maison de Venice, au bord de l'océan, «la piscine, le patio, et les murs de pierre semblent des extensions de la salle de séjour», selon l'architecte. Cette ouverture contraste avec les murs d'enceinte qui assurent une certaine intimité dans l'environnement semi-urbain assez chaotique de Venice. Bien que la forme générale reste fidèle aux tendances modernistes d'Ehrlich, les chaudes couleurs organiques et la finition en crépi semblent évoquer le rapport intime que la Californie du Sud entretient avec ses traditions hispaniques, importées du Mexique au tout début de son histoire. La surface de cette maison est de 220 m².

Pages 82/83: Not only the color scheme, but also the strong, block-shaped forms of the house, contribute to an association with the southwestern tradition of adobe architecture.

Seite 82/83: Nicht nur das Farbschema, sondern auch die kraftvollen, blockartigen Formen dieses Hauses erinnern an die traditionelle Adobearchitektur des amerikanischen Südwestens.

Pages 82/83: La coloration, mais également les formes massives, en «blocs», de la maison évoquent les constructions traditionnelles en adobe du Sud-Ouest américain.

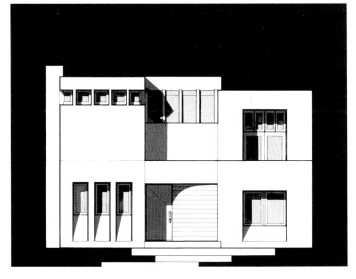

Pages 84/85: The warmth of the exterior colors finds a natural translation to the comfortable interior. The crowded architectural hodgepodge which makes up the reality of Venice is in no way evident in these images. Unlike Frank O. Gehry's nearby Norton House which makes an overt statement, architect and client here seem to agree on a much more private, isolated approach.

Seite 84/85: Die warmen Farben der Fassade finden ein natürliches Pendant in der ansprechenden Innenausstattung. Das für Venice so typische architektonische Durcheinander sucht man in diesen Bildern vergeblich. Im Gegensatz zu Frank O. Gehrys nahegelegenem Norton House, das eine eindeutige Aussage darstellt, scheinen Architekt und Kunde bei diesem Gebäude einem privaten, isolierten Ansatz den Vorzug gegeben zu haben.

Pages 84/85: Les couleurs chaleureuses des façades se retrouvent naturellement dans ce confortable intérieur. Le méli-mélo architectural de Venice ne transparaît pas vraiment sur ces images. A la différence de la toute proche Norton House de Gehry qui proclame sa différence, l'architecte et son client semblent ici s'être mis d'accord sur une approche plus retenue, plus intime.

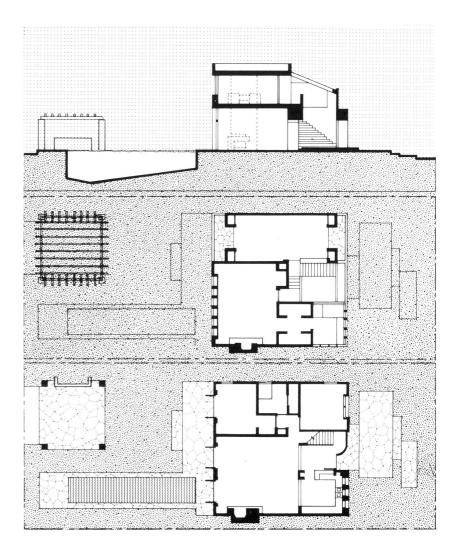

Frank O. Gehry

Frank O. Gehry

Schnabel House, Brentwood, 1986–89, view of the pool and garden pavilion.

Schnabel House, Brentwood, 1986–89, Blick auf den Teich und den Gartenpavillon.

Schnabel House, Brentwood, 1986–89, vue sur le bassin et le pavillon du jardin.

Born in Toronto, Canada in 1929, Frank O. Gehry is one of the more influential architects working today. Not only has he successfully called into question the forms which modern architecture has taken for granted, but he has done the same for materials of construction. It is not that steel and concrete are absent from his work, but rather that chain link, corrugated aluminum, or utility grade construction board are present. Gehry seems to be as much at ease building a giant fish (Fishdance Restaurant, Kobe, Japan, 1984), as he is with an office building whose facade incorporates a huge pair of binoculars (designed by Claes Oldenburg for Chiat/Day, Venice, C.A., 1989). His largest project to date, the Disney Concert Hall in Los Angeles, has been halted for the moment for lack of fundraising and budgetary reasons. Ongoing work includes: the Guggenheim Museum, Bilbao, Spain; the Samsung Museum, Seoul, Korea; commercial projects in Prague, Czech Republic, Düsseldorf, Hannover, Germany; the Mighty Ducks Rink, L.A., and an administration building for Disneyland in California.

Der 1929 in Toronto, Kanada, geborene Frank O. Gehry ist einer der einflußreichsten Architekten der heutigen Zeit. Er stellte nicht nur die Formen, sondern auch die Baumaterialien in Frage, die die moderne Architektur als selbstverständlich voraussetzte. Gehry baut zwar nicht ohne Stahl und Beton, aber im Vordergrund seiner Arbeiten stehen Wellblech und Fertigbauteile. Darüber hinaus scheint er ein ebenso großes Vergnügen daran zu haben, einen gewaltigen Fisch zu bauen (Fishdance Restaurant, Kobe, Japan, 1984) wie ein Bürogebäude, das ein riesiges Fernglas ziert (1989 von Claes Oldenburg für Chiat/Day, Venice, Kalifornien, entworfen). Bei seinem bisher größten Projekt, der Disney Concert Hall in Los Angeles, erfolgte ein budgetbedingter Baustopp mangels Fundraising. Zu Gehrys derzeitigen Arbeiten zählen das Guggenheim Museum, Bilbao, Spanien, das Samsung Museum, Seoul, gewerbliche Projekte in Prag, Düsseldorf und Hannover, das Eisstadion der Mighty Ducks in Los Angeles, und ein Verwaltungsgebäude für Disneyland, Kalifornien.

Né en 1929 à Toronto, au Canada, Frank O. Gehry est l'un des architectes les plus influents du moment. Il a brillamment remis en question à la fois les formes que l'architecture moderne avait pris pour acquises et les matériaux de construction. Dans son œuvre, le béton et l'acier se retrouvent facilement associés au treillage métallique, à la tôle ondulée d'aluminium, ou aux planches. Gehry semble aussi à l'aise pour construire un poisson géant (Fishdance Restaurant, Kobé, Japon, 1984) que pour édifier un immeuble de bureaux dont la façade intègre une paire de jumelles géantes (dessinée par Claes Oldenburg pour Chiat/Day, Venice, Californie, en 1989). Son plus important projet à ce jour, le Disney Concert Hall, L.A., est pour l'instant arrêté pour des raisons budgétaires, et à cause de l'insuffisance des fonds recueillis. Parmi ses autres projets en cours: Le Guggenheim Museum de Bilbao (Espagne), le musée Samsung à Séoul, des projets d'immeubles commerciaux à Prague, Düsseldorf et Hanovre, le Mighty Ducks Rink, L.A., et le bâtiment administratif de Disneyland en Californie.

Schnabel House, Brentwood
1986–89

In retrospect, it might be said that this 550 m² house represents the work of Frank Gehry at the height of his powers. Although the so-called Deconstructivist movement was short-lived, the exploration of the inspiration provided by the Russian Constructivist architects and artists, combined here with specific references to Wright's Barnsdall House, make the Schnabel House a concentrated résumé of Gehry's accomplishments. In the apparently chaotic appearance of this house, an underlying order, and indeed a comfort befitting its scale and location are combined in what can be called a work of art without any exaggeration. At once open and yet appropriately shielded from the strong sun, the Schnabel House also manages not to betray the socially oriented concept of the architect, as formulated through his use of ordinary materials, first seen in his 1978 house in Santa Monica.

Rückblickend wird man vielleicht sagen, daß dieses 550 m² große Haus Frank O. Gehry auf der Höhe seines Schaffens repräsentiert. Obwohl die sogenannte dekonstruktivistische Bewegung von kurzer Dauer war, stellt das Schnabel House aufgrund der Anregungen durch die russischen konstruktivistischen Architekten und Künstler, und aufgrund der gezielten Anspielungen auf Wrights Barnsdall House ein Résumé von Gehrys Schaffen dar. Trotz des chaotisch anmutenden Erscheinungsbildes wurden hier eine zugrundeliegende Ordnung und ein dem Maßstab und Standort des Hauses angemessener Komfort zu einem Konzept kombiniert, das man wohl ohne Übertreibung als ein Kunstwerk bezeichnen kann. Für das Schnabel House wählte der Architekt eine offene und zugleich vor der starken Sonne schützende Konstruktionsweise; auch blieb er bei diesem Projekt seinen sozial orientierten Prinzipien treu, die sich in der Verwendung von herkömmlichen Materialien zeigen und erstmals 1978 in seinem Haus in Santa Monica zum Ausdruck kamen.

Rétrospectivement, on peut dire de cette maison de 550 m² qu'elle représente le style d'un Gehry au sommet de sa puissance créatrice. Même si le mouvement déconstructiviste n'a guère vécu, l'exploration des recherches des constructivistes russes, combinée ici à des références spécifiques à la Barnsdall House de F.L. Wright, font de la Schnabel House un concentré des réalisations de Gehry. Sous une apparence chaotique, se retrouvent un ordre et un sens du confort adaptés à la taille et au site, qui permettent de qualifier cette maison d'œuvre d'art. A la fois ouverte et protégée du soleil, elle arrive à rester fidèle au concept social proposé par l'architecte dans sa maison personnelle de Santa Monica (1978), à travers l'utilisation de matériaux ordinaires.

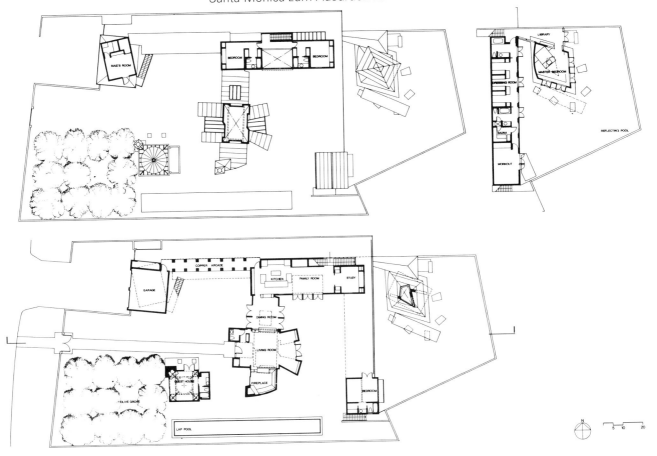

Disney Concert Hall, Los Angeles 1988–89 (project)

"Disney Hall, which I won in close competition with Stirling, Hollein and Boehm, is the first big thing I've been given to do in my home town," says Frank O. Gehry. "In Los Angeles, despite all its freedom to experiment, the avant-garde remains peripheral to the mainstream of most of what's being built." Situated near Arata Isozaki's Museum of Contemporary Art, this home for the L.A. Philharmonic Orchestra should be clad in limestone, like the American Center in Paris. Its form has been compared to an "exploding rose," and this complex shape led to a certain amount of criticism. Due to projected cost overruns and the inability of fund-raisers to find a complement to the $50 million given in 1987 by Walt Disney's widow Lillian B. Disney, it has been suggested that the building might be clad in gray titanium as opposed to the more expensive limestone. As of March 1995, with a budgetary shortfall estimated between $80 million and $120 million (according to *Newsweek*), the construction of the concert hall had not advanced beyond the underground garage level.

»Die Disney Concert Hall, deren Ausschreibung ich in einem harten Wettbewerb gegen Stirling, Hollein und Boehm gewann, ist der erste große Auftrag, den man mir in meiner Heimatstadt erteilte«, erklärte Frank O. Gehry. »In Los Angeles befindet sich die Avantgarde, trotz allem Mut zum Experiment, immer noch an der Peripherie der Architekturströmungen.« Dieses neue Gebäude für das L.A. Philharmonic Orchestra liegt in der Nähe von Arata Isozakis Museum of Contemporary Art und soll wie das American Center in Paris eine Kalksteinverkleidung erhalten. Seine komplexe Form, die mit einer »explodierenden Rose« verglichen wurde, gab bereits Anlaß zu heftiger Kritik, und aufgrund der zu erwartenden enormen Kosten und dem Mangel an potentiellen Geldgebern für den Gegenbetrag zu den 1987 von Walt Disneys Witwe, Lillian B. Disney, gestifteten 50 Millionen Dollar kam bereits der Vorschlag, das Gebäude statt mit teurem Kalkstein mit grauem Titan zu verkleiden. Infolge eines geschätzten Budgetdefizits in Höhe von 80 bis 120 Millionen Dollar (laut »Newsweek«) konnten bis zum März 1995 lediglich die unterirdischen Parkflächen fertiggestellt werden.

«Disney Hall, que j'ai remporté à l'issue d'un concours avec Stirling, Hollein et Boehm, est la première commande importante que l'on m'ait confié dans ma ville.» déclare Frank O. Gehry. «A Los Angeles, malgré notre apparente liberté d'expérimentation, l'avant-garde reste écartée des grands chantiers.» Implantée près du Museum of Contemporary Art d'Arata Isozaki, cette salle destinée au Los Angeles Philarmonic devrait être revêtue de pierre calcaire, comme l'American Center de Paris. Sa forme complexe, comparée à une «rose en explosion», a été assez critiquée. Du fait de dépassements de devis et de l'incapacité de compléter les 50 millions de $ offerts par la veuve de Walt Disney, Lillian B. Disney, on songe à remplacer la coûteuse pierre du revêtement par du titane gris. En mars 1995, il manquait encore de 80 à 120 millions de $ (selon «Newsweek») et la construction n'a pas dépassé le stade des parkings souterrains.

Page 90: On the wall of Frank O. Gehry's Santa Monica offices, a series of proposed computer-generated configurations for the interior of the Disney Concert Hall.

Seite 90: An der Wand von Frank O. Gehrys Büro befindet sich eine Reihe im Computer entworfener Konfigurationen einer Innenausstattung der Disney Concert Hall.

Page 90: Au mur des bureaux de Frank O. Gehry à Santa Monica, une série de possibilité de configurations de l'intérieur du Disney Concert Hall réalisées par ordinateur.

Pages 92/93: A photograph of the project model gives an idea of the full sculptural impact of the structure, in a neighborhood where most buildings, aside from Isozaki's MoCA, are in an uninspired modern style.

Seite 92/93: Das Modell des Gebäudes vermittelt einen Eindruck von der skulpturalen Aussagekraft der Concert Hall, die in einer Umgebung liegt, in der sich die meisten Bauten (mit Ausnahme von Isozakis MoCA) durch einen phantasielosen modernen Stil auszeichnen.

Pages 92/93: La maquette donne une idée de la présence sculpturale du bâtiment, dans un quartier où la plupart des immeubles sont d'un style moderne sans inspiration, excepté le MoCA d'Isozaki.

Joan **Hallberg**

Joan Hallberg

Sonoma Coast Residence, Stewarts Point, 1990–92, interior view.

Sonoma Coast Residence, Stewarts Point, 1990–92, Innenansicht.

Sonoma Coast Residence, Stewarts Point, 1990–92, vue intérieure.

Joan Hallberg is an unusual architect in that she eschews the usual tendency to list her own achievements. The Sonoma Coast Residence published here, despite the evident mastery of architecture which it confirms, is only her third built work. The house is essentially the product of what Joan Hallberg says at the time was a "one person office." She did work with a structural engineer (James Meacham, MKM & Associates) and a landscape specialist (Mary Rhyne). Joan Hallberg has designed nine other projects since opening her own practice in 1987, including houses in Gualala, Anchor Bay, and Sea Ranch, and a Volunteer Fire Station in Manchester. Five of these projects are currently in progress – three under construction in 1995 and two in 1996. Most of this work, with the exception of the Mountain House in Truckee and the Forest House in Taylorsville, is located on the Northern California Coast.

Joan Hallberg ist insofern eine ungewöhnliche Architektin, als daß sie die übliche Auflistung der eigenen Errungenschaften scheut. Die hier vorgestellte Sonoma Coast Residence ist trotz der architektonischen Meisterschaft, die das Gebäude dokumentiert, erst ihr drittes ausgeführtes Bauprojekt. Das Haus ist im Grunde das Produkt einer Zeit, in der Joan Hallberg als »Ein-Mann-Büro« auftrat. Allerdings arbeitete sie mit einem Ingenieur (James Meacham, MKM & Associates) und einer Landschaftsarchitektin (Mary Rhyne) zusammen. Seit der Gründung ihres Architekturbüros 1987 entwarf Joan Hallberg neun weitere Projekte, u.a. Häuser in Gualala, Anchor Bay und Sea Ranch sowie das Gebäude der Freiwilligen Feuerwehr in Manchester. Fünf dieser Projekte befinden sich zur Zeit in der Entwicklung – drei sind seit 1995 im Bau, und bei zwei Projekten beginnen die Bauarbeiten 1996. Die meisten dieser Arbeiten (mit Ausnahme des Mountain House in Truckee und des Forest House in Taylorsville) liegen an der nordkalifornischen Küste.

A la différence de beaucoup de ses confrères, Joan Hallberg refuse de faire un inventaire de ses réussites. La Sonoma Coast Residence publiée ici, malgré l'évidente maîtrise qu'elle confirme, n'est que sa troisième réalisation. Elle est essentiellement le résultat de ce que l'architecte avoue avoir été à l'époque «une agence individuelle». Elle a travaillé avec un ingénieur (James Meacham, MKM & Associates) et une paysagiste, Mary Rhine. Elle a conçu neuf autres projets depuis l'ouverture de son agence en 1987, dont des maisons à Gualala, Anchor Bay et Sea Ranch, et un poste de pompiers volontaires à Manchester. Cinq de ces projets sont en cours de réalisation, trois en 1995 et deux pour 1996. La plupart des réalisations de Hallberg, à l'exception de Mountain House, à Truckee, et de Forest House, à Taylorsville, se trouvent sur la côte de la Californie du Nord.

Sonoma Coast Residence, Stewarts Point 1990–92

The architect calls this project "somewhat medieval" and compares it to a castle. Located on a 100 hectare property 200 kilometers north of San Francisco, it is on a cliff almost 100 meters above the Pacific Ocean. In clear weather, it is possible to see more than 100 kilometers down the rugged coastline. This ample house (650 m² including the decks and catwalks) is intended by the owner to receive a large number of guests, which explains the division of the plan into three "pods," one of which is a sort of connected guest house, with the whole united by a "floating roof." Extreme climatic conditions such as high winds, and energy code requirements which limited the glass-to-floor-area ratio, rendered the design more complex. Despite the necessarily high level of sophistication, materials such as timber open-web trusses, redwood shiplap siding or industrial galvanized steel fireplace stacks give the whole of this remarkable house a strong appearance well-suited to its spectacular site.

Hallberg nennt dieses Projekt auf einem 100 Hektar großen Grundstück, 200 Kilometer nördlich von San Francisco auf einer fast 100 Meter über dem Pazifik aufragenden Klippe, »irgendwie mittelalterlich« und vergleicht es mit einer Burg. Bei klarem Wetter kann man von hier aus mehr als 100 Kilometer der zerklüfteten Küstenlinie sehen. Das geräumige Haus (650 m² inklusive Flachdächern und Stegen) soll viele Gäste aufnehmen können, was die Unterteilung des Gebäudes in drei "Kokons" erklärt, von denen einer als eine Art Gästehaus dient. Das Ganze ist unter einer »schwebenden Dachkonstruktion« vereint. Aufgrund extremer klimatischer Bedingungen (z.B. kräftiger Wind) und erforderlicher Energiesparmaßnahmen, die das Verhältnis von Glas zur Grundfläche stark einschränkten, fiel das Design des Gebäudes relativ dicht aus. Trotz des notwendigerweise hohen Niveaus an technischem Raffinement verleihen Materialien wie das Holz des Fachwerkbinders, die Außenwandverschalung aus Redwood-Spundbrettern sowie die Kaminschächte aus verzinktem Stahl diesem außergewöhnlichen Haus ein kraftvolles Erscheinungsbild, das hervorragend zu seiner aufsehenerregenden Lage paßt.

Décrivant cette réalisation implantée sur un terrain de 100 hectares à 200 km au nord de San Francisco sur une falaise à 100 m au dessus du Pacifique, son architecte parle de «caractère un peu médiéval» et la compare à un château. Par temps clair, la vue porte à 100 km à la ronde sur la côte découpée. Cette grande maison (650 m², y compris ponts et coursives) est destinée à recevoir de nombreux invités, ce qui explique sa division en trois «cosses», dont l'une est une maison d'amis, le tout unifié sous un «toit flottant». Les conditions climatiques extrêmes (des vents violents) et une réglementation énergétique limitant le rapport vitrage/surface au sol ont compliqué la réalisation. Intégrés dans un ensemble très sophistiqué, les matériaux humbles comme la poutraison apparente en bois, les bardeaux en séquoia ou la cheminée en tôle d'acier galvanisé industriel confèrent à cette maison une apparence de puissance, bien adaptée à ce site spectaculaire.

Although it does not have the menacing aspect of a medieval castle, the dominating situation of this house, together with its clustered appearance, do give an impression of a fortification, especially as viewed in the northern and southern elevations (page 97).

Obwohl dieses Haus nicht die drohende Ausstrahlung einer mittelalterlichen Burg besitzt, vermittelt es aufgrund seiner dominanten Lage und dem gedrängten Erscheinungsbild dennoch den Eindruck einer Wehranlage – wie der nördliche und südliche Aufriß zeigen (Seite 97).

Si elle n'a pas l'aspect menaçant d'un château médiéval, la situation dominante de cette maison et son apparence fermée font penser à une fortification, surtout dans ses élévations nord et sud (page 97).

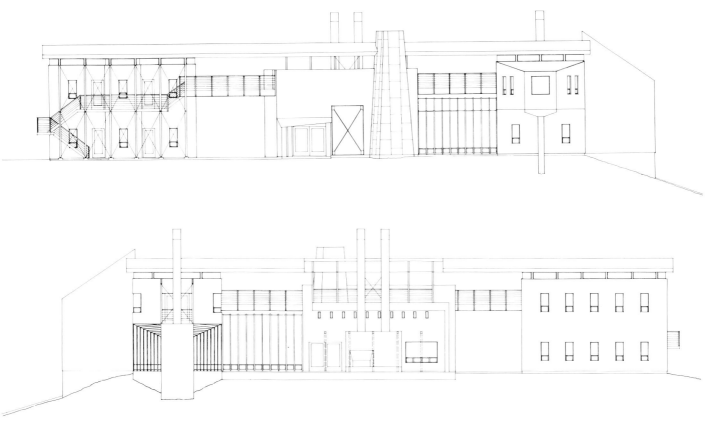

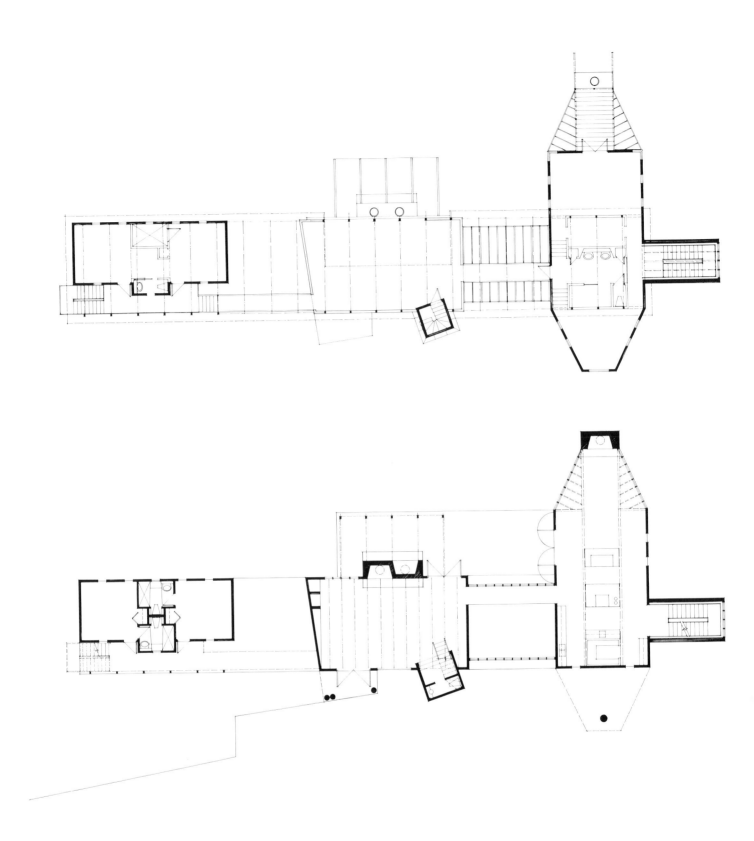

Pages 98/99: The three sections of the Sonoma Coast Residence are not joined at ground level, affording a good deal of privacy to each area. They are connected at the upper level by open-air steel-grate catwalks which are sheltered by the upper roof.

Seite 98/99: Die drei Gebäudeteile der Sonoma Coast Residence gestatten jedem Bereich ein hohes Maß an Privatsphäre. Lediglich im oberen Geschoß sorgen Lichtroste, die von dem oberen Dach geschützt werden, für eine Verbindung.

Pages 98/99: Les trois parties de la Sonoma Coast Residence sont indépendantes au niveau du sol, ce qui assure à chaque zone de vie une excellente intimité. Elles sont connectées au niveau supérieur par des passerelles à découvert en grille métallique, protégées par le toit.

Pages 100/101: Interior views show that structural elements are left apparent while not giving too technical an atmosphere. Rather, in spite of the heavy materials used, this house retains a transparency and a lightness which form an interesting tension. The heaviness of large wooden beams seem well suited to the isolated location, or even the high winds on this site, while the lightness is a tribute to a magnificent view.

Seite 100/101: Die Innenansichten zeigen, daß die strukturellen Elemente des Gebäudes zwar weitestgehend sichtbar blieben, aber dennoch keine allzu technisch anmutende Atmosphäre entstand. Trotz der schweren, massiven Materialien zeichnet sich das Haus durch Transparenz und Leichtigkeit aus, wodurch ein interessantes Spannungsfeld entsteht. Die Wucht der großen Holzbalken scheint sowohl der isolierten Lage des Hauses als auch den heftigen Windböen auf diesem Baugelände angemessen, während die Leichtigkeit einen Tribut an den spektakulären Ausblick darstellt.

Pages 100/101: Les éléments structurels sont laissés apparents, sans pour autant créer une atmosphère trop technique. La robuste présence des matériaux n'empêche pas cette maison de jouer la transparence et la légèreté, et génère même une tension intéressante. La masse des poutres de bois semble bien adaptée à l'isolement de cette construction, ainsi qu'aux fréquents vents de tempête, tandis que la transparence permet de profiter d'une superbe vue.

Hodgetts + Fung

Craig Hodgetts
Hsin-Ming Fung

Craig Hodgetts is a graduate of Oberlin College and of Yale University School of Art and Architecture. He has worked extensively in exploring the synthesis between architecture and entertainment technology, as exemplified in projects such as the Tokyo Disneyland Gate 11 Main Street, or the Panasonic Pavilion at MCA Universal's Citywalk. A professor at the UCLA Graduate School of Architecture and Planning, Craig Hodgetts is the Creative Director of Hodgetts + Fung. His partner, Hsin-Ming Fung, is Director of Design for the firm, which was created in 1984. She was born in China, raised in Vietnam, and received her M. Arch. degree from UCLA in 1980. Current projects include "Sun Power", a permanent solar exhibition at EMR's Bad Oeynhausen facility, renovation and new construction for the Craft and Folk Art Museum in Los Angeles as well as the interior architecture and installation design for the California State Archives Museum in Sacramento.

Craig Hodgetts studierte am Oberlin College und an der Yale University School of Art and Architecture. Er beschäftigt sich intensiv mit einer möglichen Synthese zwischen Architektur und Unterhaltungstechnologie, wie sie sich in solchen Projekten wie dem Tokyo Disneyland Gate 11 Main Street oder dem Panasonic Pavilion am MCA Universal's Citywalk manifestiert. Hodgetts ist Professor an der UCLA Graduate School of Architecture and Planning und der Creative Director von Hodgetts + Fung. Seine Partnerin, Hsin-Ming Fung, ist Director of Design der 1984 gegründeten Firma. Fung wurde in China geboren, wuchs in Vietnam auf und erhielt 1980 ihren Master of Architecture an der UCLA. Zu den derzeitigen Projekten zählen die Solar-Installation »Sun Power« auf dem EMR-Gelände in Bad Oeynhausen, das Craft and Folk Art Museum in Los Angeles sowie die innenarchitektonische Gestaltung und Montage des California State Archives Museum in Sacramento.

Craig Hodgetts est diplômé de Oberlin College et de Yale, University School of Art and Architecture. Il a beaucoup travaillé sur une possiblité de synthèse entre l'architecture et les technologies du spectacle, comme le montre, par exemple, sa Porte 11 sur Main Street à Disneyland Tokyo, ou le Panasonic Pavilion à MCA Universal's Citywalk. Professeur à l'école d'architecture et d'urbanisme de UCLA, il est directeur de la création de Hodgetts + Fung. Son associée Hsin-Ming Fung est directeur des projets de leur agence, créée en 1984. Née en Chine, elle a été élevée au Vietnam, et a obtenu sa maîtrise en architecture à UCLA en 1980. Parmi les projets actuels: le «Sun Power», exposition-installation solaire permanente à l'EMR de Bad Oeynhausen, la rénovation et l'extension du Craft and Folk Art Museum de Los Angeles, et l'aménagement intérieur du California State Archives Museum à Sacramento.

Towell Temporary Library, UCLA, Los Angeles, 1991–93, interior view.

Towell Temporary Library, UCLA, Los Angeles, 1991–93, Innenansicht.

Towell Temporary Library, UCLA, Los Angeles, 1991–93, vue intérieure.

Towell Temporary Library, UCLA, Los Angeles
1991–93

Situated in the midst of UCLA's Brentwood campus, this structure was intended as a temporary replacement for Powell Library, the main undergraduate facility which was to undergo a three to five year closure for seismic renovation. According to the architects, "the complex consists of four linked tented forms conceived to look different and unpredictable from all directions." Using a white and gold polyester skin, cinder block walls, off-the-shelf lighting, or exposed sprinkler pipes, the architects succeeding in completing the building which receives 500 students at a time for the low, budget price of $3.5 million. Known for their projects related to the entertainment industry, Craig Hodgetts and Ming Fung, who have taught at SCI-Arc since 1987 encouraged the idea with this building that informal, low cost temporary structures can also be well designed, a concept which is of interest, for example, to the city of Los Angeles because of its large homeless population.

Dieses Gebäude liegt inmitten des Brentwood Campus der UCLA (University of California, Los Angeles). Es wurde als zeitweiliges Domizil für die zentrale Powell Library errichtet, die für etwa drei bis fünf Jahre wegen Sicherung gegen Erdbeben geschlossen werden mußte. Nach Aussage der Architekten »besteht dieser Komplex aus vier miteinander verbundenen zeltartigen Gebilden, die so entworfen sind, daß sie aus allen Richtungen unterschiedlich und unvorhersehbar erscheinen«. Mit Hilfe von Außenwandversteifungen aus weißem und goldfarbenem Polyester, Wänden aus Schlackbetonstein, vorgefertigten Beleuchtungssystemen und den über Putz verlegten Röhren der Sprinkleranlagen gelang es den Architekten, das Gebäude, das 500 Studenten aufnehmen kann, ohne Überschreitung des relativ geringen Budgetrahmens in Höhe von 3,5 Millionen Dollar fertigzustellen. Craig Hodgetts und Ming Fung, die durch ihre Projekte für die Unterhaltungsindustrie bekannt wurden und seit 1987 am SCI-Arc lehren, unterstrichen mit diesem Gebäude die These, daß auch informelle, zeitweilige Konstruktionen mit geringem Budget nicht auf sorgfältiges Design verzichten müssen – eine These, die beispielsweise für die Stadt Los Angeles mit ihren vielen Obdachlosen von großem Interesse sein könnte.

Situé au milieu du campus de UCLA (University of California, Los Angeles) à Brentwood, ce bâtiment remplace provisoirement la Powell Library, la bibliothèque principale qui devait être restaurée après les dégâts du tremblement de terre. Selon l'architecte, «l'ensemble est composé de quatre éléments en forme de tentes, dessinés de façon à être perçus de façon différente et surprenante de toutes les directions». Avec ses toitures recouvertes de polyester blanc et or, ses murs en parpaings, ses éclairages de série, et ses tuyauteries d'incendie apparentes, le bâtiment, qui peut accueillir 500 étudiants, a pu être construit sans dépasser le modeste budget prévu (3,5 millions de $). Connus pour leurs réalisations pour l'industrie du spectacle, Craig Hodgetts et Ming Fung, qui enseignent à SCI-Arc depuis 1987, ont ainsi fait progresser peu coûteuses l'idée que des constructions provisoires peu coûtenses peuvent être bien conçues, concept séduisant pour une ville qui compte une importante population de sans-logis.

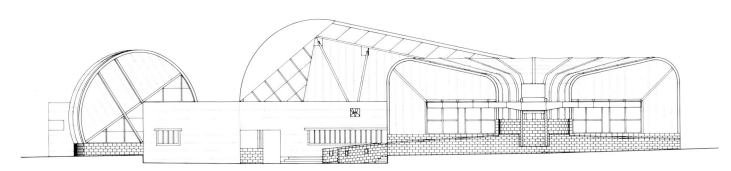

Pages 104/105: Described as "rough tech" this very efficient temporary structure uses glazed, overlapping sheets of corrugated or clear fiberglass, and low-height brick colored concrete masonry walls to anchor the tent superstructure. Through the use of dynamic forms and colors, the fundamentally low budget nature of this project becomes less a handicap than an advantage.

Seite 104/105: Dieses als »rough tech« bezeichnete, effiziente, provisorische Domizil der Bibliothek besteht aus verglasten, einander überlappenden Panelen aus geriffeltem oder klarem Fiberglas und niedrigen, ziegelsteinfarbenen Wänden aus Betonmauerwerk, die dem zeltartigen Aufbau Halt geben. Die so entstandenen dynamischen Formen und Farben lassen das ursprünglich als Nachteil betrachtete niedrige Budget dieses Projektes als Vorteil erscheinen.

Pages 104/105: Qualifiée de «rough tech» (techno brut), cette construction provisoire et bien pensée pour son usage est recouverte de plaques de fibre de verre ondulées ou transparentes vernissées. Les murets en béton teinté ancrent la superstructure en forme de tente. Grâce à un usage dynamique des formes et des couleurs, le budget serré de cette opération a été moins un handicap qu'un avantage.

Pages 106/107: The use of old furniture from Powell Library emphasizes the make-shift aspect of the project, but also gives a certain warmth. Simple lighting fixtures and off-the-shelf materials are used in such original ways that their rough aspect contributes to an overall aesthetic.

Seite 106/107: Die Verwendung des alten Mobiliars der Powell Library unterstreicht den Übergangscharakter dieses Projektes, vermittelt aber auch eine gewisse Wärme. Einfache Beleuchtungssysteme und vorgefertigte Materialien wurden auf so originelle Weise eingesetzt, daß ihr ungeschliffenes Erscheinungsbild zur Gesamtästhetik des Gebäudes beiträgt.

Pages 106/107: La réutilisation du vieux mobilier de la Powell Library met l'accent sur l'aspect économique du projet, mais lui confère aussi une certaine chaleur. Un système d'éclairage simple et des matériaux courants sont utilisés de façon tellement originale que leur aspect brut finit par créer un certain style.

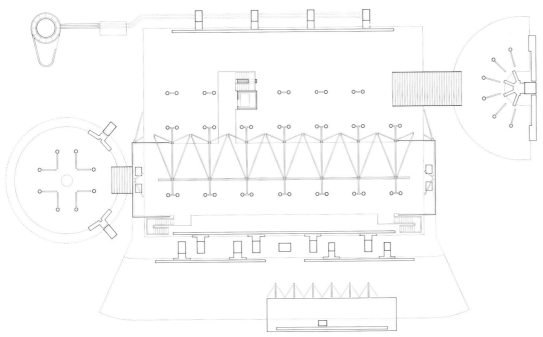

BUILDING PLAN

0 10 20   40

N

Franklin **Israel**

Franklin Israel

Goldberg-Bean Residence,
Hollywood Hills, 1991, entrance.

Goldberg-Bean Residence,
Hollywood Hills, 1991, Eingang.

Goldberg-Bean Residence,
Hollywood Hills, 1991, entrée.

Franklin Israel is certainly one of the more promising architects to emerge from the generation which followed the pioneering California work of Frank O. Gehry. Born in 1945 in New York, he has often made an effort to bring architecture and the culture of Hollywood into an intriguing form of dialogue. He has done renovation work (Bright and Associates, Venice, 1991; Limelight Productions, Los Angeles, 1991), additions to existing structures (Goldberg-Bean Residence, published here; Woo Fong Pavilion, Silver Lake, 1992), and more recently moved with partners Barbara Callas and Annie Chu into the very different questions revolving around much larger projects such as the U.C. Riverside Building (also published here). His very personal mastery of form, color and space place him in a distinct category amongst California architects. Although he has engaged in a synthesis of elements of local culture, his maturing style could certainly permit him to build elsewhere than the Los Angeles region.

Franklin Israel zählt zu den vielversprechendsten Architekten einer Generation, die den kalifornischen Pionierarbeiten Frank O. Gehrys folgte. Der 1945 in New York geborene Israel bemüht sich seit Jahren darum, die Architektur und Kultur Hollywoods zu einem faszinierenden Dialog zusammenzubringen. Zu seinen Arbeiten gehören Sanierungsaufträge (Bright and Associates, Venice, 1991; Limelight Productions, Los Angeles, 1991) und Erweiterungsbauten (die hier beschriebene Goldberg-Bean Residence; Woo Fong Pavilion, Silver Lake, 1992). Seit einiger Zeit beschäftigt er sich gemeinsam mit seinen Partnern Barbara Callas und Annie Chu auch mit den Problemen, die weit größere Bauprojekte (das ebenfalls hier beschriebene U.C. Riverside Building) aufwerfen. Israels sehr persönlicher, meisterhafter Umgang mit Form, Farbe und Raum läßt ihn aus der Masse der kalifornischen Architekten deutlich herausragen, und obwohl er sich um eine Synthese der Elemente regionaler Kultur bemüht, würde es ihm sein reifer Stil durchaus gestatten, auch außerhalb des Einzugsgebiets von Los Angeles tätig zu werden.

Franklin Israel est certainement l'un des architectes les plus prometteurs de la génération de l'après-Frank O. Gehry. Né en 1945 à New York, il a souvent tenté des rapprochements étonnants entre l'architecture et la culture hollywoodienne. Il a réalisé des projets de rénovation (Bright & Associates, Venice, 1991; Limelight Productions, Los Angeles, 1991), agrandi des bâtiments existants (Goldberg-Bean Residence, reproduite ici; Woo Fong Pavilion, Silver Lake, 1992), et plus récemment s'est attaqué à des sujets très différents avec ses associées Barbara Callas et Annie Chu, à l'occasion de projets plus vastes comme le Riverside Building de l'Université de Californie (également reproduit). Sa maîtrise très personnelle de la forme, de la couleur et de l'espace le distingue de beaucoup d'architectes californiens. Bien qu'il soit très engagé dans la recherche de la synthèse des éléments de la culture locale, son style, en pleine maturation, lui permettra certainement de construire ailleurs qu'à Los Angeles.

Pages 110/111: Franklin Israel added a gallery to the original house, reclad the structure and complemented the whole with a master bedroom tower to create a more coherent whole. Case Study prototypes are cited by the architect as an inspiration for the open relationship between interior and exterior.

Seite 110/111: Franklin Israel baute eine Galerie an das ursprüngliche Haus an, versah die gesamte Konstruktion mit einer neuen Verkleidung und schuf durch den Schlafzimmerturm ein kohärentes Ganzes. Die Case Study Prototypen dienten dem Architekten als Inspirationsquelle für das offene Verhältnis zwischen Innen- und Außenbereichen.

Pages 110/111: Franklin Israel a ajouté un galerie à la maison d'origine, posé un nouveau revêtement de façade, et complété l'ensemble par une chambre principale en forme de tour, qui rend le plan plus cohérent. L'architecte a déclaré que les Case Study prototypes lui avaient inspiré cette relation ouverte entre l'intérieur et l'extérieur.

Goldberg-Bean Residence, Hollywood Hills 1991

This is an addition to a 1950s ranch-style house located in an area where a number of different architectural styles jostle each other for attention, a typical situation in Los Angeles. Franklin Israel has responded with a sculptural composition which calls on a variety of materials such as plaster, cedar plywood, sheet metal or cinder blocks. A tilting steel and glass canopy marks the entrance to the house, whose curves and rectilinear forms play against the existing house and the nearby curved road. Within, features like the four gray metal posts which serve to support an elevated studio and at the same time create a canopy chamber for a bed below, show the inventiveness of the architect without ever lapsing into self-indulgent design quirks. Through its choice of color and materials, as well as through its sculptural forms, this house confirms the artistic talent of Israel.

Hier handelt es sich um den Erweiterungsbau eines Hauses im Ranchstil aus den 50er Jahren, das in einer Gegend liegt, in der viele unterschiedliche Architekturströmungen miteinander um Aufmerksamkeit ringen – eine typische Situation in Los Angeles. Franklin Israels Antwort ist eine skulpturale Konstruktion, die auf eine Vielzahl von Materialien wie Putz, Zedernspanplatten, Blech und Schlackenbetonstein zurückgreift. Den Eingang des Hauses markiert ein schrägstehendes Kragdach aus Stahl und Glas, dessen geschwungene und rechtwinklige Formen auf das bereits existierende Haus und die nahegelegene, kurvenreiche Straße Bezug nehmen. Im Inneren des Gebäudes zeugen besondere Kennzeichen wie die vier grauen Metallpfeiler, die ein höher gelegenes Atelier tragen und zugleich einen Baldachin für das daruntergelegene Bett bilden, von der Erfindungsgabe des Architekten, der jedoch bewußt auf jeglichen selbstverliebten Designschnickschnack verzichtete. Durch die Wahl der Farben und Materialien sowie seine skulpturalen Formen dokumentiert dieses Haus Israels künstlerisches Talent.

Il s'agit de l'extension d'une maison années 50 d'esprit «ranch», située dans un quartier où se bousculent les styles architecturaux, comme souvent à Los Angeles. Franklin Israel répond au contexte par cette composition sculpturale qui fait appel à des matériaux aussi variés que le plâtre, le contreplaqué de cèdre, la tôle ou les parpaings. Un auvent inclinable en verre et acier marque l'entrée de la maison, dont les courbes et les formes droites jouent en contrepoint de la partie ancienne et du virage de la route. A l'intérieur, des trouvailles, comme les quatre piliers en métal gris qui soutiennent un atelier surélevé et encadrent une alcôve au niveau inférieur, montrent que la créativité de l'architecte ne tombe jamais dans la complaisance ou la bizarrerie. Le choix des matériaux et des couleurs, la sculpture des formes, confirment le talent artistique de Israel.

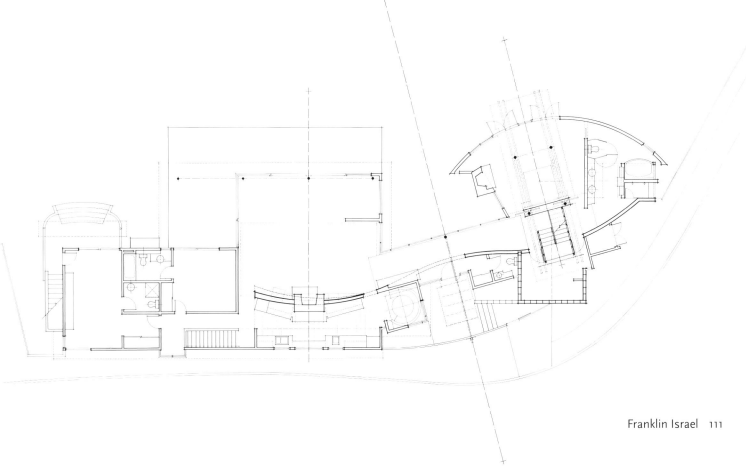

Pages 112/113: Plans reveal the extent to which the addition to the Goldberg-Bean Residence is architecturally different from the original.

Seite 112/113: Die Baupläne zeigen, in welchem Maße sich der Anbau der Goldberg-Bean Residence von der Architektur des ursprünglichen Hauses unterscheidet.

Pages 112/113: Le plan montre à quel point l'extension de la Goldberg-Bean Residence se différencie de la construction originale.

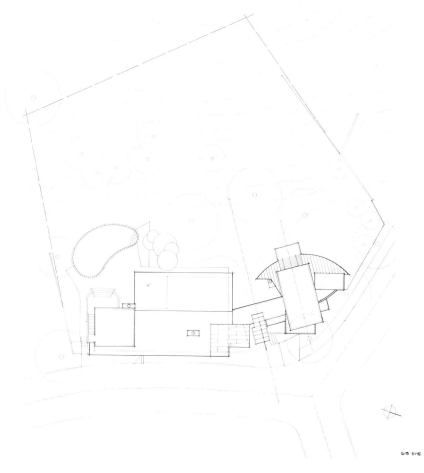

Art Pavilion, Beverly Hills
1991

Located in an exclusive residential area, this 1100m² freestanding pavilion is next to the large home of the client, and connected to it by an underground passage. Intended to house his art collection and two floors of studio space, the structure is likened by the architect to a "great ark, containing an important collection of abstract expressionist art, yet empowered by its contents to become a piece of art in the terraced sculpture garden." The most spectacular space is undoubtedly the 8.5 meter high top floor with its large timber trusses. The materials used are fiberglass reinforced concrete for the upper, outside walls, with stucco below, chosen to create a harmony with the original house. The roof is covered in sheet metal and tile. A surprising exterior feature is a protruding boat-shaped balcony. As the architect says, "a smaller version of the great ark, it is intended to appear as if it were being raised from the garden below."

Dieser 1100 m² große, freistehende Pavillon in einer exklusiven Wohngegend von Los Angeles liegt direkt neben dem großen Anwesen des Kunden und ist durch eine unterirdische Passage damit verbunden. Da der Pavillon eine Kunstsammlung aufnehmen und auf zwei Etagen Atelierräume beherbergen soll, wurde er von dem Architekten »mit einer großen Arche« verglichen, »die eine bedeutende Sammlung abstrakter expressionistischer Kunst enthält, wobei der Inhalt sie selbst zu einem Kunstwerk in dem terrassenartigen Skulpturengarten werden läßt.« Der spektakulärste Raum ist zweifellos das 8,5 Meter hohe oberste Geschoß mit seinen großen Holzträgern. Außerdem verwendete der Architekt Glasfaserbeton für die oberen Außenwände und Putz für den Bereich darunter, um mit dem ursprünglichen Haus zu harmonieren. Das Dach ist mit Blech und Dachziegeln gedeckt. Einen interessanten Blickfang bildet der herausragende, bootsförmige Balkon, den der Architekt als »eine kleinere Version der großen Arche« beschrieb, »die den Eindruck erweckt, als würde sie aus dem daruntergelegenen Garten hochgezogen.«

Situé dans un élégant quartier résidentiel, ce pavillon indépendant de 1100 m² s'élève non loin de la demeure de son propriétaire. Il lui est relié par un passage souterrain. Destiné à accueillir une collection d'art et deux niveaux d'atelier, il est comparé par l'architecte à «une grande arche, contenant une importante collection d'art expressionniste abstrait, et destinée par son contenu à devenir une œuvre d'art en soi dans un jardin de sculptures en terrasses». L'espace le plus spectaculaire est sans aucun doute le niveau supérieur, de 8,5 m de haut, et son énorme charpente de bois. Les revêtements des façades (béton renforcé de fibre de verre pour le niveau supérieur et crépi au rez-de-chaussée) s'harmonisent avec la maison. Le toit est recouvert de tôles et de tuiles. Sur la façade, l'avancée d'un balcon en forme de nef surprend. L'architecte a voulu créer «une version réduite de la grande arche», et donner l'impression qu'elle émerge du jardin en contrebas.

Pages 114/115: In the main gallery, works by Andy Warhol, Morris Louis, Frank Stella and George Segal create an ambiance which is not unlike that of a museum or a major private art gallery, recalling a loft-type structure.

Seite 114/115: In der Galerie lassen Werke von Andy Warhol, Morris Louis, Frank Stella und George Segal ein loftähnliches Ambiente entstehen, das sich kaum von der Atmosphäre eines Museums oder einer bedeutenden Privatsammlung unterscheidet.

Pages 114/115: Dans la grande salle, des œuvres d'Andy Warhol, Morris Louis, Frank Stella et George Segal et un esprit de loft créent une ambiance qui n'est pas très différente de celle d'un musée ou d'une galerie privée.

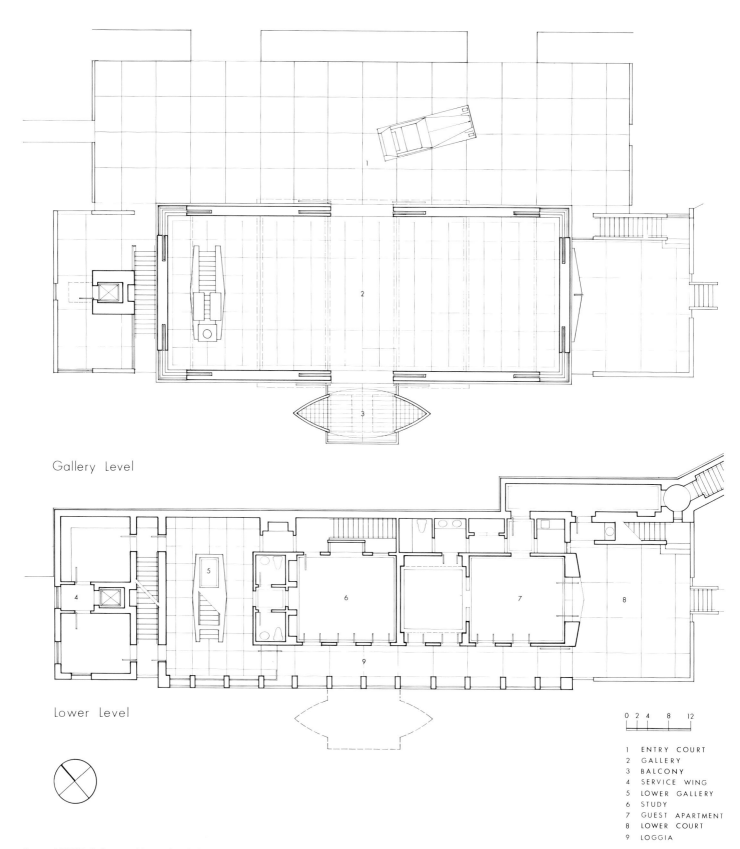

Gallery Level

Lower Level

0 2 4 8 12

1 ENTRY COURT
2 GALLERY
3 BALCONY
4 SERVICE WING
5 LOWER GALLERY
6 STUDY
7 GUEST APARTMENT
8 LOWER COURT
9 LOGGIA

Pages 116/117: Gallery and lower level plans, together with a view of a large work by Roy Lichtenstein, and the stairway connecting the two floors, give an idea both of the juxtaposition of spaces and of works of art in this exceptional private gallery.

Seite 116/117: Die Pläne der Galerie und der unteren Ebenen sowie der Blick auf ein großes Gemälde von Roy Lichtenstein und die Verbindungstreppe zwischen den beiden Geschossen vermitteln einen Eindruck davon, wie in dieser außergewöhnlichen Privatgalerie Raum und Kunst nebeneinander gestellt wurden.

Pages 116/117: Les plans de la galerie et du niveau inférieur, la forte présence d'un grand tableau de Roy Lichtenstein, et l'atelier qui réunit les deux niveaux, donnent une idée de la façon dont s'imbriquent les espaces et les œuvres d'art de cet exceptionnel musée privé.

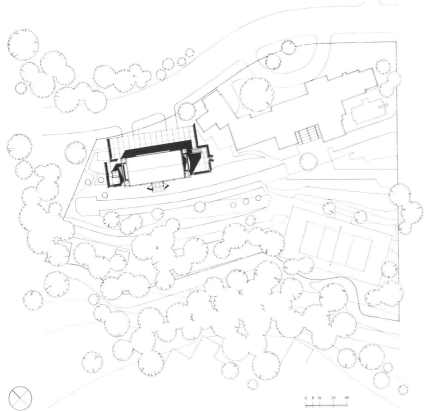

Pages 118/119: An overall site plan explains the relationship of the gallery to the main private house. Moveable walls in the gallery make it possible to use it as a reception or lecture space. The most surprising feature remains the boat-shaped balcony.

Seite 118/119: Der Lageplan verdeutlicht die Beziehung zwischen der Galerie und dem Privathaus. Dank der versetzbaren Trennwände ist eine zusätzliche Nutzung der Galerieräume für Empfänge oder Lesungen möglich. Aber das überraschendste Element dieses Gebäudes bleibt der bootsförmige Balkon.

Pages 118/119: Le plan de situation explique la relation entre la galerie et la maison principale. Des cloisons mobiles permettent de transformer la galerie en salle de réception ou de conférence. Le balcon en forme de bateau est la caractéristique la plus étonnante.

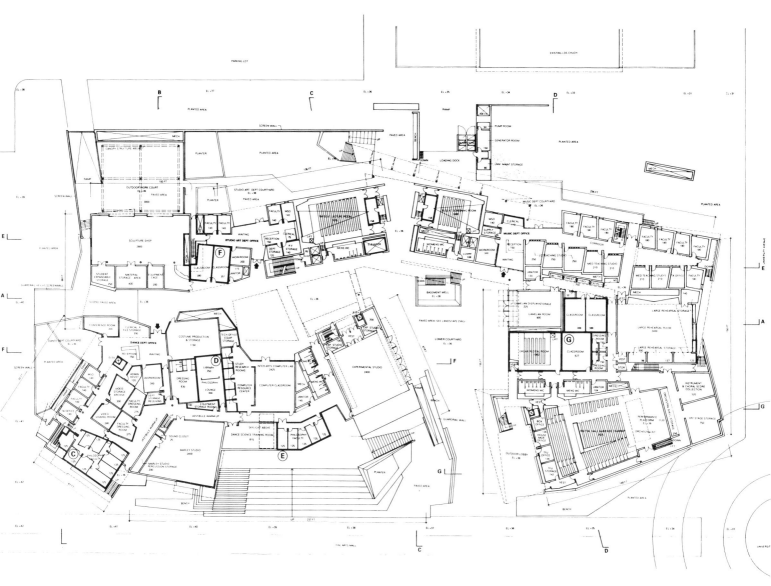

Fine Arts Building, University of California, Riverside 1994 (project)

This is the first major public commission given to Frank Israel with his partners on this project Barbara Callas and Annie Chu. Located 100 kilometers east of Los Angeles, the 13000m² Riverside building, whose budget is $33 million, began construction in 1995. Designed as a gateway to the campus on a site facing a major freeway to the west, with the San Bernardino mountains beyond, the complex is intended to bring together the disciplines of dance, music, studio art, art history, creative writing and film with the hope of creating some interaction. The main construction materials will be stucco, brick and concrete, used in rapport with the sparse desert landscape of the region to create "an organic response to the site." According to the architect, "The entire building is designed as a series of kinetic sculpture volumes implying movement and encouraging the users to explore the building's plazas, rooftops, terraces and extensive outdoor circulation that envelope and penetrate the building forming both 'tunnels' and 'bridges' throughout the complex."

Bei diesem Gebäude handelt es sich um Franklin Israels ersten großen, öffentlichen Bauauftrag. Bei diesem Projekt arbeitet er mit Barbara Callas und Annie Chu zusammen. Mit den Bauarbeiten für das 13000 m² große Riverside-Gebäude, das sich etwa 100 Kilometer östlich von Los Angeles befindet und ein Budget von 33 Millionen Dollar umfaßt, wurde 1995 begonnen. Der Gebäudekomplex, der als Zugang zum Universitätsgelände dienen soll und auf einem Gelände liegt, das im Westen an einer der Hauptverkehrsstraßen liegt (mit den dahinterliegenden San Bernardino Mountains), wurde mit der Absicht entworfen, so unterschiedliche Disziplinen wie Tanz, Musik, bildende Kunst, Kunstgeschichte, Schriftstellerei und Film unter einem Dach zu vereinen, in der Hoffnung, daß diese sich gegenseitig inspirieren. Zu den vorherrschenden Baumaterialien zählen Putz, Ziegelsteine und Beton, die in Übereinstimmung mit der kahlen Wüstenlandschaft dieser Region verwendet werden, um »eine organische Antwort auf das Gelände« zu geben. Nach Aussage des Architekten »ist das gesamte Gebäude als eine Reihe kinetischer Skulpturräume konzipiert, die Bewegung bedeuten und die Besucher dazu ermutigen, die Plätze, Dächer, Terrassen und ausgedehnten Außenanlagen wie Treppen und Gänge zu erforschen, die den Gebäudekomplex umgeben, durchdringen und mit 'Tunneln' und 'Brücken' versehen.«

Ce bâtiment de 13000 m² et de 33 millions de $ est la première grande commande publique passée à Frank Israel et à ses associées pour ce projet Barbara Callas et Annie Chu. Il a été conçu en commun par son agence, Israel Callas Chu, et BOORA Architects. Le chantier a commencé en 1995. Porte du campus, face à une importante autoroute et sur le fond des montagnes de San Bernardino, ce complexe implanté à une centaine de kilomètres à l'est de Los Angeles devrait faciliter des rapprochements et si possible des interactions entre des disciplines comme la danse, la musique, la peinture et la sculpture, l'histoire de l'art, l'écriture et le cinéma. Les matériaux – brique, béton, revêtements au montier de ciment – se veulent «une réponse organique au site» désertique de la région. Selon l'architecte «tout l'ensemble est conçu comme une suite de volumes sculpturaux cinétiques qui invitent au mouvement et encouragent les utilisateurs à explorer les plazzas, les toits, les terrasses et le système de circulation extérieure qui entoure et pénètre le bâtiment par des 'tunnels' et des 'ponts'.»

Page 120: The UC Riverside Fine Arts Building is a project of BOORA Architects with Israel Callas Chu Design Associates. A plan and model photograph give an idea of the complexity of the design.

Seite 120: Bei dem UC Riverside Fine Arts Building handelt es sich um ein Projekt des Büros BOORA Architects in Zusammenarbeit mit Israel Callas Chu Design Associates. Bauplan und Modell vermitteln ein Gefühl für die Komplexität des Designs.

Page 120: Le Fine Arts Buildings de l'Université de Californie à Riverside est un projet de BOORA Architects et d'Israel Callas Chu Design Associates. Le plan et la maquette donnent une idée de la complexité de ce projet.

Wes Jones

Wes Jones

Wes Jones has rapidly become one of the most influential forces in the debate about a technological approach to contemporary architecture. He is a graduate of the University of California, Berkeley (BA in Architecture) and Harvard (M. Arch.). He worked with the ELS Design Group in Berkeley, and Eisenman/Robertson in New York before becoming Director of Design for Holt & Hinshaw, and then a principal for the same firm, renamed Holt Hinshaw Pfau Jones. His most noted accomplishments are undoubtedly the UCLA Chiller Plant/Facilities Complex and the Astronauts' Memorial at Kennedy Space Center in Florida. Current projects include the 565 seat San Jose Repertory Theater, the Confluence Point Interpretive Center in San Jose's Guadalupe River Park, the Edenscape Masterplan and the Zimmer Stair Folly at the University of Cincinnati, and the Hesselink Residence in Hope Valley, California.

Wes Jones wurde innerhalb kürzester Zeit einer der einflußreichsten Teilnehmer in der Debatte um einen technologischen Ansatz der zeitgenössischen Architektur. Er studierte an der University of California, Berkeley (Bachelor of Architecture) sowie in Harvard (Master of Architecture) und arbeitete mit der ELS Design Group in Berkeley und Eisenman/Robertson in New York zusammen, bevor er bei Holt & Hinshaw als Director of Design tätig war. Danach machte man ihn zum Teilhaber dieser Firma, die in Holt Hinshaw Pfau Jones umbenannt wurde. Zu seinen bemerkenswertesten Projekten gehören zweifellos der UCLA Chiller Plant/Facilities Complex und das Astronauts' Memorial im Kennedy Space Center in Florida. Seine derzeitigen Bauvorhaben umfassen das 565 Sitze zählende San Jose Repertory Theater, das Confluence Point Interpretive Center in San Joses Guadalupe River Park, den Bebauungsplan von Edenscape und das Zimmer Stair Folly an der University of Cincinnati sowie die Hesselink Residence in Hope Valley, Kalifornien.

Wes Jones est rapidement devenu l'un des plus influents participants du débat sur l'approche technologique dans l'architecture contemporaine. Il est diplômé en architecture (BA University California, Berkeley et M. Arch à Harvard). Il a travaillé avec le ELS Design Group à Berkeley, et Eisenman/Robertson à New York avant de devenir directeur des projets pour Holt & Hinshaw, puis associé de cette agence, devenue Holt Hinshaw Pfau Jones. Ses réussites les plus remarquées sont incontestablement la centrale thermique d'UCLA et le Mémorial des astronautes au Kennedy Space Center en Floride. Parmi ses projets récents: le Repertory Theater de San José (565 places), le Confluence Point Interpretive Center, au San José Guadalupe River Park, le plan pilote d'Edenscape, la Zimmer Stair Folly à l'Université de Cincinnati, et Hesselink Residence à Hope Valley, en Californie.

UCLA Chiller Plant/Facilities Complex, Los Angeles, 1987–94, façade.

UCLA Chiller Plant/Facilities Complex, Los Angeles, 1987–94, Frontfassade.

UCLA Chiller Plant/Facilities Complex, Los Angeles, 1987–94, façade principale.

UCLA Chiller Plant/Facilities Complex, Los Angeles 1987–94

Located not far from the Towell Temporary Library on the UCLA campus, this impressive structure takes a very different approach to the problems of design and function. The central plant which supplies steam, chilled water and electricity to the entire campus, the facility is 140 meters long and 40 meters high. Its total area is 17 000m², and it was built for a budget of $ 180 million. "A testament to the power of technology," the building nonetheless calls into question the mechanical paradigm praised by Modernist architecture. The protruding stacks and pipes of the design represent the intrusion of an industrial vocabulary into an otherwise tranquil university street. The architect Wes Jones is very interested in the implications of technological development for the future of architecture, but he maintains that even in an "electronic society," mechanical forms will remain a necessary adjunct in order to "give the electronic substance."

Dieser nicht weit von der Towell Temporary Library auf dem Gelände der UCLA (University of California, Los Angeles) gelegene Gebäudekomplex zeigt eine völlig andere Einstellung zur Frage von Design und Funktion. Die Heizanlage, die das gesamte Universitätsgelände mit Wasserdampf, Kühlwasser und Strom versorgt, ist 140 Meter lang, 40 Meter hoch und besitzt eine Gesamtfläche von 17 000 m² (bei einem Budget von 180 Millionen Dollar). Dieses »Zeugnis für die Macht der Technik« stellt dennoch das von der modernistischen Architektur gelobte Paradigma der maschinellen Fertigung in Zweifel. Seine herausragenden Kamine und Röhren repräsentieren das Eindringen der industriellen Formensprache in eine ansonsten ruhige Universitätsstraße. Der Architekt Wes Jones interessiert sich sehr für die Implikationen, die die technische Entwicklung für die Zukunft der Architektur mit sich bringt, aber er vertritt die Meinung, daß selbst in einer »elektronischen Gesellschaft« mechanische Formen ein notwendiges Zubehör bleiben werden, um »der Elektronik Substanz zu verleihen«.

Située non loin de la bibliothèque provisoire Towell, sur le campus de UCLA (University of California, Los Angeles), l'impressionnante réalisation de Wes Jones pour Holt Hinshaw Pfau Jones, est très différente de celle-ci, autant par sa fonction que par son approche conceptuelle. Unité centrale qui approvisionne le campus en vapeur, eau réfrigérée et électricité, elle mesure 140 m de long sur 40 de haut. Sa surface totale est de 17 000 m², et elle représente un investissement de 180 millions de $. «Tout en témoignant de la puissance de la technologie, le bâtiment n'en remet pas moins en question le paradigme mécaniste de l'architecture moderniste. Le bourgeonnement de tuyaux et de cheminées représente l'intrusion d'un vocabulaire industriel dans cette tranquille rue de l'université. L'architecte Wes Jones s'intéresse à la portée du progrès technologique pour l'avenir de l'architecture, mais soutient que même dans une «société électronique», les formes mécaniques resteront pour donner la «substance de l'électronique».

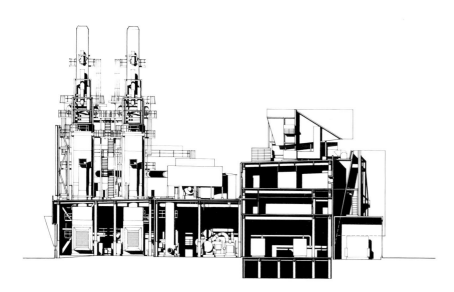

Pages 124/125: Situated in a very visible part of the UCLA campus, the Chiller Plant impresses first of all by its sheer size. The brick veneer surfaces echo nearby classroom buildings, but the industrial imagery of the superstructure quickly shifts the attention of passersby upward. This is a massive technical building with a "civilized" face.

Seite 124/125: Die in einem weithin sichtbaren Teil des UCLA-Campus gelegene Heizanlage beeindruckt schon aufgrund ihrer Größe. Während die Ziegelverblendung die Fassade der nahegelegenen Klassenräume noch einmal aufnimmt, lenkt das industrielle Erscheinungsbild der darüberliegenden Konstruktion die Aufmerksamkeit des Betrachters schnell in die Höhe. Bei diesem Gebäude handelt es sich um ein massives technisches Bauwerk mit einer »zivilisierten« Fassade.

Pages 124/125: Situé dans une partie très visible du campus d'UCLA, le Chiller Plant impressionne au premier abord par ses imposantes dimensions. Les murs recouverts de brique rappellent les bâtiments d'enseignement voisins, mais l'œil est immédiatement attiré par les installations industrielles qui couronnent l'édifice. Cette ambitieuse réalisation a su garder un visage «civilisé».

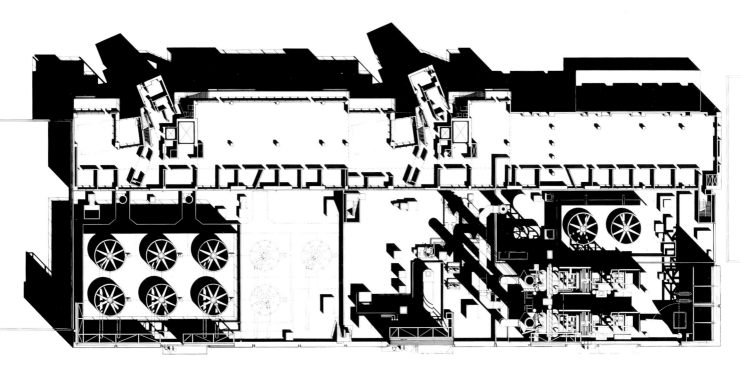

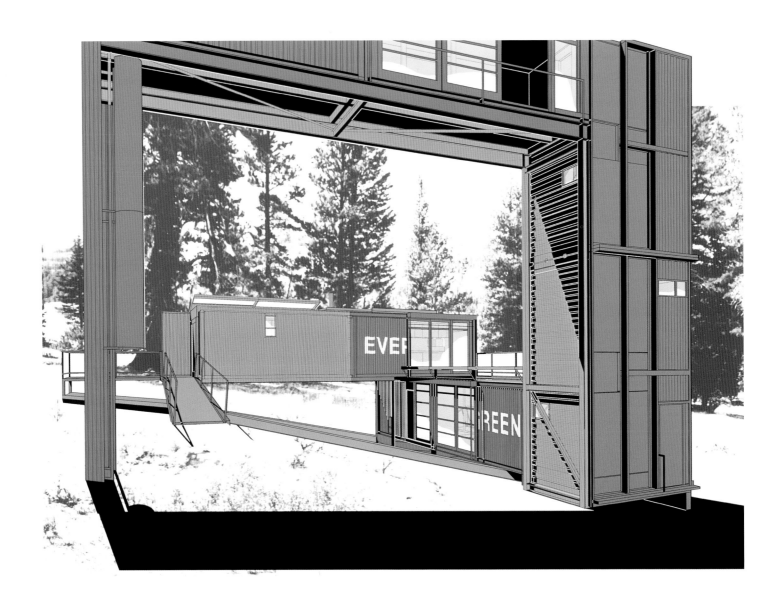

High Sierras Cabins, Hope Valley
1994 (project)

This remarkable project is to be assembled from six meter long shipping containers on a 160 hectare property bordered on all sides by non-developable federal land. Designed for two Stanford University professors, the containers will be airlifted by Sky Crane helicopters to the mountain site. Describing this innovative use of prefabricated elements, the architect write, "Their provenance in transportation technology ensures that the container-cabins will sit lightly on the land – ensures, in fact, that they could get up and walk away... the cabins make no absurd claims of ownership or dominion over these rocks and trees." It would be difficult to find an attitude more distant from that displayed by Frank Lloyd Wright for example in his famous "Falling Water." Young and inventive, Wes Jones is seeking a vocabulary for a new world, which California often seems closer to than Europe or the East Coast of America.

Dieses bemerkenswerte Bauprojekt besteht aus sechs Meter langen Containern auf einem 160 Hektar großen Grundstück, das auf allen Seiten von nicht erschließbarem Bundesgebiet umgeben ist. Die für zwei Professoren der Stanford University entwickelten Container sollen mit Hilfe eines Sky Crane-Helikopters durch die Luft auf ihren Gebirgs-Standort transportiert werden. Bei seiner Beschreibung dieser innovativen Verwendung von vorgefertigten Bauelementen bemerkte der Architekt: »Ihr Ursprung aus dem Transportwesen gewährleistet, daß die Container nur leicht auf dem Land aufsitzen – eigentlich könnten sie sich erheben und einfach weggehen... Die Container stellen keine absurden Besitzansprüche oder Eigentumsrechte an diese Felsen und Bäume.« Es wäre schwierig, eine Haltung gegenüber der Natur zu finden, die sich noch weiter von Frank Lloyd Wrights Einstellung entfernt (welche beispielsweise in Wrights berühmtem Bauwerk »Falling Water« zum Ausdruck kommt). Der junge und innovative Architekt Wes Jones sucht nach einer Formensprache für eine neue Welt, die Kalifornien häufig näher zu sein scheint als Europa oder die Ostküste Amerikas.

Ce remarquable projet conçu pour deux professeurs de l'Université de Stanford, devrait être réalisé sur une propriété de 160 ha entourée de terrains fédéraux non constructibles, à partir de l'assemblage de conteneurs maritimes de 6 m de long. Les conteneurs seront apportés par hélicoptères. L'architecte décrit ainsi cette utilisation d'éléments préfabriqués inhabituels : «Leur origine – la technologie des transports – garantit que ces conteneurs-cabines reposeront avec légèreté sur le sol, et que l'on pourra donc éventuellement les emporter ailleurs. Ces cabines n'ont aucune prétention absurde à la propriété ou à la domination de ces rochers et de ces arbres.» Il serait difficile de trouver une attitude plus opposée à celle de Frank Lloyd Wright, par exemple, pour sa fameuse maison de la cascade, «Falling Water». Jeune et créatif, Wes Jones recherche un vocabulaire nouveau pour un monde nouveau, dont la Californie semble souvent plus proche que la Côte Est des U.S.A. ou l'Europe.

Pages 126/127: Although shipping containers would not appear to be the most "ecological" form of construction, the fact that they can presumably be removed as easily as they were installed makes this an environmentally "friendly" project.

Seite 126/127: Obwohl die Container auf den ersten Blick nicht als »ökologischste« Konstruktionsform erscheinen, handelt es sich hier dennoch um ein umweltfreundliches Projekt – einfach aufgrund der Tatsache, daß sie sich so schnell wieder entfernen lassen, wie sie aufgebaut wurden.

Pages 126/127: Bien que les conteneurs métalliques ne soient pas la forme de construction la plus écologique, le fait qu'ils se déplacent aussi facilement qu'ils s'installent rend le projet tout à fait viable du point de vue de l'environnement.

Morphosis

Thom Mayne

The "modernist penchant for unification and simplification must be broken," writes Morphosis principal Thom Mayne. The work of his group, originally created with Michael Rotondi, has emphasized the importance of societal changes, such as the growing role of electronic communications, and the "breakdown of a conventional notion of community." Although beginning from a different analysis, Morphosis, like certain Japanese architects, has insisted on breaking down the boundaries between the interior and the exterior of buildings. Since its first projects, Morphosis has placed a great deal of importance on the process which leads after a complex, introspective analysis to construction. Elaborate models have continued to play a role in this transformative investigation.

»Die moderne Vorliebe für Vereinheitlichung und Vereinfachung muß zerstört werden« schreibt der Leiter von Morphosis, Thom Mayne. Die Arbeiten dieser Gruppe, die Mayne ursprünglich zusammen mit Michael Rotondi gründete, betonen die Dominanz sozialer Veränderungen wie die wachsende Bedeutung elektronischer Kommunikation und der »Zusammenbruch der gewohnten Vorstellung vom Zusammenleben«. Obwohl sie von unterschiedlichen Standpunkten ausgehen, beharren die Mitglieder von Morphosis genau wie verschiedene japanische Architekten darauf, die Grenzen des Innen und Außen von Gebäuden aufzuheben. Seit den ersten Projekten legt Morphosis großen Wert auf den Entwicklungsprozeß, der nach einer komplexen, introspektiven Analyse zur Bauphase führt. Kunstvolle Modelle spielen nach wie vor eine bedeutende Rolle bei dieser transformativen Untersuchung.

Le «penchant moderniste pour l'unification et la simplification doit être aboli», écrit l'associé principal de Morphosis, Thom Mayne. Le travail de ce groupe, fondé à l'origine avec Michael Rotondi, met l'accent sur l'importance de changements sociaux comme le rôle grandissant de la communication électronique et «la crise de la notion conventionnelle de communauté». Bien que partant d'une analyse différente, Morphosis insiste, comme certains architectes japonais, sur l'abolition de la cêsure intérieur/extérieur. Depuis ses premiers projets, Morphosis attache une grande importance au processus complexe d'analyse introspective qui aboutit à la construction. Les maquettes, très travaillées, jouent un grand rôle dans cette recherche.

Blades Residence, Goleta, 1992 (project), aerial view.

Blades Residence, Goleta, 1992 (Projekt), Vogelperspektive.

Blades Residence, Goleta, 1992 (projet), vue aerienne.

Blades Residence, Goleta
1992 (project)

As is often the case with the projects of Morphosis, this 750 m² house has been in design for some time, with elaborate models giving the best impression of its appearance. The architect's words describe as well as any his intentions in the case of the Blades Residence: "A large exterior room has been created within which the house is situated. This room embraces an augmented natural landscape conveying a sense of sanctuary... Through the fusion of the exterior and interior worlds, the individual gradually becomes oriented... learns to keep balance... The building arrangement, while alluding to the specific characteristics of this site, ultimately demonstrates its tentativeness to fixity by making overt reference to our temporary status as occupants." Although the idea of an exploded room as origin of the architectural forms seems relatively clear in the model, the idea of an intellectual archeology of sorts, of a time before existing time, also prevails.

Wie so häufig bei Morphosis befindet sich auch dieses 750 m² große Haus bereits seit längerem in Planung, wobei kunstvolle Modelle einen sehr guten Eindruck vermitteln. Der Architekt beschreibt seine diesbezüglichen Intentionen: »Zuerst wurde ein großer Außenraum geschaffen, in dem das Haus liegt. Dieser umfaßt eine erweiterte natürliche Umgebung mit dem Hauch eines Heiligtums... Durch die Fusion der Innen- und Außenwelten erhält das Individuum schrittweise eine Orientierung... es lernt, das Gleichgewicht zu halten... Während das Gebäudearrangement auf die Charakteristika des Geländes anspielt, demonstriert es im Grunde seinen experimentellen Charakter gegenüber Beständigkeit, indem es unverhohlen auf unseren nur temporären Status als Bewohner hinweist.« Obwohl die These eines in Einzelteile aufgelösten Raumes als Ursprung der architektonischen Formen im Modell relativ deutlich ist, spielt auch der Gedanke an eine Art intellektueller Archäologie hinein, an eine Zeit vor der existierenden Zeit.

Comme c'est souvent le cas dans les projets de Morphosis, la conception de cette maison de 750 m² a duré un certain temps, des maquettes poussées précisant à chaque étape le propos. Voici comment l'architecte décrit cette réalisation : «Une grande pièce extérieure a été créée, à l'intérieur de laquelle se développe la maison. Cette pièce embrasse un paysage naturel, qui lui confère un sens de sanctuaire... Grace à la fusion des univers extérieur et intérieur, l'individu est peu à peu orienté... il apprend à trouver son équilibre... l'aménagement de la construction, tout en s'appuyant sur les caractéristiques du site, affirme enfin sa tendance à la permanence, à travers une référence appuyée à notre statut temporaire d'occupants.» L'idée de pièce éclatée, à l'origine de la forme architecturale, ressort clairement de la maquette, ainsi que celle d'une sorte d'archéologie rêvée, d'une époque «avant».

Eric Owen **Moss**

Eric Owen Moss

The architect Philip Johnson has called Eric Owen Moss, born in Los Angeles in 1943 "a jeweller of junk." In his work built to date, this young California architect has placed an emphasis on unusual materials. Old chains, broken trusses and other incongruous elements take their place in his buildings, much as they might participate in a modern sculpture. The visual arts have acquired a freedom which seemed forbidden to architecture because of the constraints of practicality and building codes, but also because of peoples' expectations. Like the Austrian Wolf Prix, principal of the Coop Himmelblau firm who praises his work, Eric Owen Moss is in the process of exploring the ways in which architecture can be de-constructed. His own particularity, as evidenced in the buildings he has completed in Culver City, California, remains his extensive and unexpected experimentation with materials and forms.

Der Architekt Philip Johnson bezeichnete den 1943 in Los Angeles geborenen Eric Owen Moss als »Juwelier des Schrotts«. Dieser junge kalifornische Architekt legte in seinen bisherigen Bauten den Schwerpunkt vor allem auf ungewöhnliche Materialien. In seinen Entwürfen finden sich alte Ketten, gebrochene Balken und andere scheinbar deplazierte Elemente, die genauso auch zu einer modernen Skulptur passen könnten. Die bildenden Künste haben eine Freiheit erworben, die für die Architektur sowohl aufgrund der Durchführbarkeit und der Baubestimmungen als auch aufgrund der Erwartungen ihrer Klientel undenkbar schien. Eric Owen Moss sucht ebenso nach neuen Wegen, auf denen die Architektur de-konstruiert werden kann, wie der Österreicher Wolf Prix von Coop Himmelblau, der von Moss' Arbeiten begeistert ist. Sein Kennzeichen ist der intensive und experimentelle Umgang mit Materialien und Formen wie in seinen Bauten in Culver City, Kalifornien.

L'architecte Philip Johnson a pu qualifier Eric Owen Moss, né en 1943 à Los Angeles, de «joaillier de la ferraille». En effet, cet architecte californien s'intéresse beaucoup aux matériaux insolites. Vieilles chaînes, poutres brisées et autres éléments inattendus trouvent leur place dans ses constructions, un peu comme dans la sculpture contemporaine. Les arts plastiques ont conquis une liberté que les contraintes pratiques et les réglementations, mais également les attentes des clients, semblaient interdire à l'architecture. Comme l'Autrichien Wolf Prix, associé principal de Coop Himmelblau et qui apprécie son travail, Eric Owen Moss explore les diverses manières dont l'architecture peut se déconstruire. Son originalité, mise en valeur dans ses rénovations de Culver City (Californie), réside dans des expériences aussi poussées qu'originales sur les formes et les matériaux.

The Box, Culver City, 1990–94, stairway.

The Box, Culver City, 1990–94, Treppenaufgang.

The Box, Culver City, 1990–94, les escaliers.

The Box, Culver City
1990–94

Whereas the neighboring IRS Building (pages 138–141) was modified through a hollowing out and reemergence of existing elements, The Box consists essentially of an addition, in the form of a "bronco attic" sitting at an unusual angle on the roof of the existing building. Originally intended as a private room for a restaurant, this protuberance is reached through a stairway which is partially inside and partially outside. Since the restaurant did not in fact install itself here, the usefulness of the box itself would appear to be limited, but it is an arresting design feature which in itself serves as a signature in the indifferent industrial environment of Culver City. Eric Owen Moss is clearly interested in the recognition of passersby, since he recounts his pleasure when, as a result of the 1994 Los Angeles earthquake, a substantial amount of freeway traffic was diverted onto National Boulevard, permitting thousands of drivers a day to see his work. As in the neighboring structures, the internal layout of the building, aside from Moss's addition, has been kept very straightforward.

Während das benachbarte IRS Building (Seite 138–141) durch teilweise Entkernung und Neuverwendung bereits vorhandener Bauelemente abgewandelt wurde, besteht The Box im Grunde aus einem Anbau in Form eines Dachgeschosses, das in einem ungewöhnlichen Neigungswinkel auf dem Dach sitzt. Dieser ursprünglich als Séparée eines Restaurants gedachte Höcker ist über einen Aufgang zu erreichen, der teilweise innen und teilweise außen verläuft. Da das Restaurant jedoch nicht hier untergebracht wurde, stellt sich nun die Frage nach der Verwendung dieses Aufsatzes. Aber es ist ein interessantes Designelement, ein herausragendes Kennzeichen in der ansonsten eintönigen industriellen Umgebung von Culver City. Eric Owen Moss legt Wert auf einen hohen Wiedererkennungswert seiner Arbeiten; er selbst berichtete, daß zu seiner großen Freude täglich Tausende von Autofahrern sein Werk sehen konnten, als die Stadt in Folge des Erdbebens von 1994 einen Großteil des Autobahnverkehrs an seinem Bauwerk vorbei auf den National Boulevard umleitete. Genau wie bei den benachbarten Häusern wurde die Innenaufteilung dieses Gebäudes – abgesehen von Moss' Aufsatz – sehr geradlinig und unkompliziert gehalten.

Alors que l'IRS Building (pages 138–141) avait été modifié par creusement, fouille, et reprise d'éléments préexistants, The Box consiste essentiellement en une extension, une sorte de grenier-observatoire, posé à un angle inhabituel sur le toit d'un bâtiment existant. Cette «protubérance» devait à l'origine abriter le salon privé d'un restaurant. On y accède par un escalier intérieur/extérieur. Le restaurant ne s'étant finalement pas installé à cet endroit, la «boîte» a perdu sa raison, mais elle n'en reste pas moins une sorte de signature dans l'environnement industriel monotone de Culver City. Eric Owen Moss aime susciter l'intérêt des passants. Il raconte avec délectation qu'à la suite du tremblement de terre de Los Angeles en 1994, une bonne partie de la circulation de l'autoroute était détournée par le National Boulevard, permettant à des milliers d'automobilistes d'apercevoir son travail. Comme dans les constructions voisines, le plan intérieur de l'immeuble, en dehors de l'addition de Moss, reste très classique.

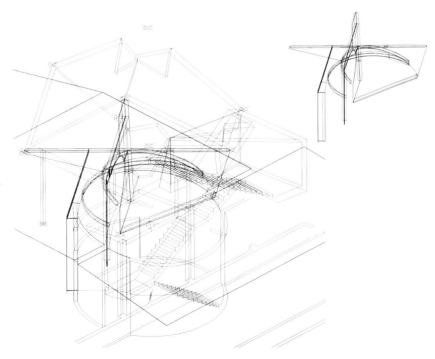

Pages 134/135: Located near the other National Boulevard projects of Eric Owen Moss, The Box shows the penchant of the architect for unusual geometries, in this instance in the context of a rather straightforward converted warehouse space.

Seite 134/135: Das in der Nähe von Eric Owen Moss' anderen National Boulevard-Projekten gelegene Gebäude The Box dokumentiert die Vorliebe des Architekten für ungewöhnliche geometrische Formen, die hier im Zusammenhang mit einem eher konventionell umgewandelten Lagerhaus zum Tragen kam.

Pages 134/135: Situé non loin d'un autre de ses projets sur National Boulevard, The Box d'Eric Owen Moss illustre le penchant de l'architecte pour des géométries originales, même dans le contexte de la reconversion d'un entrepôt assez banal.

Pages 136/137: A ground floor view shows how Eric Owen Moss introduces the very original geometry of the structure of The Box itself to an otherwise rectilinear volume.

Seite 136/137: Die Ansicht des Erdgeschosses zeigt, auf welche Weise Eric Owen Moss die originelle Geometrie von The Box in eine ansonsten rechtwinklige Konstruktion integrierte.

Pages 136/137: Une vue du rez-dechaussée montre la manière dont Eric Owen Moss a greffé la construction géométrique très originale qu'est The Box sur un volume par ailleurs rectiligne.

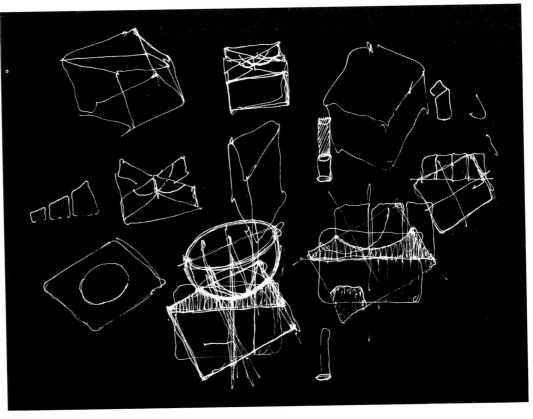

IRS Building, Culver City
1993–94

Located on a corner of a main thoroughfare in Culver City, this structure is next to the 8522 National Boulevard Building and the Goalen Group which Eric Owen Moss restructured in 1988–90. The IRS Building, together with The Box, are located in the so-called Hayden Tract, which Moss and the developer Frederick Norton Smith have been rehabilitating for most of the past ten years. Intended for a music company (and not the Internal Revenue Service) the 2500m² office area creates the sort of unusual juxtapositions between the existing warehouse architecture and newly added features for which Moss has become well-known. The most spectacular aspect of his intervention is the entrance area where he has hollowed out the corner and created a sculpture with structural steel elements extracted from the old building and clear acrylic. This confrontation of the new and the old, turned to a different purpose, is a signature element of Moss's work and sets him apart both in terms of style and approach.

Dieses an einer der Hauptverkehrsstraßen von Culver City gelegene Eckgebäude befindet sich direkt neben dem 8522 National Boulevard Building und der Goalen Group, die Eric Owen Moss zwischen 1988 und 1990 umbaute. Das IRS Building liegt zusammen mit The Box im sogenannten Hayden-Gebiet, das Moss und der Stadtplaner Frederick Norton Smith während der vergangenen zehn Jahre saniert haben. Dieses ursprünglich für eine Plattenfirma geplante, 2500 m² große Bürogebäude weist die Art von ungewöhnlichen Gegensätzen zwischen der bereits existierenden Lagerhaus-Architektur und den neu hinzugefügten Bauteilen auf, für die Moss berühmt wurde. Der aufregendste Aspekt seiner Eingriffe ist der Eingangsbereich, bei dem er die Ecke aushöhlte und mit Baustahlelementen aus dem alten Gebäude sowie durchsichtigem Acryl eine Skulptur schuf. Die Konfrontation von Neuem und Altem, das einem anderen Verwendungszweck zugeführt wird, ist ein typisches Element in Moss' Werken und hebt ihn sowohl in Fragen des Stils als auch der Konzeption aus der Masse hervor.

Cette construction posée au coin d'un des principaux axes de circulation de Culver City est voisine de l'immeuble du 8522 National Boulevard et du Goalen Group qu'Eric Moss a restructuré en 1988–90. Le IRS Building et The Box se trouvent sur le Hayden Tract que Moss et le promoteur Frederick Norton Smith réhabilitent depuis une dizaine d'années. Réalisé pour une compagnie de disques, cet immeuble de bureaux de 2 500 m² juxtapose curieusement d'anciens entrepôts à des additions contemporaines, qui ont rendu Moss célèbre. Les éléments les plus spectaculaires de son intervention sont l'entrée, creusée dans un angle, et dont il a fait une sorte de sculpture à partir de poutres d'acier récupérées dans l'ancien bâtiment et d'acrylique transparent. Cette confrontation du nouveau et de l'ancien, ce bouleversement des fonctions, est l'une des composantes les plus notables de l'approche stylistique originale de Moss.

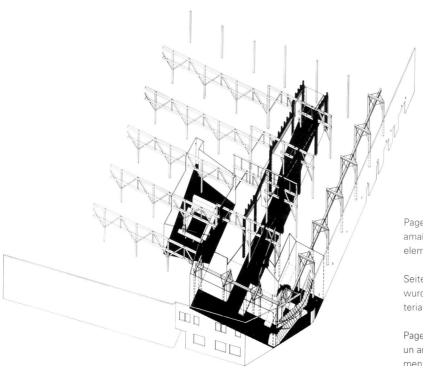

Pages 138/139: The spectacular sculptural entrance to the IRS Building is an amalgamation of steel elements extruded from the old structure and new elements. The plan shows the corner location of this entrance.

Seite 138/139: Bei dem spektakulären Eingangsbereich des IRS Building wurden Stahlelemente aus dem ursprünglichen Gebäude mit neuen Baumaterialien kombiniert.

Pages 138/139: Spectaculaire et sculpturale, l'entrée de l'IRS Building est un amalgame d'éléments d'acier récupérés dans l'ancien bâtiment et d'éléments neufs. Le plan montre l'implantation en coin de cette entrée.

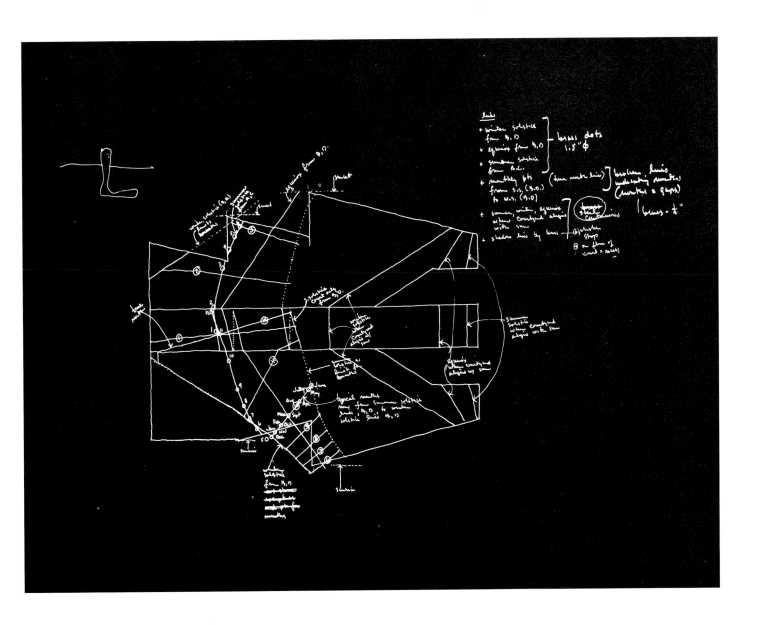

Pages 140/141: Whereas The Box represents the addition of an unusual architectural volume to a rectangular space, the IRS is perhaps more closely related to a sculptural gesture in its extrusion of existing structural elements. Here steel and plexiglas are associated with a very unexpected external stairway.

Seite 140/141: Während The Box die Angliederung einer ungewöhnlichen architektonischen Konstruktion an ein rechteckiges Bauwerk repräsentiert, überrascht das IRS Building dank der Neuverwendung vorhandener Bauelemente durch seine skulpturalen Aspekte. Stahl und Plexiglas ergänzen sich hier zu einer völlig unerwarteten Außentreppe.

Pages 140/141: Si The Box est l'ajout d'un volume architectural étonnant sur un bâtiment rectangulaire. IRS se rapproche davantage du geste sculptural. L'acier et le plexiglass se retrouvent associés dans un escalier extérieur inattendu.

Edward R. **Niles**

Edward R. Niles

Born in 1935 and raised in Los Angeles, Edward Niles attended the University of Southern California, where he obtained his M. Arch. degree in 1961. He created his own practice in 1967, and has been an associate professor of architecture and USC since that date. Influenced early in his career by Wright, Robert Maillart, Le Corbusier and Niemeyer, he says, "I have difficulty with consistency and order for order's love. I am philosophically at ease with the unknown, and with the anarchy of the search." A majority of his built work is in the area of private residences, but he has also designed offices for Ziff Davis Publishing Corporation, or the Descience Corporation. Current work includes the Klein, McClellan, McKay, and Schneider residences in Malibu, the Luskin Residence in Brentwood, and the Malibu Jewish Center.

Der 1935 in Los Angeles geborene und aufgewachsene Edward Niles studierte an der University of Southern California, an der er 1961 seinen Master of Architecture erhielt. 1967 gründete er sein eigenes Architekturbüro und ist seit dieser Zeit auch als außerordentlicher Professor für Architektur an der USC tätig. Anfangs von Wright, Robert Maillart, Le Corbusier und Niemeyer stark beeinflußt, meint er: »Ich habe Schwierigkeiten mit Gleichmaß und Ordnung um der Ordnung willen. Ich fühle mich auf philosophischer Ebene im Einklang mit dem Unbekannten und mit dem Chaos des Forschens.« Bei einem Großteil seiner errichteten Werke handelt es sich um Privathäuser, aber Niles entwarf auch Bürogebäude für die Ziff Davis Publishing Corporation und die Descience Corporation. Zu seinen derzeitigen Arbeiten gehören die Häuser Klein, McClellan, McKay und Schneider in Malibu, die Luskin Residence in Brentwood sowie das Malibu Jewish Center.

Né en 1935 et élevé à Los Angeles, Edward Niles obtient sa maîtrise d'architectures à l'University of Southern California (1961). Il ouvre son agence en 1967 et enseigne à USC en tant que professeur associé depuis cette date. Influencé en début de carrière par Wright, Robert Maillart, Le Corbusier et Niemeyer, il déclare : «J'ai des problèmes avec la cohérence et l'ordre pour l'amour de l'ordre. Je suis philosophiquement à l'aise avec l'inconnu et l'anarchie de la recherche.» Les résidences privées constituent l'essentiel de ses réalisations, mais Niles a également conçu des bureaux pour Ziff Davis Publishing Corporation, ou la Descience Corporation. Il travaille actuellement sur les résidences Klein, McClellan McKay et Schneider, à Malibu, la Luskin Residence à Brentwood, et le Malibu Jewish Center.

Sidley Residence, Malibu, 1985–91, drive way.

Sidley Residence, Malibu, 1985–91, Auffahrt.

Sidley Residence, Malibu, 1985–91, voie d'accès.

Sidley Residence, Malibu
1985–91

Located high above the Pacific Coast Highway, this 500 m² house which resembles a space station was built for a budget of $ 1700 per m². If that figure seems relatively reasonable, it is undoubtedly because the architect and his daughter became their own contractors for this project. The main steel spine of the house rests on three concrete piers, and an effort has been made, through solar collectors and heat pumps, to render the structure energy-efficient. The main loop containing the living room, dining room and kitchen is composed of translucent fiberglass and metal sheathing.

Despite the futuristic appearance of the design, Edward Niles insists that it is not a "high-tech" building. As he says, "an attempt is made to have a dialogue with the land, a respect of each other's rights or synthetic needs versus evolutionary demands. It is an attitude of an alien object, an intrusion of the 'manifest destiny of man' over the spiritual realm."

Dieses hoch über dem Pacific Coast Highway gelegene, 500 m² große Haus, das an eine Raumstation erinnert, wurde mit einem Budget von 1700 Dollar pro Quadratmeter errichtet. Die relativ preisgünstige Finanzierung hängt zweifellos damit zusammen, daß der Architekt und seine Tochter als ihre eigenen Bauunternehmer auftraten. Der Hauptstahlträger dieses Hauses ruht auf drei Betonpfeilern, und durch die Verwendung von Sonnenkollektoren und Wärmepumpen versuchte der Architekt, eine positive Energiebilanz des Gebäudes zu erreichen. Der Haupttrakt, in dem Küche, Wohn- und Eßbereich untergebracht sind, wurde aus durchscheinendem Fiberglas und Blechverkleidung gefertigt. Trotz des futuristischen Erscheinungsbildes besteht Edward Niles darauf, daß es sich nicht um ein »High-Tech«-Gebäude handelt. Nach seiner Aussage wurde »hier der Versuch unternommen, einen Dialog mit dem Land zu führen, Respekt vor den gegenseitigen Rechten, nämlich synthetische Bedürfnisse gegenüber evolutionären Anforderungen, aufzubringen. Es ist die Haltung eines fremden Objektes, ein Einmischen des 'offenkundigen Schicksals der Menschheit' in das Reich des Spirituellen.«

Au-dessus de la Pacific Coast Highway, cette maison de 500 m² qui ressemble à une station orbitale a été construite pour 1700 $ le m². Ce coût abordable s'explique aussi par le fait que l'architecte et sa fille ont joué les entrepreneurs. L'épine dorsale en acier repose sur trois piles de béton. Des réflecteurs solaires et des pompes à chaleur abaissent la consommation énergétique. L'anneau principal, qui contient la salle de séjour, la salle à manger et la cuisine, est en fibre de verre translucide et feuilles de métal. Edward Niles précise que, malgré son aspect futuriste, l'habitation n'est pas véritablement high-tech : «Je voulais un dialogue avec la terre, le respect des droits ou des attentes de chacun face à des besoins qui évoluent. C'est l'attitude d'un objet étranger, une intrusion de la 'destinée manifeste de l'homme' dans la sphère spirituelle.»

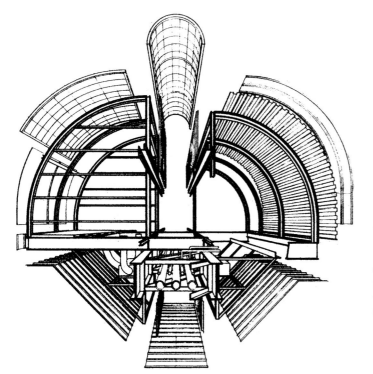

Pages 144/145: The Sidley Residence is undoubtedly the most extravagant design of Edward Niles, offering at least a formal comparison to the space vehicles of Hollywood films. Despite its large glass surfaces, the house is rendered as energy-efficient as possible.

Seite 144/145: Die Sidley Residence ist zweifellos Edward Niles' extravagantester Entwurf, gestattet sie doch zumindest einen formalen Vergleich mit den Raumschiffen der Hollywoodfilme. Trotz seiner großen Glasflächen wurde das Haus so energiesparend wie möglich konzipiert.

Pages 144/145: La Sidley Residence est certainement l'un des projets les plus extravagants d'Edward Niles. On pourrait presque la comparer aux véhicules spatiaux des films hollywoodiens. Malgré ses vastes surfaces vitrées, cette maison s'efforce d'économiser l'énergie.

Pages 146–149: with its large arched volumes, the Sidley Residence could not be said to fit into any very precise style. Its futuristic appearance is less surprising in the ambiance of Southern California where individuality and original design are accepted quantities, than it might be in the more conservative Eastern United States.

Seite 146–149: Aufgrund ihrer großen bogenförmigen Bauelemente scheint die Sidley Residence keiner Stilrichtung vollkommen zu entsprechen. Ihr futuristisches Erscheinungsbild wirkt in der südkalifornischen Architekturlandschaft, in der Individualität und originelles Design geschätzt werden, weniger überraschend als das in den eher konservativen Oststaaten der USA der Fall wäre.

Pages 146–149: Avec ses grands volumes voûtés, la Sidley Residence ne se rattache à aucun style précis. Son aspect futuriste est moins surprenant dans l'atmosphère californienne, où l'individualisme et l'originalité sont parfaitement acceptés, plus en tous cas que sur la côte Est des Etats-Unis.

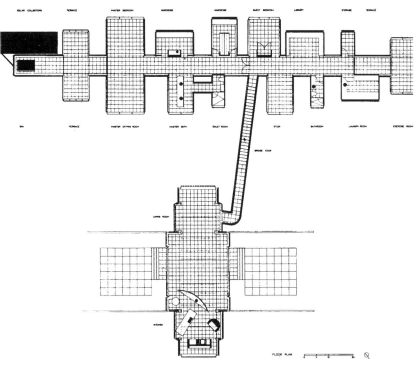

Goodson Residence, Malibu
1990–93

Located directly on the ocean front, this wedge shaped house is directly exposed to the elements in a particularly dramatic way. The rigid steel frame structure is supported by a grid of concrete caissons embedded two meters into the volcanic rock, to meet both the force of the ocean, and of potential earthquakes. Vast expanses of glass, in the form of translucent blocks to the rear and large panes in the front, admit light under all conditions, and provide a clear view of the ocean. With its three bedrooms and large living area, this house is in fact structured around its exceptional location and view, whose dynamic nature is emphasized by the wedge design.

Dieses direkt am Meer gelegene, keilförmige Haus ist dem Spiel der Elemente auf besondere Weise ausgesetzt. Seine steife Stahlskelettkonstruktion wird von einem Gitter aus Betonsenkkästen getragen, die zwei Meter tief in den vulkanischen Fels eingelassen sind, um sowohl den Kräften des Ozeans als auch potentiellen Erdbeben zu widerstehen. Riesige Glasflächen – im hinteren Bereich als Glasbausteine und vorne in Form von großen Glasscheiben – lassen stets genügend Licht einfallen und bieten eine großartige Aussicht auf das Meer. Tatsächlich wurde dieses Haus mit seinen drei Schlafzimmern und dem großen Wohnbereich, dessen dynamischer Charakter durch die Keilform noch betont wird, um diese außergewöhnliche Lage und Aussicht herum konzipiert.

Construite face à l'océan, cette maison en coin est spectaculairement exposée aux éléments. La structure rigide en poutres d'acier est posée sur une grille de caissons en béton enfoncée de deux mètres dans la roche volcanique pour résister à la force des vents et aux tremblements de terre éventuels. Avec ses trois chambres et sa vaste zone de séjour, cette maison est structurée en fonction du site et des vues, dont la nature dynamique est soulignée par le plan en coin.

Pages 150/151: The wedge-shaped design of the Goodson Residence expresses the condition of many Southern California beach houses. Restricted either by geological or urban considerations on their rear entrance side, these houses tend to open out generously on the ocean side, giving the owners views of one of the most remarkable horizons in the United States.

Seite 150/151: Das keilförmige Design der Goodson Residence verdeutlicht die Bauweise vieler südkalifornischer Strandhäuser. Während diese Häuser auf der Rückseite (Eingangsbereich) aufgrund geologischer oder urbaner Gegebenheiten häufig stark eingeschränkt sind, öffnen sie sich auf der dem Ozean zugewandten Seite und bieten ihren Bewohnern damit Ausblick auf einen der spektakulärsten Horizonte in den Vereinigten Staaten.

Pages 150/151: La conception de la Goodson Residence traduit la problématique de nombreuses maisons de plage de Californie du Sud. Limitées, pour des raisons topographiques ou urbanistiques, sur leur façade arrière qui est aussi leur entrée, elle s'ouvrent généreusement sur l'océan, offrant à leurs propriétaires quelques-uns des plus beaux panoramas des Etats-Unis.

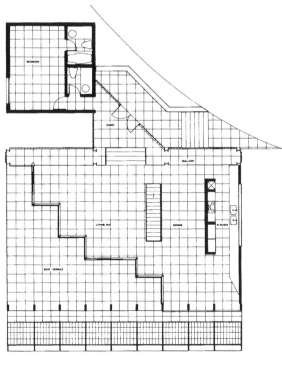

Pages 152/153: The extremely high volume of the upper, living-room deck offers not only a generous view of the Pacific, but also an unexpected occasion to hang works of art, with a Roy Lichtenstein living-room scene.

Seite 152/153: Die extreme Deckenhöhe des oberen Wohnzimmerbereichs bietet nicht nur einen wunderbaren Blick auf den Pazifik, sondern auch eine ungewöhnliche Ausstellungsfläche für Gemälde – wie hier Roy Lichtensteins Wohnraumszene.

Pages 152/153: Le volume extrêmement élevé de la salle de séjour du haut offre à la fois une vue généreuse sur le Pacifique et la possibilité d'accrocher des œuvres d'art comme ce grand Lichtenstein.

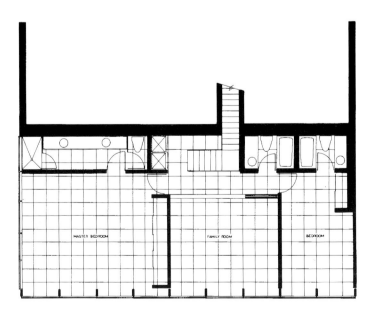

LEVEL ONE

RoTo

Michael Rotondi

Clark Stevens

Qwfk House, New Jersey, 1989–95
(project), detail of the façade.

Qwfk Hause, New Jersey, 1989–95
(Projekt), Detail der Fassade.

Qwfk Hause, New Jersey, 1989–95
(projet), détail de la façade.

Michael Rotondi co-founded Morphosis with Thom Mayne in 1979. He has been the director of SCI-Arc since 1987. Having left Morphosis with his collaborator Clark Stevens in 1991, Rotondi created with Stevens RoTo Architects in 1993. Although his approach remains as intensely intellectual as that of Mayne, he has evolved toward the idea that an architect should not maintain "singular control" over the design process. Clients and others are called to give their opinions during an open-ended interaction. As Rotondi says, "The search is for a zone, an in-between state, the confusion in the transformation from one state of rest to another, where neither dominates. The third state can still have evidence of the original two." Or again, "In nature, complex systems are layered interdependently to compose essential beauty." His projects since leaving Morphosis include the Nicola Restaurant (Los Angeles) and CDLT 1,2, Cedar Lodge Terrace, Silverlake (started in 1989).

Michael Rotondi, Mitbegründer von Morphosis, ist seit 1987 Direktor des SCI-Arc. Nachdem er Morphosis 1991 verlassen hatte, gründete er 1993 gemeinsam mit Clark Stevens RoTo Architects. Obwohl sein Ansatz so intellektuell ist wie der von Mayne, meint er, daß der Architekt nicht die »alleinige Kontrolle« über den Designprozeß haben solle; auch Klienten werden um ihre Meinung gebeten. Rotondi formulierte es so: »Die Suche richtet sich auf eine Zone, ein Zwischenstadium, die Verwirrung während der Transformation von einem Ruhezustand zum nächsten, die Phase, in der keiner von beiden dominiert. Der dritte Zustand kann natürlich Teile der beiden ursprünglichen Zustände enthalten.« Er fährt fort: »In der Natur sind komplexe Systeme so voneinander abhängig und miteinander verwoben, daß wahre Schönheit entsteht.« Seine Projekte – nach seinem Ausscheiden bei Morphosis – umfassen das Nicola Restaurant (Los Angeles) und CDLT 1,2, Cedar Lodge Terrace, Silverlake (Baubeginn 1989).

Michael Rotondi est avec Thom Mayne le co-fondateur de Morphosis en 1979. Il dirige SCI-Arc depuis 1987. Après avoir quitté Morphosis en 1991 avec son collaborateur Clark Stevens, il crée avec celui-ci RoTo Architects en 1993. Bien que son approche soit restée aussi intellectuelle que celle de Mayne, il a évolué vers l'idée que l'architecte ne devait pas exercer un «contrôle exclusif» sur le processus de conception. Le client, entre autres, doit donner son avis. Rotondi précise: «Je cherche cette zone intermédiaire, floue, qui garde encore des traces de ce qui fut et laisse déjà apparaître ce qui va être. Dans la nature, les systèmes complexes se superposent intimement pour faire naître une beauté essentielle.» Parmi ses projets depuis son départ de Morphosis : le Nicola Restaurant (Los Angeles) et CLDT 1, 2, Cedar Lodge Terrace, Silverlake (commencé en 1989).

Qwfk House, New Jersey
1989–95

Located in a rural, rather conservative area of New Jersey, not far from Richard Meier's Grotta House, this extraordinary residence has been in the process of design and construction for some time. As Michael Rotondi says, "This house explores complexity as a guide to a different kind of legibility, not based upon the conventional ordering of spaces and positioning of materials." The materials are to some extent chosen with respect to the setting. "Lead coated copper roofing parallels the gray blue skies most often found above the site. Some walls are from fractured ochre bedrock displaced in the excavation, additional walls are plaster tinted in this hue, and in the central zone, walls are surfaced in wood to express the exposed boundaries of this area," again according to the architect. Having left Morphosis with his collaborator Clark Stevens in 1991, Rotondi created with Stevens RoTo Architects in 1993. The Qwfk House is an unusual experiment which should test the viability of the most advanced concepts of California architecture in a different environment.

Diese außergewöhnliche Residenz in einer eher ländlichen, konservativen Gegend von New Jersey (in der Nähe von Richard Meiers Grotta House) befindet sich bereits seit längerem in der Planungs- und Bauphase. Michael Rotondi beschrieb es so: »Dieses Haus erforscht die Komplexität als Richtlinie für eine unterschiedliche Form von Lesbarkeit, die nicht auf der konventionellen Aufteilung von Räumen und Verwendung von Materialien beruht.« Die Materialien wurden zum Teil im Hinblick auf die umliegende Landschaft ausgewählt: »Die mit Blei ummantelte Kupferbedachung stellt eine Parallele zu dem graublauen Himmel dar, den man in dieser Gegend häufig vorfindet. Einige Wände bestehen aus gebrochenem ockerfarbenen Muttergestein, das bei der Ausschachtung zu Tage kam, einige andere Wände sind in diesem Farbton verputzt, und im mittleren Bereich wurden einige Wände mit Holz verkleidet, als Antwort auf die exponierte Begrenzung des Geländes.« Nachdem Michael Rotondi zusammen mit seinem Mitarbeiter Clark Stevens die Firma Morphosis 1991 verlassen hatte, gründete er gemeinsam mit Clark Stevens 1993 das Architekturbüro RoTo Architects. Das Qwfk House stellt ein ungewöhnliches Experiment dar, das die Lebensfähigkeit der fortschrittlichsten Konzepte kalifornischer Architektur in einer anderen Umgebung testet.

Cette extraordinaire résidence est en chantier depuis un certain temps déjà. Elle est située dans une région rurale et assez conservatrice du New Jersey, non loin de la Grotta House de Richard Meier. Comme l'explique Michael Rotondi, «elle introduit la complexité afin de parvenir à une lisibilité qui ne soit pas basée sur l'ordonnancement conventionnel de l'espace et la juxtaposition des matériaux». Dans une certaine mesure, les matériaux sont ici choisis en fonction du site. «Le toit en cuivre recouvert de plomb renvoie au ciel gris-bleu que l'on découvre souvent dans cette région. Certains murs ont été montés avec des blocs de tuffeau ocre excavés lors des travaux de terrassement. D'autres sont enduits de plâtre teinté dans la même nuance, et des cloisons revêtues des bois délimitent visuellement l'espace central.» Aprés avoir quitté Morphosis en 1991, accompagné de son collaborateur Clark Stevens, Michael Rotondi a créé avec celui-ci RoTo Architects en 1993. La Qwfk House est une expérience originale qui devrait tester les capacites d'acclimatation de la nouvelle architecture californienne sous d'autres cieux.

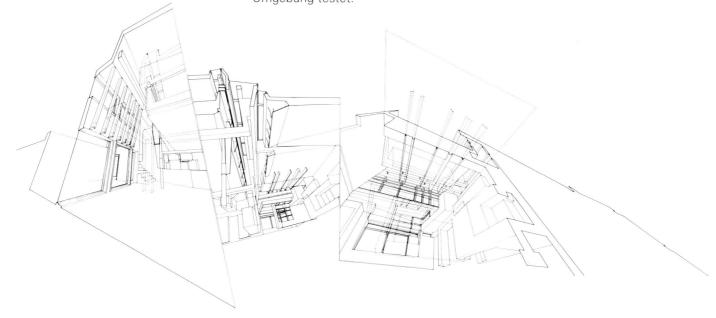

Pages 156/157: The Qwfk House displays not only its extreme complexity, but a fortress-like defiance. Built in a conservative, rural part of New Jersey, this project is an interesting test of the viability of what has been called The Santa Monica School far from its native shore.

Seite 156/157: Das Qwfk House demonstriert nicht nur seine extreme Komplexität, sondern vermittelt auch den Eindruck einer Festung. In dieser ländlichen, konservativen Gegend von New Jersey stellt es einen interessanten Test dar für die Akzeptanz der sogenannten »Santa Monica School«, weit entfernt von ihrem ursprünglichen Tätigkeitsfeld.

Pages 156/157: La Qwfk House affiche son extrême complexité et son allure de forteresse. Edifié dans un zone rurale et conservatrice du New Jersey, ce projet est un intéressant test de viabilité pour le mouvement de la «Santa Monica School» (l'École de Santa Monica), loin de sa base.

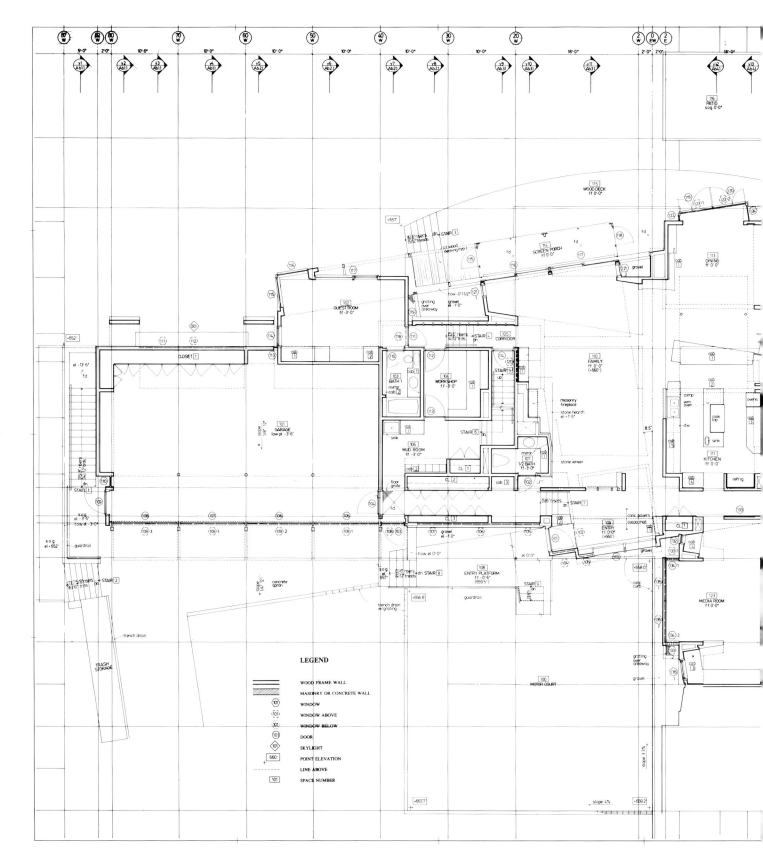

LEGEND

	WOOD FRAME WALL
	MASONRY OR CONCRETE WALL
101	WINDOW
101	WINDOW ABOVE
101	WINDOW BELOW
101	DOOR
101	SKYLIGHT
660'	POINT ELEVATION
	LINE ABOVE
101	SPACE NUMBER

Pages 158/159: With its plans modified during construction by Michael Rotondi, the Qwfk house in many respects represents an assault on the typically accepted faces of contemporary architecture. Far from the pleasant farm houses of its environment, this is the sort of challenging architecture which requires a close relationship between the client and the designer.

Seite 158/159: Das Qwfk House, dessen Pläne während der Bauzeit von Michael Rotondi überarbeitet wurden, repräsentiert in vielerlei Hinsicht einen Angriff auf die Konventionen zeitgenössischer Architektur. Weit entfernt von den adretten Farmhäusern seiner Umgebung erfordert eine solche architektonische Herausforderung die enge Zusammenarbeit von Architekt und Kunden.

Pages 158/159: Avec ses plans modifiés en cours de construction par Michael Rotondi, la Qwfk House représente à de nombreux égard un défi à certaines conventions de l'architecture contemporaine. Très éloignée dans son inspiration des agréables habitations rurales de la région, elle tient le pari d'une architecture qui associe étroitement le client à la conception du projet.

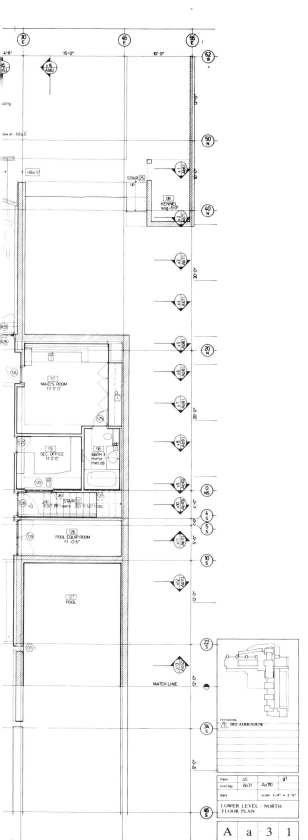

MAID'S ROOM
ff 0'-0"

SEC OFFICE
ff 0'-0"

BATH 3
mirror
med cab

STAIR

POOL EQUIP ROOM
ff -0'-6"

POOL

STAIR
up

KENNEL
sag +5'-0"

MATCH LINE

revisions
⚠ BID ADDENDUM

base	a5		g1
overlay	Aa31	Aa70	
date		scale 1/4" = 1'-0"	

LOWER LEVEL - NORTH
FLOOR PLAN

A a 3 1

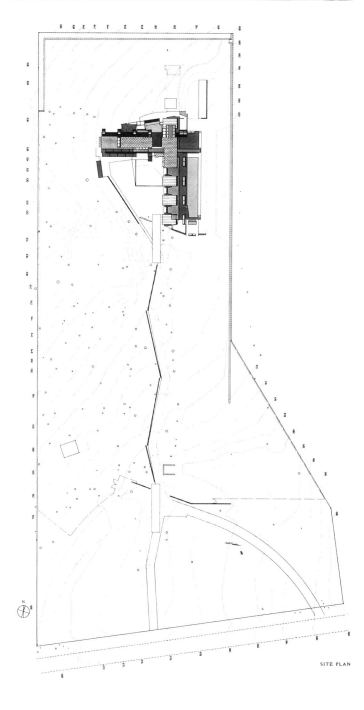

SITE PLAN

Carlson-Reges Residence, Los Angeles
1992–95

This unusual project involves the addition of a gallery and living space to an existing 1920s industrial building, on a site surrounded by a railroad. In a gesture typical of Michael Rotondi's work, one of the clients is a builder who is using materials that either existed on the site, or were taken from other buildings he has worked on. One spectacular gesture is the construction of a swimming pool almost six meters off the ground, with its axis turned toward downtown Los Angeles, "so that swimmers can look toward the city as they swim." An observation tower has been added to the roof. The living area is elevated to the mezzanine and includes a garden. Strange and incongruous in this rather industrial setting, the Carlson-Reges Residence provides further proof that Michael Rotondi is one of the most innovative architects currently working in Los Angeles.

Dieses ungewöhnliche Projekt umfaßt den Anbau einer Galerie und eines Wohnbereichs an ein Industriegebäude aus den 20er Jahren, das auf einem von Gleisen umgebenen Gelände liegt. Bei einem der Auftraggeber handelt es sich um einen Bauunternehmer, der entsprechend Michael Rotondis Vorgehensweise Materialien verwendet, die entweder bereits auf dem Gelände vorhanden waren oder aus Gebäuden stammen, an denen er zuvor arbeitete. Ganz besonders spektakulär wirkt der Swimmingpool, der fast sechs Meter hoch liegt und dessen Achse auf die Innenstadt von Los Angeles ausgerichtet ist, »damit die Schwimmer über die Stadt schauen können.« Dem Dach wurde ein Aussichtsturm hinzugefügt. Der Wohnbereich wurde ins Mezzaningeschoß verlegt und umfaßt auch einen Garten. Die in dieser eher industriellen Umgebung eigenartig und ungereimt wirkende Carlson-Reges Residence ist ein weiterer Beweis dafür, daß Michael Rotondi derzeit in Los Angeles zu den innovativsten Architekten gehört.

Ce projet original est en fait l'adjonction d'une galerie et d'une salle de séjour à un bâtiment industriel des années 20 implanté dans un site entouré d'une voie ferrée. L'un des clients est entrepreneur et a utilisé des matériaux trouvés sur le site ou récupérés sur d'autres chantiers. L'extraordinaire piscine, à presque six mètres au-dessus du sol, orientée vers le centre de Los Angeles pour que l'on puisse admirer la ville en se baignant. Une tour d'observation a été ajoutée sur le toit. La pièce de séjour est élevée en mezzanine et comprend un jardin. La Carlson-Reges Residence, dont la présence surprend dans un quartier plutôt industriel, prouve une fois encore que Michael Rotondi et son associé Clark Stevens font partie des architectes les plus créatifs de Los Angeles.

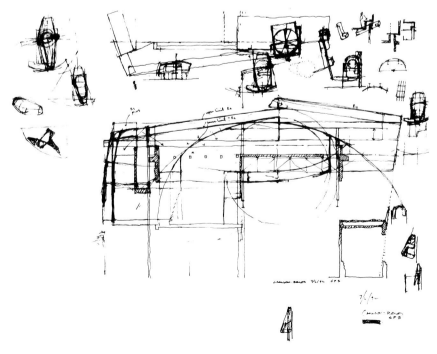

Pages 160/161: Although the intellectual process behind this design is not directly related to the images of the movie industry, the prickly additions made by Michael Rotondi to the existing structure recall the kind of makeshift war mentality described in movies like "Mad Max." This is not so much "deconstruction" as it is recon-struction in an environment of urban decay and a certain amount of fear.

Seite 160/161: Obwohl die Theorie hinter diesem Entwurf keinen direkten Zusammenhang mit den Bildern der Film-industrie aufweist, erinnern die spitzen Aufbauten, mit denen Michael Rotondi das existente Gebäude versah, an die aus der Not geborene Kriegsmentalität, wie sie in Fil-men wie »Mad Max« zum Ausdruck kommt. Hierbei han-delt es sich weniger um »Dekonstruktion« als um Rekon-struktion in einer Umgebung urbanen Verfalls und ständiger Angst.

Pages 160/161: Rotondi a hérissé le bâtiment existant d'extensions qui rappellent l'atmosphère guerrière de films comme «Mad Max». Il s'agit moins de déconstruction que de reconstruction dans un environnement marqué par la peur et la décadence urbaine.

Schweitzer BIM

Josh Schweitzer

Josh Schweitzer grew up in the Midwest (BA Pitzer College, Claremont, CA, M. Arch., University of Kansas, 1980). He worked for Spencer + Webster in London, PBNA in Kansas City and Frank O. Gehry before creating his own partnership, Schweitzer-Kellen in 1984. His own office, Schweitzer BIM opened in 1987. He has completed work in New York, Kansas City, Missouri, Honolulu and Fukuoka, Japan as well as California. He has also designed furniture and light fixtures for his projects as well as eyeglass frames, tableware, jewelry and sets for an opera. Amongst his more published work, the Border Grill 2 in Santa Monica (1990) was a collaborative project with artists. Josh Schweitzer has completed numerous renovations and store interior projects, essentially in the Los Angeles area.

Josh Schweitzer wuchs im mittleren Westen der Vereinigten Staaten auf (Bachelor of Arts, Pitzer College, Claremont, Kalifornien; Master of Architecture, University of Kansas, 1980). Er arbeitete für Spencer + Webster in London, PBNA in Kansas City und Frank O. Gehry, bevor er 1984 das Gemeinschaftsbüro Schweitzer-Kellen gründete. 1987 eröffnete er sein eigenes Architekturbüro, Schweitzer BIM. Schweitzers Werke stehen sowohl in New York, Kansas City, Missouri, Honolulu und Fukuoka (Japan) als auch in Kalifornien. Für seine Projekte entwarf er Möbel und Beleuchtungskörper, gestaltete aber auch Brillengestelle, Geschirr und Besteck, Schmuck sowie Bühnenbilder für eine Oper. Unter seinen häufig besprochenen Werken befindet sich der Border Grill 2 in Santa Monica (1990), ein Gemeinschaftsprojekt mit verschiedenen Künstlern. Josh Schweitzer übernahm zahlreiche Sanierungsarbeiten und die Gestaltung von Ladeninneneinrichtungen, hauptsächlich im Einzugsgebiet von Los Angeles.

Josh Schweitzer a grandi dans le Middle West (BA Pitzer College, Claremont, Californie, M. Arch. University of Kansas, 1980). Il a travaillé pour Spencer + Webster à Londres, PBNA à Kansas City, et Frank O. Gehry, avant d'ouvrir sa propre agence, Schweitzer-Kellen en 1984, puis Schweitzer BIM, en 1987. Il a construit à New York, Kansas City, Honolulu, Fukuoka (Japon), et en Californie. Il a également conçu des meubles et des luminaires à l'occasion de ses projets d'architecture, ainsi que des montures de lunettes, des services de table, des bijoux et des décors pour un opéra. L'un de ses projets les plus reproduits, le Border Grill 2, à Santa Monica (1990), a été réalisé avec des artistes. Josh Schweitzer a réalisé de nombreuses rénovations et aménagements de magasins, essentiellement dans la région de Los Angeles.

The Monument, Joshua Tree, 1987–90, interior view.

The Monument, Joshua Tree, 1987–90, Innenansicht.

The Monument, Joshua Tree, 1987–90, vue intérieure.

The Monument, Joshua Tree
1987–90

The Joshua Tree National Monument is a desert area located three hours by car outside of Los Angeles. This small (90 m²) house, intended for the use of the architect and five friends is located on a 4 hectare site within the confines of the park. It is an assemblage of one room buildings, each containing a separate function. There is an orange, porch-like structure which is a shaded outdoor space. The olive green pavilion contains a 3.5 meter high living room, while a blue-violet volume contains a dining area, kitchen and sleeping spaces. Built with painted stucco walls, exposed aggregate concrete floors and windows framed with redwood, The Monument is an homage to its surroundings, imbued with a "monastic solemnity." As the architect says, "Its colors are the colors of the desert." He also cites Rudolph Schindler's ideal of the house as a "permanent camp" as an inspiration for this structure.

Das Joshua Tree National Monument ist ein Wüstengebiet, das in einer dreistündigen Autofahrt von Los Angeles aus zu erreichen ist. Das kleine (90 m²) Haus für den Architekten und fünf Freunde liegt auf einem 4 Hektar großen Gelände innerhalb des Nationalparks und besteht aus einer Ansammlung von Einraum-Gebäuden, die alle eine unterschiedliche Funktion besitzen. Eine orangefarbene, verandaähnliche Konstruktion dient als schattiger Raum im Freien; der olivgrüne Pavillon enthält den 3,50 Meter hohen Wohnbereich, während ein violettblaues Gebäude den Eßbereich, die Küche und die Schlafgelegenheiten umfaßt. The Monument mit seinen gestrichenen Putzwänden, Waschbetonböden und den mit Redwoodrahmen versehenen Fenstern ist eine Hommage an seine Umgebung, erfüllt von »klösterlicher Feierlichkeit«. Der Architekt formulierte es so: »Seine Farben sind die Farben der Wüste«. Darüber hinaus vermerkt er, daß Rudolph Schindlers Idealbild eines Hauses als »permanentes Zeltlager« ihm als Inspirationsquelle diente.

Le Parc National de Joshua Tree est une zone désertique, à trois heures de voiture de Los Angeles. Cette petite maison (90 m²) destinée à l'architecte et à ses amis est située sur un terrain de 4 ha, aux confins du parc. C'est un assemblage de petites constructions d'une pièce, chacune remplissant une fonction. La structure orange en forme de porche délimite un espace extérieur ombragé. Le pavillon olive abrite une salle de séjour de 3,5 m de haut. L'espace bleu-violet regroupe la salle à manger, la cuisine et les coins repos. Avec ses murs en crépi, ses sols en béton à granulat apparent et ses châssis de fenêtre en séquoia, The Monument rend à son environnement un hommage empreint de «solennité monacale». «Ses couleurs sont celles du désert, explique l'architecte, qui cite également parmi ses sources d'inspiration le «campement permanent» cher à Rudolph Schindler.

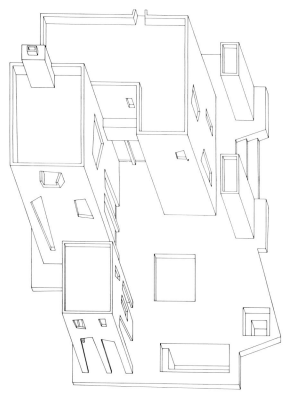

THE MONUMENT

Pages 164/165: Sculptural and painterly in this desert setting, The Monument is a reminder that California architecture is profoundly related to its spectacular natural settings. With its unusual door and window angles, together with a rather blocky formalism, The Monument might be described as a cross between adobe architecture and Surrealism.

Seite 164/165: Das in dieser Wüstengegend skulpturhaft und malerisch wirkende Monument erinnert daran, daß die kalifornische Architektur immer in engem Zusammenhang mit ihrer spektakulären natürlichen Umgebung stand. Aufgrund der ungewöhnlichen Tür- und Fensterneigungen sowie dem eher blockartigen Formalismus ließe sich The Monument auch als Mischung von Adobe-Architektur und Surrealismus bezeichnen.

Pages 164/165: Œuvre de sculpteur et de peintre au milieu du désert, The Monument rappelle que l'architecture californienne est profondément liée à son spectaculaire environnement naturel. Avec ses portes et ses fenêtres insolites et le formalisme de ses masses, The Monument semble né d'un croisement entre l'architecture en pisé et le surrélisme.

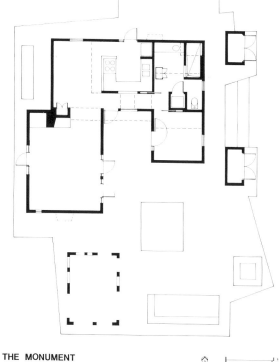

THE MONUMENT

Pages 166-169: Spare, with numerous openings to the desert environment, The Monument is an affirmation of architecture in the face of spectacular scenery. Not so much a defiance of the grandeur of the setting as it is an affirmation of the power of art, The Monument stands apart from other California architecture, if only because of its location.

Seite 166-169: Mit seinem kargen Erscheinungsbild und den zahlreichen Öffnungen zur wüstenartigen Umgebung stellt The Monument eine Bestätigung der Architektur im Angesicht einer spektakulären Szenerie dar. Dabei handelt es sich weniger um eine Herausforderung an die grandiose Umgebung als um die Bekräftigung der Macht der Kunst. The Monument hebt sich deutlich von der übrigen Architektur Kaliforniens ab – und sei es nur aufgrund seiner Lage.

Pages 166-169: A la fois fermé et ouvert sur son environnement désertique, The Monument est une affirmation de l'architecture face à un panorama spectaculaire. Défi à la grandeur du site mais davantage encore affirmation de la puissance de l'art, il occupe, ne serait-ce que par son site, une place à part dans l'architecture californienne.

Biographies
Biographien

Asymptote

Lise Anne Couture was born in Montreal in 1959. She received her B. Arch. from Carleton University, Canada, and M. Arch from Yale. She is presently on the faculty of the Department of Architecture at Parsons School of Design, New York. Hani Rashid received his M. Arch degree from the Cranbrook Academy of Art, Bloomfield Hills, Michigan. He is currently Adjunct Associate Professor at the Columbia University Graduate School of Architecture, New York. They created Asymptote in 1987. Projects include their 1989 4th place entry for the Alexandria Library, a commissioned housing project for Brig, Switzerland, and their participation in the 1993 competition for an art center in Tours, France (1993).

Lise Anne Couture wurde 1959 in Montreal geboren. Sie erhielt ihren Bachelor of Architecture an der Carleton University (Kanada) und ihren Master of Architecture in Yale. Zur Zeit ist sie als Designrezensentin am Master of Architecture-Programm der Parsons School of Design (New York) tätig. Hani Rashid erhielt seinen Master of Architecture an der Cranbrook Academy of Art in Bloomfield Hills (Michigan). Er arbeitet zur Zeit als Professor an der Columbia University Graduate School of Architecture, New York. Gemeinsam gründeten sie 1987 das Büro Asymptote. Zu ihren Projekten zählen ihr Wettbewerbsbeitrag für die Alexandria Library (1989), der auf dem vierten Platz landete, ein städtisches Wohnungsbauprojekt in Brig (Schweiz) und ihre Teilnahme an der Ausschreibung für das Kunstzentrum in Tours, Frankreich (1993).

Lise Anne Couture est née à Montréal en 1959. B. Arch. de Carleton University, au Canada, et M. Arch. de Yale, elle est actuellement critique de projets pour le program-me du master d'architecture de la Parsons School of Design, à New York. Hani Rashid a reçu son M. Arch. à la Cranbrook Academy of Art, Bloomfield Hills, Michigan. Il est actuellement professeur à l'école d'architecture de Columbia University, New York. Après avoir créé Asymptote en 1987, Couture et Rashid remportent la quatrième place au concours pour la bibliothèque d'Alexandrie (1989), la commande d'un immeuble de bureaux à Brig, en Suisse, et participent au concours pour un centre artistique à Tours (1993).

Asymptote Architecture
36 West 15th Street, 3 rd floor
New York, NY 10011
Tel: (212) 645-335
Fax: (212) 255-4989

Central Office of Architecture

The three principals of Central Office of Architecture received their B. Arch. degrees from the California Polytechnic State University, San Luis Obispo in 1981. Ron Golan received his M. Arch. at the Southern California Institute of Architecture, Santa Monica in 1986. Both Eric A. Kahn and Russell N. Thomsen worked at SuperStudio in Florence before creating COA. Eric A. Kahn also worked with Morphosis and Skidmore Owings and Merrill, while Russell N. Thomsen worked in the offices of Mark Mack and Richard Meier. Their work includes the Kahn Residence (Pacific Palisades, 1988) and the Summers Residence (Laguna Beach, 1991).

Die drei Leiter des Central Office of Architecture erhielten 1981 ihren Bachelor of Architecture an der California Polytechnic State University, San Luis Obispo. Ron Golan bekam 1986 seinen Master of Architecture am Southern California Institute of Architecture, Santa Monica. Sowohl Eric A. Kahn als auch Russell N. Thomsen waren bei SuperStudio in Florenz tätig, bevor sie das COA gründeten. Eric A. Kahn arbeitete auch mit Morphosis und Skidmore Owings and Merrill zusammen, während Russell N. Thomsen für Mark Mack und Richard Meier tätig war. Zu ihren Arbeiten zählen die Kahn Residence (Pacific Palisades, 1988) und die Summers Residence (Laguna Beach, 1991).

Les trois associés principaux du Central Office for Architecture sont tous diplômés (B.Arch.) de la California Polytechnic State University, San Luis Obispo, (1981). Ron Golan a passé son M. Arch. au Southern Institute of Architecture de Santa Monica, en 1986. Eric A. Kahn et Russell N. Thomsen ont travaillé pour SuperStudio à Florence avant de fonder le COA. Eric A. Kahn a également collaboré avec Morphosis, et Skidmore Owings and Merrill; Thomsen avec Mark Mack et Richard Meier. Ils ont réalisé, entre autres, Kahn Residence (Pacific Palisades, 1988), et Summers Residence (Laguna Beach, 1991).

Central Office of Architecture
1056 S. Sierra Bonita Avenue
Los Angeles,
CA 90019-2571
Tel: (213) 936-9210
Fax: (213) 936-1590

Cigolle & Coleman

Mark Cigolle (born in 1949 in La Salle, Illinois, BA and M. Arch., Princeton) and Kim Coleman (born in 1955 in New York, BA Smith College, M. Arch. University of Virginia) are a husband and wife team who created their own firm in 1982. Their completed work includes the Cloud Lane House (Los Angeles, 1985–86), the Socoloske House (Calabasas, 1985–88), a Faculty Club Expansion and Renovation for the University of Southern California, Los Angeles (1983–88), their Canyon House, and Renovations for the Wildwood School (Culver City, 1992–93). Work in progress includes the Marks/Klar House (Beverly Hills), the Sky Ranch House (Carmel Valley), and the Old Ranch Road House (Los Angeles).

Mark Cigolle (1949 in La Salle, Illinois, geboren, Bachelor of Arts und Master of Architecture, Princeton) und Kim Coleman (1955 in New York geboren, Bachelor of Arts, Smith College; Master of Architecture, University of Virginia) sind nicht nur Geschäfts-, sondern auch Ehepartner. 1982 gründeten sie ihre eigene Firma. Zu ihren fertiggestellten Arbeiten zählen das Cloud Lane House (Los Angeles, 1985-86), das Socoloske House (Calabasas, 1985-88), eine Renovierung mit Erweiterungsbau des Faculty Club der University of Southern California, Los Angeles (1983-88), ihr Canyon House sowie Renovierungsarbeiten an der Wildwood School (Culver City, 1992-93). Ihre derzeitigen Projekte umfassen das Marks/Klar House (Beverly Hills), das Sky Ranch House (Carmel Valley) und das Old Ranch Road House (Los Angeles).

Mark Cigolle (né en 1949 à La Salle, Illinois, B.A. et M. Arch. à Princeton), et Kim Coleman (née en 1955 à New York, B.A. Smith College et MA University of Virginia) sont mari et femme. Ils créent leur agence en 1982. Parmi leurs réalisations: la Cloud Lane House (Los Angeles, 1985–86), la Socoloske House (Calabasas, 1985–88), l'extension et la rénovation du Club des professeurs pour l'University of Southern California Los Angeles (1983–88), leur propre maison, Canyon House, et rénovations à l'école de Wildwood (Culver City, 1992–93). Parmi leurs projets en cours : Marks/Klar House (Beverly Hills), Sky Ranch House (Carmel Valley), et Old Ranch Road House (Los Angeles).

Cigolle & Coleman, Architects
455 Upper Mesa Road
Santa Monica, CA 90402
Tel: (310) 454-3684
Fax: (310) 454-2843

Steven Ehrlich

Born in New York in 1946, Steven Ehrlich received his B. Arch. degree from the Rensselaer Polytechnic Institute, Troy, New York in 1969. He studied indigenous vernacular architecture in North and West Africa from 1969 to 1977. He has completed numerous private residences, including the Friedman Residence (1986), the Ehrman-Coombs Residence (1989–91, Santa Monica), and the Schulman Residence (Brentwood, 1989–92), all in the Los Angeles area. Other built work includes the Shatto Recreation Center (1991) and Sony Music Entertainment Campus (Santa Monica, 1993).

Steven Ehrlich wurde 1946 in New York geboren und erhielt 1969 seinen Bachelor of Architecture am Rensselaer Polytechnic Institute, Troy, New York. Zwischen 1969 und 1977 beschäftigte er sich intensiv mit der Architektur Nord- und Westafrikas. Danach errichtete Ehrlich zahlreiche Privathäuser, einschließlich der Friedman Residence (1986), der Ehrman-Coombs Residence (Santa Monica, 1989-91) und der Schulman Residence (Brentwood, 1989-92), die sich alle im Gebiet von Los Angeles befinden. Zu seinen weiteren Werken zählen das Shatto Recreation Center (1991) und der Sony Music Entertainment Campus (Santa Monica, 1993).

Né à New York en 1946, Ehrlich passe son B. Arch. au Rensselaer Polytechnic Institute (Troy, New York) en 1969, puis étudie l'architecture indigène vernaculaire en Afrique du Nord et de l'Ouest de 1969 à 1977. Il a réalisé de nombreuses demeures privées dans la région de Los Angeles, dont Friedman Residence (1986), Ehrman-Coombs Residence (Santa Monica, 1989–91), et Schulman Residence (Brentwood, 1989–92). Il est également auteur du Shatto Recreation Center (1991), et du Sony Music Entertainment Campus (Santa Monica, 1993).

Steven Ehrlich Architects
2210 Colorado Avenue,
Santa Monica, CA 90404
Tel: (310) 828-6700
Fax: (310) 828-7710

Frank O. Gehry

Born in Toronto, Canada in 1929, Frank O. Gehry, studied at the University of Southern California, Los Angeles (1949–51), and at Harvard (1956–57). Principal of Frank O. Gehry and Associates, Inc., Los Angeles, since 1962, he received the 1989 Pritzker Prize. Some of his main projects are, the Loyola Law School, Los Angeles (1981–84); the Norton House, Venice, California (1982–84); California Aerospace Museum, Los Angeles (1982–84); Schnabel House, Brentwood (1986–89); Festival Disney, Marne-la-Vallée, France (1988–92); University of Toledo Art Building, Toledo, Ohio (1990–92); American Center, Paris, France (1988–93); Disney Concert Hall, Los Angeles (construction temporarily halted), and the Guggenheim Museum, Bilbao Spain (under construction).

Frank O. Gehry wurde 1929 in Toronto, Kanada, geboren und studierte an der University of Southern California, Los Angeles (1949-51) sowie in Harvard (1956-57). Als Leiter von Frank O. Gehry and Associates, Inc., Los Angeles (seit 1962) erhielt er 1989 den Pritzker-Preis. Zu seinen wichtigsten Projekten gehören die Loyola Law School, Los Angeles (1981-84); Norton House, Venice, Kalifornien (1982–84); California Aerospace Museum, Los Angeles (1982-84); Schnabel House, Brentwood (1986–89); Festival Disney, Marne-la-Vallée, Frankreich (1988-92); University of Toledo Art Building, Toledo, Ohio (1990-92); American Center, Paris (1988–93); Disney Concert Hall, Los Angeles (zeitweiliger Baustopp) sowie das Guggenheim Museum, Bilbao, Spanien (im Bau befindlich).

Né en 1929 à Toronto au Canada, Frank O. Gehry étudie l'architecture à l'University of Southern California, Los Angeles (1949–51), et Harvard (1956–57). Responsable de Frank O. Gehry and Associates, Inc., Los Angeles, depuis 1962, il reçoit le Pritzker Prize en 1989. Parmi ses principales réalisations: Loyola Law School, Los Angeles (1981–84); Norton House, Venice, Californie (1982–84); le California Aerospace Museum, Los Angeles (1982–84); Schnabel House, Brentwood (1986–89); Festival Disney, Marne-la-Vallée, France (1988–92); le bâtiment des Arts, University of Toledo, Toledo, Ohio (1990–92); l'American Center à Paris, France (1988–93); le Disney Concert Hall, Los Angeles (construction momentanément arrêtée), et le Guggenheim Museum, Bilbao, Espagne (en construction).

Frank O. Gehry and Associates, Inc.
1520-B Cloverfield Blvd.
Santa Monica, CA 90404
Tel: (310) 828-6088
Fax: (310) 828-2098

Joan Hallberg

Born in Moline, Illinois in 1950, Joan Hallberg received her B. Design/Arch. degree from the University of Florida in 1981, M. Arch., Harvard, 1983. At Harvard, she studied under Helmut Jahn, Michael McKinnell and Stanley Tigerman. While in Boston she worked with Don Hisaka and Schwartz/Silver Architects and taught design at the Boston Architectural Center. She moved to California in 1985, worked with Ratcliff Architects in Berkeley and opened her own office in 1987 near Sea Ranch.

Joan Hallberg wurde 1950 in Moline, Illinois, geboren und erhielt 1981 ihren Bachelor of Design/Architecture an der University of Florida. 1983 machte sie ihren Master of Architecture in Harvard, wo sie bei Helmut Jahn, Michael McKinnell und Stanley Tigerman hörte. In Boston arbeitete sie mit Don Hisaka und Schwartz/Silver Architects zusammen und lehrte Design am Boston Architectural Center. 1985 zog sie nach Kalifornien, arbeitete mit Ratcliff Architects in Berkeley und gründete 1987 ihr eigenes Architekturbüro in der Nähe von Sea Ranch.

Née en 1950 à Moline, Illinois, Joan Hallberg passe son B. Arch. et design à l'University of Florida en 1981, et son M. Arch. à Harvard en 1983, où elle suit les cours d'Helmut Jahn, Michael McKinnel et Stanley Tigerman. A Boston, elle travaille avec Don Hisaka et Schwartz/Silver Architects, et enseigne le dessin au Boston Architectural Center. Elle s'installe en 1985 en Californie, où elle collabore avec Ratcliff Architects à Berkeley et ouvre son agence en 1987, près de Sea Ranch.

Joan Hallberg, Architect
Post Office Box 295
The Sea Ranch, CA 95497
Tel: (707) 785-2080
Fax: (707) 785-2080

Hodgetts + Fung

The principals of Hodgetts + Fung, created in 1984, are Craig Hodgetts (BA Oberlin College, M. Arch. Yale) and Hsin-Ming Fung (M. Arch. UCLA). Aside from the Towell Temporary Library at UCLA, their work includes the Click & Flick Agency (Hollywood), a permanent solar exhibition environment at EMR's Bad Oeynhausen facility, L.A. Arts Park in the Sepulveda Basin, Hemdale Film Corporation Office facility, L.A., the Viso Residence (Hollywood). They designed the exhibition "Blueprints for Modern Living" at the MOCA/Temporary Contemporary, and are currently working on a traveling exhibition of the work of Charles and Ray Eames scheduled to open in Washington in 1997.

Craig Hodgetts (Bachelor of Arts, Oberlin College; Master of Architecture, Yale) und Hsin-Ming Fung (Master of Architecture, UCLA) sind die Leiter des 1984 gegründeten Architekturbüros Hodgetts + Fung. Neben ihrer Arbeit an der Towell Temporary Library der UCLA umfassen ihre Projekte die Click & Flick Agency in Hollywood, eine Solar-Installation auf dem EMR-Gelände in Bad Oeynhausen, den L.A. Arts Park im Sepulveda Basin, das Hemdale Film Corporation Bürogebäude in L.A. sowie die Viso Residence (Hollywood). Hodgetts + Fung gestalteten die »Blueprints for Modern Living«-Ausstellung im MOCA/Temporary Contemporary und arbeiten zur Zeit an einer Wanderausstellung der Arbeiten von Charles und Ray Eames, die 1997 in Washington stattfinden soll.

Les associés de Hodgetts + Fung, agence créée en 1984, sont Craig Hodgetts (BA Oberlin College, M. Arch. Yale), et Hsin-Ming Fung (M. Arch. UCLA). Outre la bibliothèque provisoire Towell pour UCLA, ils ont réalisé la Click & Flick Agency à Hollywood, une exposition-installation solaire permanente à l'EMR de Bad Oeynhausen, l'L.A. Arts Park du Sepulveda Basin, l'immeuble de la Hemdale Film Corporation (Los Angeles), Viso Residence (Hollywood), Schrage/Butler Residence (Santa Monica), et Goetz Residence (Laurel Canyon). Ils ont conçu l'exposition «Blueprints for Modern Living» au MOCA/Temporary Contemporary, et préparent actuellement une exposition itinérante sur l'œuvre de Charles et Ray Eames, qui devrait être inaugurée à Washington en 1997.

Hodgetts + Fung
1750 Berkeley Street,
Santa Monica, CA 90404
Tel: (310) 829-1969
Fax: (310) 829-5942

Franklin Israel

Born in 1945 in New York, Franklin Israel was educated at the University of Pennsylvania, Yale and Columbia. He received the Rome Prize in Architecture in 1973 and worked with Giovanni Pasanella in New York, and Llewelyn-Davies, Weeks, Forestier-Walker and Bor in London and Teheran before becoming an art director at Paramount Pictures (1978–79), participating in film projects in Los Angeles, China and the Philippines. He created his own firm, Franklin D. Israel Design Associates in 1983. His completed projects include offices for Propaganda Films in Hollywood, and Virgin Records in Beverly Hills. Confirming his close connections to the movie industry, he has also designed a Malibu beach house for Robert Altman.

Franklin Israel wurde 1945 in New York geboren und studierte an der University of Pennsylvania, in Yale und in Columbia. 1973 erhielt er den Rome Prize für Architektur und arbeitete zusammen mit Giovanni Pasanella in New York und Llewelyn-Davies, Weeks, Forestier-Walker and Bor in London und Teheran, bevor er zwischen 1978 und 1979 als Art-director von Paramount Pictures tätig war und an Filmprojekten in Los Angeles, China und auf den Philippinen teilnahm. 1983 gründete er seine eigene Firma, Franklin D. Israel Design Associates. Seine fertiggestellten Projekte umfassen u.a. Bürogebäude für Propaganda Films in Hollywood und Virgin Records in Beverly Hills. Darüber hinaus entwarf er in Malibu ein Strandhaus für Robert Altman, was seine enge Verbindung zur Filmindustrie unterstreicht.

Né en 1945 à New York, Franklin Israel a étudié à l'University of Pennsylvania, à Yale et Columbia. Il a reçu le Prix de Rome d'architecture en 1973, et a travaillé avec Giovanni Pasanella à New York et Llewelyn-Davies, Weeks, Forestier-Walker and Bor à Londres et Téhéran. Directeur artistique de Paramount Pictures (1978–79), il participe à des projets de films à Los Angeles, en Chine et aux Philippines. En 1983, il crée sa propre agence, Franklin D. Israel Design Associates. Parmi ses projets achevés: des bureaux pour Propaganda Films à Hollywood, et Virgin Records à Beverly Hills. Très proche du monde du cinéma, il a également dessiné la maison de plage de Robert Altman à Malibu.

Franklin D. Israel Design Associates, Inc.
254 So Robertson Blvd.
Suite 205
Beverly Hills, CA 90211
Tel: (310) 652-8087
Fax: (310) 652-3383

Wes Jones

Wes Jones, born in 1958 in Santa Monica, attended the United States Military Academy at West Point, the University of California at Berkeley (BA) and the Harvard Graduate School of Design (M. Arch.). A recipient of the Rome Prize in Architecture, he has served as a visiting Professor at Harvard, Rice, Tulane and Columbia Universities. He worked with Eisenman/Robertson, Architects in New York before becoming Director of Design at Holt & Hinshaw in San Francisco. As partner in charge of design at Holt Hinshaw Pfau Jones, he completed the Astronauts' Memorial at Kennedy Space Center in Florida and the UCLA Chiller Plant/Facilities Complex.

Wes Jones wurde 1958 in Santa Monica geboren und besuchte die United States Military Academy in West Point, die University of California in Berkeley (Bachelor of Arts) sowie die Harvard Graduate School of Design (Master of Architecture). Als Empfänger des Rome Prize für Architektur war er als Gastprofessor an den Universitäten von Harvard, Rice, Tulane und Columbia tätig. Bevor er bei Holt & Hinshaw in San Francisco zum Director of Design ernannt wurde, arbeitete er mit Eisenman/Robertson, Architects in New York zusammen. Als jetziger Teilhaber und Hauptverantwortlicher für den Bereich Design bei Holt Hinshaw Pfau Jones vollendete er das Astronauts' Memorial im Kennedy Space Center in Florida und den UCLA Chiller Plant/Facilities Complex.

Né en 1958 à Santa Monica, Wes Jones fait ses études à l'Académie militaire de West Point, à l'University of California (B. Arch.) et à l'Harvard Graduate School of Design (M. Arch.). Titulaire du Prix de Rome d'architecture, il est professeur invité aux universités de Harvard, Rice, Tulane et Columbia. Il travaille avec Eisenman/Robertson, Architects, New York avant de devenir directeur des projets chez Holt & Hinshaw à San Francisco. Associé chargé de la mise en forme des projets chez Holt Hinshaw Pfau Jones, il vient d'achever le Mémorial des astronautes au Kennedy Space Center en Floride, et le UCLA Chiller Plant/Facilities Complex.

Jones, Partners: Architecture
461 2nd Street
Suite 458
San Francisco,
CA 94107-1416
Tel: (415) 957-0530
Fax: (415) 957-0513

Morphosis

Morphosis principal Thom Mayne, born in Connecticut in 1944, received his B. Arch. in 1968 (USC), and his M. Arch. degree at Harvard in 1978. He created Morphosis in 1979. Some of the main buildings of Morphosis are: the Lawrence House (1981); Kate Mantilini Restaurant, Beverly Hills (1986); Cedar's Sinai Comprehensive Cancer Care Center, Beverly Hills (1987); Los Angeles Arts Park, Performing Arts Pavilion, Los Angeles, competition (1989); Crawford Residence, Montecito, (1987–92); Yuzen Vintage Car Museum, West Hollywood, project (1992), as well as the more recent Blades Residence (Goleta, 1992–) and projects for schools in California (La Jolla Country Day School, La Jolla, Pomona Unified School District, competition, 1993).

Thom Mayne, der Leiter von Morphosis, 1944 in Connecticut geboren, erhielt 1968 seinen Bachelor of Architecture (USC) und 1978 seinen Master of Architecture in Harvard. Er gründete 1979 das Architekturbüro Morphosis. Die wichtigsten Arbeiten der Firma Morphosis umfassen u.a. das Lawrence House (1981); das Kate Mantilini Restaurant, Beverly Hills (1986); Cedar's Sinai Comprehensive Cancer Care Center, Beverly Hills (1986); Los Angeles Arts Park, Performing Arts Pavilion, Los Angeles (Wettbewerb 1989); die Crawford Residence, Montecito (1987-92); das Yuzen Vintage Car Museum, West Hollywood (Projekt 1992) sowie die entworfene Blades Residence, (Goleta-Projekt, 1992) und Projekte für Schulen in Kalifornien.

Directeur de Morphosis, Thom Mayne, né en 1944 dans le Connecticut, a passé son B. Arch. en 1968 (USC) et son M. Arch. à Harvard en 1978. Il crée Morphosis en 1979. Installé à Santa Monica, en Californie, Morphosis compte parmi ses réalisations: Lawrence House (1981), le Kate Mantilini Restaurant, Beverly Hills (1986), le Cedar's Sinai Comprehensive Cancer Care Center, Beverly Hills (1987), le Los Angeles Park, Performing Arts Pavilion, Los Angeles (concours, 1989); Crawford Residence, Montecito, (1987–92); le Yuzen Village Car Museum, West Hollywood (projet, 1992), Blades Residence, Goleta (1992); et des projets d'écoles en Californie.

Morphosis
Mr. Thom Mayne
2041 Colorado Avenue
Santa Monica, CA 90404
Tel: (310) 453-2247
Fax: (310) 829-3270

Eric Owen Moss

Born in Los Angeles, California in 1943, Eric Owen Moss received his BA degree from UCLA in 1965, and his M. Arch. in 1968. He also received a M. Arch. degree at Harvard in 1972. He has been a Professor of Design at the Southern California Institute of Architecture since 1974. He opened his own firm, in Culver City in 1976. His built work includes the Central Housing Office, University of California at Irvine, Irvine (1986–89) ; Lindblade Tower, Culver City, (1987–89) ; Paramount Laundry, Culver City, (1987–89) ; Gary Group, Culver City, (1988–90), The Box, Culver City (1990–94) and the IRS Building, also in Culver City (1993–94).

Eric Owen Moss wurde 1943 in Los Angeles geboren und erhielt 1965 seinen Bachelor of Arts und 1968 seinen Master of Architecture an der UCLA sowie 1972 seinen Master of Architecture in Harvard. Seit 1974 ist Moss als Professor of Design am Southern California Institute of Architecture tätig. 1976 gründete er in Culver City seine eigne Firma. Zu seinen Arbeiten zählen das Central Housing Office, University of California at Irvine, Irvine (1986–89); Lindblade Tower, Culver City (1987–89); Paramount Laundry, Culver City (1987–89); Gary Group, Culver City (1988–90); The Box, Culver City (1990–94) und das IRS Building, ebenfalls Culver City (1993–94).

Né en 1943 à Los Angeles, Eric Owen Moss est diplômé en architecture de UCLA (BA,1965) et a passé deux Masters à UCLA (1968) et Harvard (1972). Il enseigne le dessin d'architecture au SCI-Arc depuis 1974, et a créé sa propre agence à Culver City, en 1976. Parmi ses réalisations: Central Housing Office, University of California at Irvine, Irvine (1986–89); Lindblade Tower, Culver City (1987–89); Paramount Laundry, Culver City (1987–89); Gary Group, Culver City (1988–90); The Box, Culver City (1990–94) et l'IRS Building, toujours à Culver City (1993–94).

Eric Owen Moss, Architects
8557 Higuera Street
Culver City, CA 90232
Tel: (310) 839-1199
Fax: (310) 839-7922

Edward R. Niles

Born in 1935, Edward Niles has had a California State Architecture License since 1962. He created his own firm in 1967 and has built numerous private residences, mostly in Southern California, since that date. Associate Professor of Architecture at the University of Southern California since 1967, he has lectured recently at UCLA, Cal Poly San Luis Obispo, USC and at the American Institute of Architects (1992). His recent projects include the Milton Sidley Residence (Malibu), the Ziff Davis Publishing Corporation Offices (Malibu), the Alvin Toffler Residence (Malibu) and the Zuma Terrace Office building (Point Dume, Malibu).

Edward Niles wurde 1935 in Los Angeles geboren und besitzt seit 1962 die California State Architecture License. 1967 gründete er seine eigene Firma und hat seitdem zahlreiche Privathäuser errichtet, hauptsächlich in Südkalifornien. Ebenfalls seit 1967 außerordentlicher Professor der Architektur an der University of Southern California, lehrte er vor kurzem an der UCLA, der Cal Poly San Luis Obispo, an der USC und am American Institute of Architects (1992). Zu seinen jüngsten Projekten zählen die Milton Sidley Residence (Malibu), die Ziff Davis Publishing Corporation Offices (Malibu), die Alvin Toffler Residence (Malibu) und das Zuma Terrace Office Building (Point Dume, Malibu).

Né en 1935, Edward Niles exerce en tant qu'architecte depuis 1962. Il a créé sa propre agence en 1967, et a construit depuis cette date de nombreuses résidences privées, essentiellement en Californie du Sud. Professeur associé en architecture (University of Southern California) depuis 1967, il enseigne également à UCLA, Cal Poly San Luis Obispo, USC et à l'American Institute of Architects (1992). Parmi ses récents projets : Milton Sidley Residence (Malibu), les bureaux de Ziff Davis Publishing Corporation (Malibu), la maison d'Alvin Toffler (Malibu), et l'immeuble de bureaux Zuma Terrace (Point Dume, Malibu).

Edward R. Niles, Architect
29350 Pacific Coast Highway
Suite 9
Malibu, CA 90265
Tel: (310) 457-3602
Fax: (310) 457-3376

RoTo

Born in 1949 in Los Angeles, Michael Rotondi received his B. Arch. from the Southern California Institute of Architecture (SCI-Arc) in 1973. He worked with DMJM in Los Angeles (1973–76), and collaborated with Peter de Bretteville and Craig Hodgetts from 1974 to 1976. He was Director of the Graduate Design Faculty at SCI-Arc from 1976 to 1987. Founding principal of Morphosis with Thom Mayne, Michael Rotondi has been the Director of SCI-Arc since 1987. He left Morphosis in 1991 and created his present firm, RoTo in 1993 with Partner Clark Stevens. Ongoing projects include the Nicola Restaurant (Los Angeles) and CDLT 1,2, Cedar Lodge Terrace, Silverlake (started in 1989) and the Qwfk House. A recently designed project is Warehouse C, a 210 meter long structure to be built on landfill in the harbor of Nagasaki, Japan.

Michael Rotondi wurde 1949 in Los Angeles geboren und erhielt 1973 seinen Bachelor of Architecture am Southern California Institute of Architecture (SCI-Arc). Zwischen 1973 und 1976 war er für DMJM in Los Angeles tätig und arbeitete von 1974 bis 1976 mit Peter de Bretteville und Craig Hodgetts zusammen. Zwischen 1976 und 1987 war er Direktor der Graduate Design Faculty am SCI-Arc, und als Gründungsmitglied von Morphosis (zusammen mit Thom Mayne) ist Michael Rotondi seit 1987 Direktor vom SCI-Arc. 1991 verließ er Morphosis und gründete 1993 gemeinsam mit Clark Stevens RoTo. Zu seinen derzeitigen Projekten zählen das Nicola Restaurant (Los Angeles) und CDLT 1,2, Cedar Lodge Terrace, Silverlake (Baubeginn 1989) sowie das Qwfk House. Vor kurzem entwarf Rotondi das Warehouse C, eine 210 Meter lange Konstruktion, die auf einem aufgeschütteten Gelände im Hafen von Nagasaki (Japan) entstehen soll.

Né en 1949 à Los Angeles, Michael Rotondi est diplômé du SCI-Arc (1973). Il travaille à Los Angeles pour DMJM (1973–76), et collabore avec Peter de Bretteville et Craig Hodgetts de 1974 à 1976. Il dirige le département de design du SCI-Arc, de 1976 à 1987. Principal fondateur de Morphosis avec Thom Mayne, il dirige le SCI-Arc depuis 1987. Après avoir quitté Morphosis en 1991, il crée deux ans plus tard son agence actuelle, RoTo, avec Clark Stevens. Parmi ses projets en cours figurent le Nicola Restaurant (Los Angeles), et CDLT 1,2, Cedar Lodge Terrace, Silverlake (commencé en 1989), et Qwfk House. Il a récemment conçu le projet Warehouse C, un bâtiment de 210 m de long qui sera construit sur un terrain récupéré sur la mer dans le port de Nagasaki, au Japon.

RoTo Architects
600 Moulton Avenue, Suite 305
USA–Los Angeles, CA 90031
Tel: (213) 226-1112
Fax: (213) 226-1105

Schweitzer BIM

Born in 1953 in Cincinnati, Ohio, Josh Schweitzer (BA Pitzer College, Claremont, CA, M. Arch., University of Kansas, 1980), worked for Spencer + Webster in London, PBNA in Kansas City and Frank O. Gehry in Santa Monica before creating his own partnership, Schweitzer-Kellen in 1984, and his own office, Schweitzer BIM opened in 1987. Besides The Monument, his completed work includes restaurants such as Venue (Kansas City, 1993), or the California Chicken Cafe (Los Angeles, 1992). He recently completed the Big Life Sports Bar in Fukuoka, Japan, and has begun work on a 450 hectare Water Park/Hotel complex in southern Japan. Also recently completed, the Mossimo sports wear store at South Coast Plaza (Costa Mesa, CA).

Josh Schweitzer wurde 1953 in Cincinnati, Ohio, geboren (Bachelor of Arts, Pitzer College, Claremont, Kalifornien; Master of Architecture, University of Kansas, 1980) und arbeitete für Spencer + Webster in London, PBNA in Kansas City und Frank O. Gehry in Santa Monica, bevor er 1984 das Gemeinschaftsbüro Schweitzer-Kellen und 1987 sein eigenes Architekturbüro, Schweitzer BIM gründete. Zu seinen fertiggestellten Arbeiten zählen – neben The Monument – verschiedene Restaurants wie etwa das Venue (Kansas City, 1993) oder das California Chicken Cafe (Los Angeles, 1992). Erst vor kurzem entstanden die Big Life Sports Bar in Fukuoka (Japan) und das Sportbekleidungsgeschäft Mossimo am South Coast Plaza (Costa Mesa, Kalifornien). Zur Zeit arbeitet Schweitzer an einem 450 Hektar großen Water Park/Hotel-Komplex im Süden Japans.

Né en 1953 à Cincinnati, Ohio, Josh Schweitzer (BA Pitzer College, Claremont, Californie, M. Arch. University of Kansas, 1980). Il a travaillé pour Spencer + Webs-ter à Londres, PBNA à Kansas City et Frank O.Gehry, avant d'ouvrir sa propre agence, SchweitzerKellen en 1984, puis Schweitzer BIM, en 1987. Outre The Monument, ses réalisations comprennent des restaurants comme Venue (Kansas City, 1993), ou le California Chicken Café (Los Angeles, 1992). Il vient d'achever le Big Life Sports Bar à Fukuoka (Japon), le magasin de vêtements de sport Mossimo à South Coast Plaza (Costa Mesa, Californie). Il travaille actuellement à un ensemble parc aquatique /hôtel de 450 hectares dans le Sud du Japon.

Schweitzer BIM
5441 West Washington Blvd.
Los Angeles, CA 90016
Tel: (213) 936-6163
Fax: (213) 936-5327

Bibliography
Bibliographie

Cook, Peter, and George Rand. *Morphosis, Buildings and Projects*. New York: Rizzoli, 1989.

Eric Owen Moss, Buildings and Projects. New York: Rizzoli, 1991.

Eric Owen Moss. Architectural Monographs N°20. London: Academy Editions, 1993.

Escher, Frank, ed. *John Lautner, Architect*. München: Artemis, 1994.

Franklin D. Israel. Architectural Monographs N°34. London: Academy Editions, 1994.

Futagawa, Yukio, ed. *Frank O. Gehry*. GA Architect 10. Tokyo: A.D.A. Edita, 1993.

Gebhard, David, and Robert Winter. *Los Angeles. An Architectural Guide*. Salt Lake City, Gibbs-Smith, 1994.

Hines, Thomas, and Franklin Israel. *Franklin D. Israel*. New York: Rizzoli, 1992.

Hines, Thomas: *Richard Neutra and the Search for Modern Architecture*. Berkeley: University of California Press, 1994.

Jencks, Charles. *Heteropolis, Los Angeles. The Riots and the Strange Beauty of Hetero-Architecture*. London: Academy Editions, 1993.

LA Lost & Found. New York: Sam Hall Kaplan, Crown Trade Paperbacks, 1987.

Lacy, Bill ed. *Angels and Franciscans, Innovative Architecture from Los Angeles and San Francisco*. New York: Rizzoli, 1992.

Los Angeles. World Cities. London: Academy Editions, 1994.

"Los Angeles." *Abitare,* May 1994, n°329.

Los Angeles Architecture. The Contemporary Condition. London: James Steele, Phaidon Press, 1993.

McGrew, Patrick, and Robert Julian. *Landmarks of Los Angeles*. New York: Harry Abrams, 1994.

Polledri, Paolo, ed. *Visionary San Francisco*. Munich: Prestel-Verlag, 1990.

Steele, James: *Eames House, Charles and Ray Eames*. London: Phaidon, 1994.

Weinstein, Richard. *Morphosis, Buildings and Projects. 1989-92*. New York: Rizzoli 1994.

Index

Photographic credits
Fotonachweis
Crédits photographiques

The publisher and editor wish to thank each of the architects and photographers for their kind assistance.

p. 2	© Photo: Tom Bonner
p. 6	© Photo: Universal City Studios
p. 8-9	© Photo: Timothy Hursley
p. 13	© Photo: Julius Shulman
p. 14-15	© Photo: Richard Barnes
p. 16-28	© Photo: Julius Shulman
p. 31	© Photo: Grant Mudford
p. 32	© Photo: Tim Street-Porter/ Esto
p. 33	© Frank O. Gehry
p. 34-35	© Photo: Arcaid/ Natalie Tepper
p. 36	© Photo: Arcaid/ John Edward Linden
p. 37	© Photo: Timothy Hursley
p. 39	© Photo: Alfred Wolf
p. 40-41	© Photo: Arnaud Carpentier
p. 42	© Photo: RoTo Architects, Inc.
p. 44-45	© Photo: Tom Bonner
p. 46	© Photo: Grant Mudford
p. 47	© Photo: Tom Bonner
p. 48 top	© Photo: Arcaid/ Richard Bryant
p. 48 bottom	© The J. Paul Getty Trust and Richard Meier & Partners, Photo: Jock Pottle/ Esto
p. 49-51	© Photo: Richard Barnes
p. 52	© Photo: Tom Bonner
p. 54	© Photo: Arnaud Carpentier
p. 55	© Photo: Erich Koyama
p. 58	© Photo: Asymptote Architecture
p. 59	© Asymptote Architecture
p. 60-61	© Photo: Asymptote Architecture
p. 62	© Photo: Hawkes Photo Studio
p. 63-64	© Central Office of Architecture
p. 65 top	© Photo: Tom Bonner
p. 65 bottom	© Central Office of Architecture
p. 66	© Photo: Erhard Pfeiffer
p. 67-68	© Cigolle & Coleman
p. 69	© Photo: Erhard Pfeiffer
p. 70	© Photo: Grey Crawford
p. 71	© Nancy Ellison
p. 72	© Steven Ehrlich
p. 73-75	© Photo: Grey Crawford
p. 76	© Steven Ehrlich
p. 77-81 top	© Photo: Tom Bonner
p. 81 bottom	© Steven Ehrlich
p. 82	© Steven Ehrlich
p. 83-84	© Photo: Grey Crawford
p. 84 bottom	© Steven Ehrlich
p. 85	© Photo: Grey Crawford
p. 86	© Photo: Timothy Hursley
p. 87-88	© Frank O. Gehry
p. 89	© Photo: Timothy Hursley
p. 90-93	© Photo: Arnaud Carpentier
p. 94	© Photo: Alan Weintraub
p. 95	© Joan Hallberg
p. 96-97 top	© Photo: Alan Weintraub
p. 97 bottom	© Joan Hallberg
p. 98	© Joan Hallberg
p. 99-101	© Photo: Alan Weintraub
p. 102	© Photo: Grant Mudford
p. 103	© Photo: Steve Broaddus
p. 104	© Hodgetts + Fung
p. 105-107 top	© Photo: Grant Mudford
p. 107 bottom	© Hodgetts + Fung
p. 108	© Photo: Tom Bonner
p. 109	© Franklin Israel
p. 110	© Photo: Tom Bonner
p. 111	© Franklin Israel
p. 112 top	© Photo: Tom Bonner
p. 112 bottom	© Franklin Israel
p. 112/113	© Photo: Tom Bonner
p. 115	© Photo: Grant Mudford
p. 116	© Franklin Israel
p. 117-119 top	© Photo: Grant Mudford
p. 119 bottom	© Franklin Israel
p. 120 top	© Photo: Tom Bonner
p. 120 bottom	© Franklin Israel
p. 122	© Photo: Erich Koyama
p. 123-124	© Wes Jones
p. 125 top	© Photo: Erich Koyama
p. 125 bottom	© Wes Jones
p. 126-127	© Photo: Wes Jones
p. 128	© Photo: Tom Bonner
p. 129	© Thom Mayne
p. 130-131 top	© Photo: Tom Bonner
p. 131 bottom	© Morphosis
p. 132	© Photo: Tom Bonner
p. 133-134	© Eric Owen Moss
p. 135-136 top	© Photo: Tom Bonner
p. 136 bottom	© Eric Owen Moss
p. 137	© Photo: Tom Bonner
p. 138	© Eric Owen Moss
p. 139-140	© Photo: Tom Bonner
p. 141	© Eric Owen Moss
p. 142	© Photo: Eric Chan
p. 143-144	© Edward Niles
p. 145	© Photo: Wayne Fujii
p. 146 top	© Photo: Marvin Rand
p. 146 bottom	© Edward Niles
p. 147 top	© Photo: Wayne Fujii
p. 147 bottom	© Photo: Alan Weintraub
p. 148/149	© Photo: Eric Chan
p. 150-151 top	© Photo: Alan Weintraub
p. 151 bottom	© Edward Niles
p. 152-153 top	© Photo: Alan Weintraub
p. 153 bottom	© Edward Niles
p. 154-156	© Photo: RoTo Architects, Inc.
p. 157	© Photo: Assassi Productions
p. 158/159	© RoTo Architects, Inc.
p. 158 top	© Photo: RoTo Architects, Inc.
p. 158 bottom	© RoTo Architects, Inc.
p. 160	© Photo: Assassi Productions
p. 161 top	© Photo: RoTo Architects, Inc.
p. 161 bottom	© RoTo Architects, Inc.
p. 162	© Photo: Timothy Hursley
p. 163-164	© Joseph Schweitzer
p. 165 -167 top	© Photo: Timothy Hursley
p. 167 bottom	© Joseph Schweitzer
p. 168/169	© Photo: Timothy Hursley